From Here to the Horizon

Photographs in Honor of Barry Lopez

From Here to the Horizon

Photographs in Honor of Barry Lopez

Edited by
Toby Jurovics

With contributions by
Debra Gwartney
Robert Macfarlane
Wally Mason

Sheldon Museum of Art

Barry Lopez Foundation
for Art & Environment

Distributed by
Trinity University Press

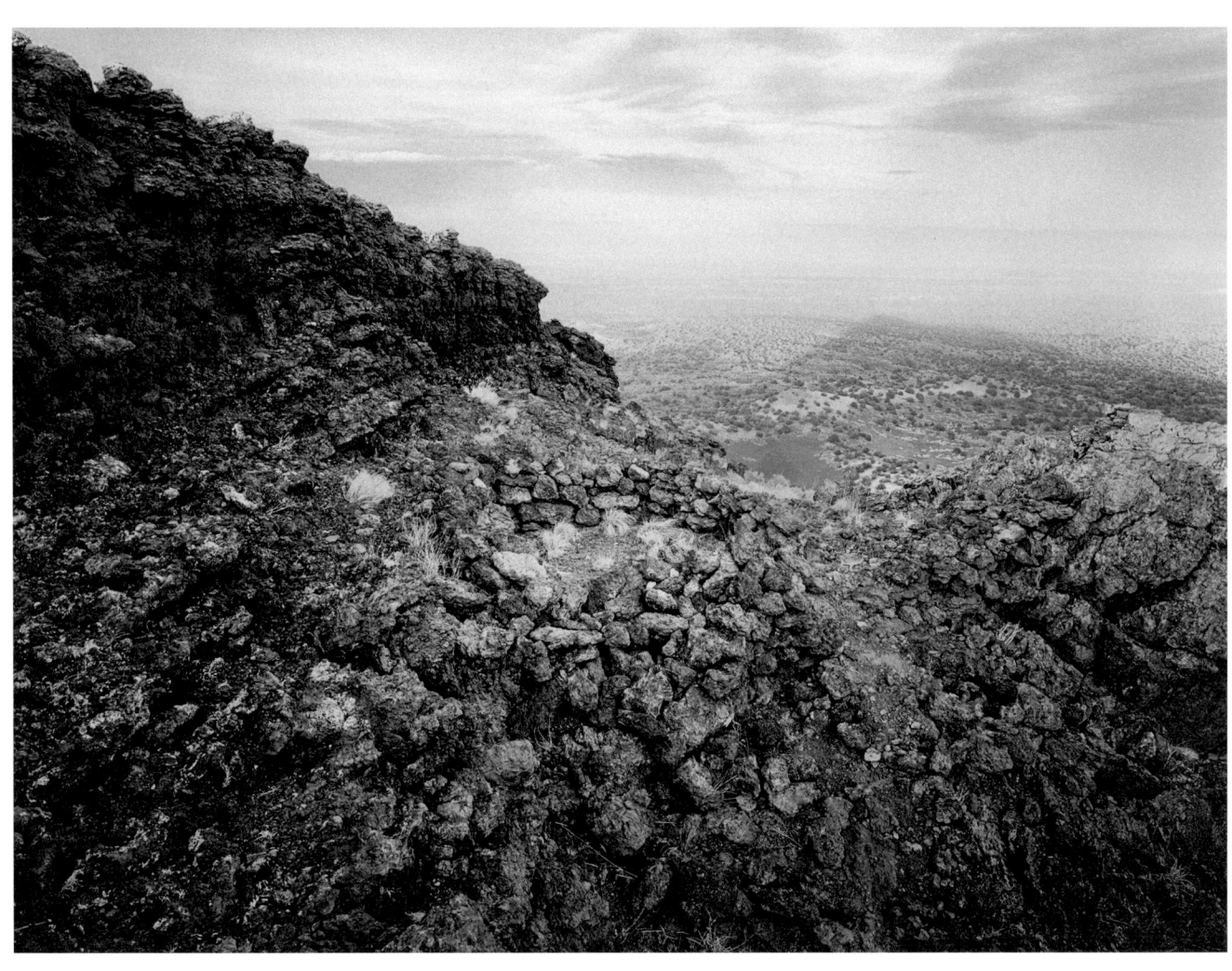

William Sutton
Strawberry Crater, Coconino National Forest, Arizona, 1989
Sheldon Museum of Art, the Home Ground Collection

Crater

Contents

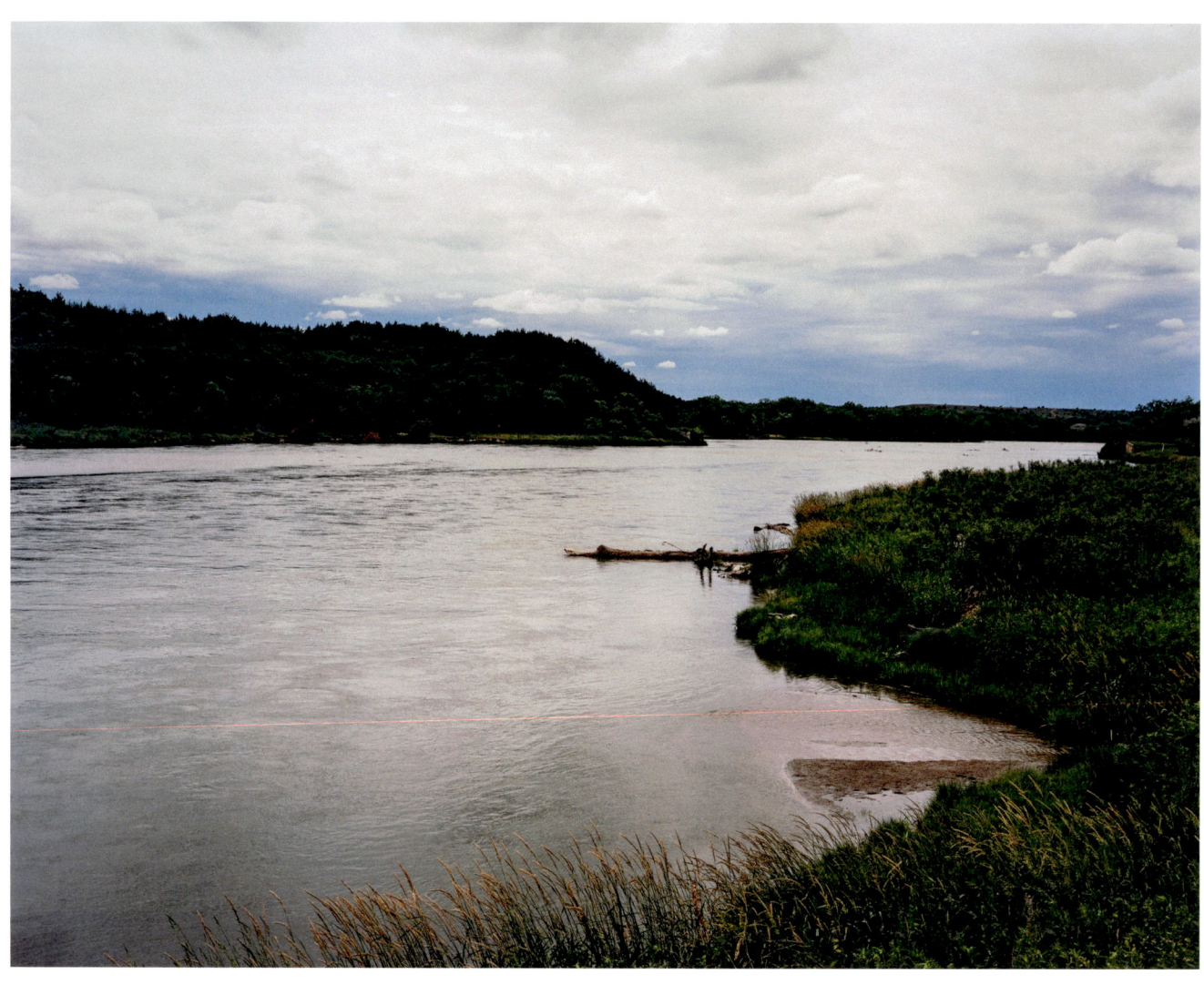

Mary Peck
Following the Route of the Keystone XL, Niobrara National Scenic
River North of Newport, Nebraska, 2017
Sheldon Museum of Art, the Home Ground Collection

Ecotone

Director's Foreword

As a writer, Barry Lopez eloquently focused our attention on the intersection of nature and human culture. As an advocate for both the environment and the arts, he encouraged us to use our individual creativity and collective actions to engage in essential discussions about the future of our planet. At Sheldon Museum of Art, we view the opportunity to house and exhibit the Home Ground Collection as a means to honor Barry's legacy and stay true to our connections to the natural world and one another.

The ubiquity of photographic images and cameras that allows us our own firsthand experience behind the lens gives audiences unprecedented familiarity with making pictures of the landscape. Even the most rudimentary awareness of image making provides insight into the fact that the photographers in this collection do much more than simply click the shutter. As one looks from picture to picture, it becomes increasingly evident that these veteran practitioners seamlessly elevate both their passions for the subject and their processes of physically creating prints. Their reverence for Barry's work and willingness to generously donate their own can never be underestimated, and we will never be able to thank them sufficiently.

Sheldon Museum of Art began collecting photography in 1943 after receiving a gift from the Works Progress Administration (WPA). Since then, each of the museum's directors has shown a passion for the medium, adding significant works to our holdings. Currently twenty percent of the museum's 13,000 objects are photographs. Relationships with photographers such as Harry Callahan and a series of invitational exhibitions of photography beginning in the 1960s enabled the museum to be an early collector of works by Robert Adams, Lewis Baltz, and Imogen Cunningham, among many others. Past collaborations with Toby Jurovics and respect for this project also made it easy to welcome this important group of pictures into the collection. Many of these photographers are already represented in Sheldon's

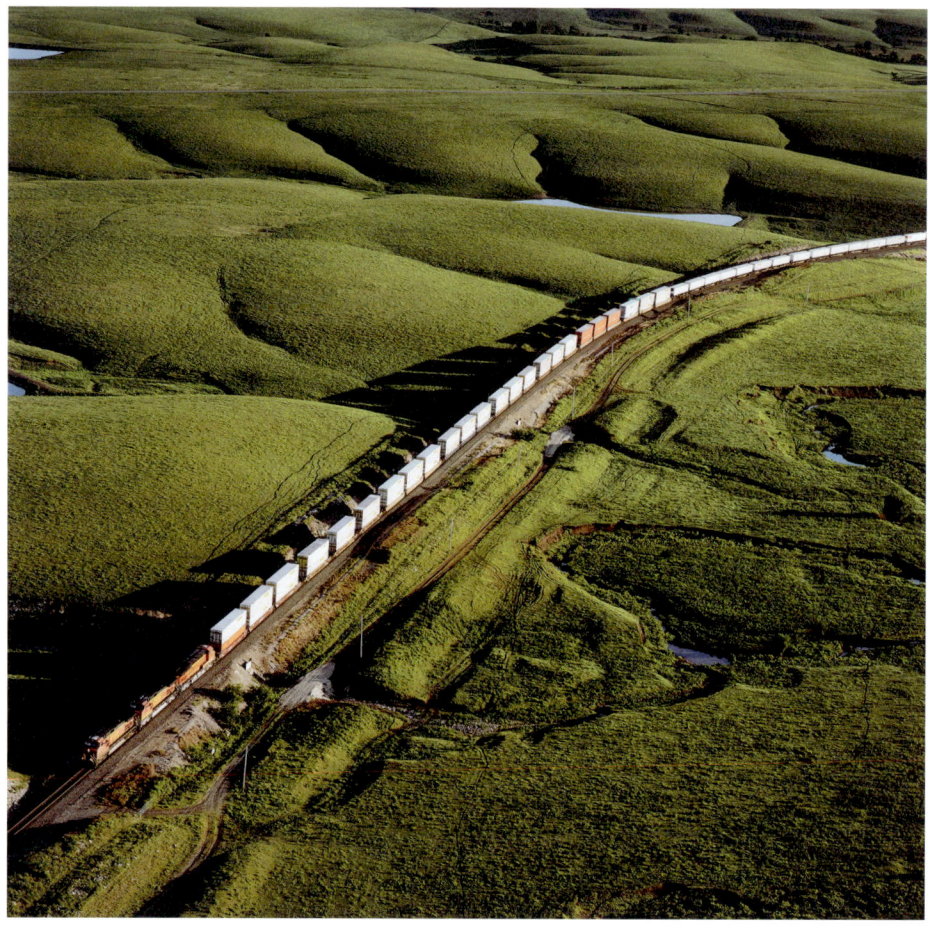

Terry Evans
*Train North of Matfield Green,
Chase County, Kansas, July
2009,* 2009
Sheldon Museum of Art, the
Home Ground Collection

Prairie

holdings, and as an object-based teaching museum, we are thrilled to augment existing pictures with these additions. They contribute to our ability to present art that intersects with curriculum, and the exhibition derived from this collection, *From Here to the Horizon,* supports discussions in fields of study throughout the university.

Projects of this scope depend on the resources of many talented individuals. Our thanks go to Stacey Walsh, registrar; Genevieve Ellerbee, associate registrar; Natalie Yates, associate registrar for collections and exhibitions; Erin Hanas, curator of academic engagement; Saraphina Masters, assistant curator of engagement; Ann Gradwohl, public relations and marketing manager; and Laura Reznicek, director of development. We also wish to acknowledge the generosity of Philippe Laumont of Laumont Photographics, a high school classmate of Barry's, for mounting several of the works in the exhibition.

Toby Jurovics, director of the Barry Lopez Foundation for Art & Environment, and I would also like to acknowledge the Sheldon Art Association. Since its founding in the late nineteenth century, this organization has been dedicated to the visual education of the people of Nebraska, tirelessly securing the resources required for the museum to collect art, operate as an academic art museum, and prosper. The current officers enthusiastically embraced this project and, along with the full board, secured funding for the publication and touring exhibition. Support has been generously provided by Phyllis Acklie, Assurity, Kristen and Geoff Cline, D F Dillon Foundation, Duncan Family Trust, Melanie and Jon Gross, Institute of Museum and Library Services, Kathy and Marc LeBaron, Patricia and Joel Meier, Nebraska Arts Council and Nebraska Cultural Endowment, Peck Stacpoole Foundation, Roseann and Phil Perry, Rhonda Seacrest, and Lisa and Tom Smith. The Charles Engelhard Foundation provided significant funding to support publication of the exhibition catalogue, for which we are most grateful.

We would also like to thank Tom Payton and Trinity University Press, the original publisher of *Home Ground: A Guide to the American Landscape*, which provided the framework for this collection, for joining us in the publication and distribution of *From Here to the Horizon*.

Toby Jurovics is a colleague and friend for whom I have the greatest respect. Much of my knowledge of the medium of photography has derived from long conversations and lots of listening. It has been a pleasure working on this project. Thank you.

Wally Mason
Director and Chief Curator
Sheldon Museum of Art

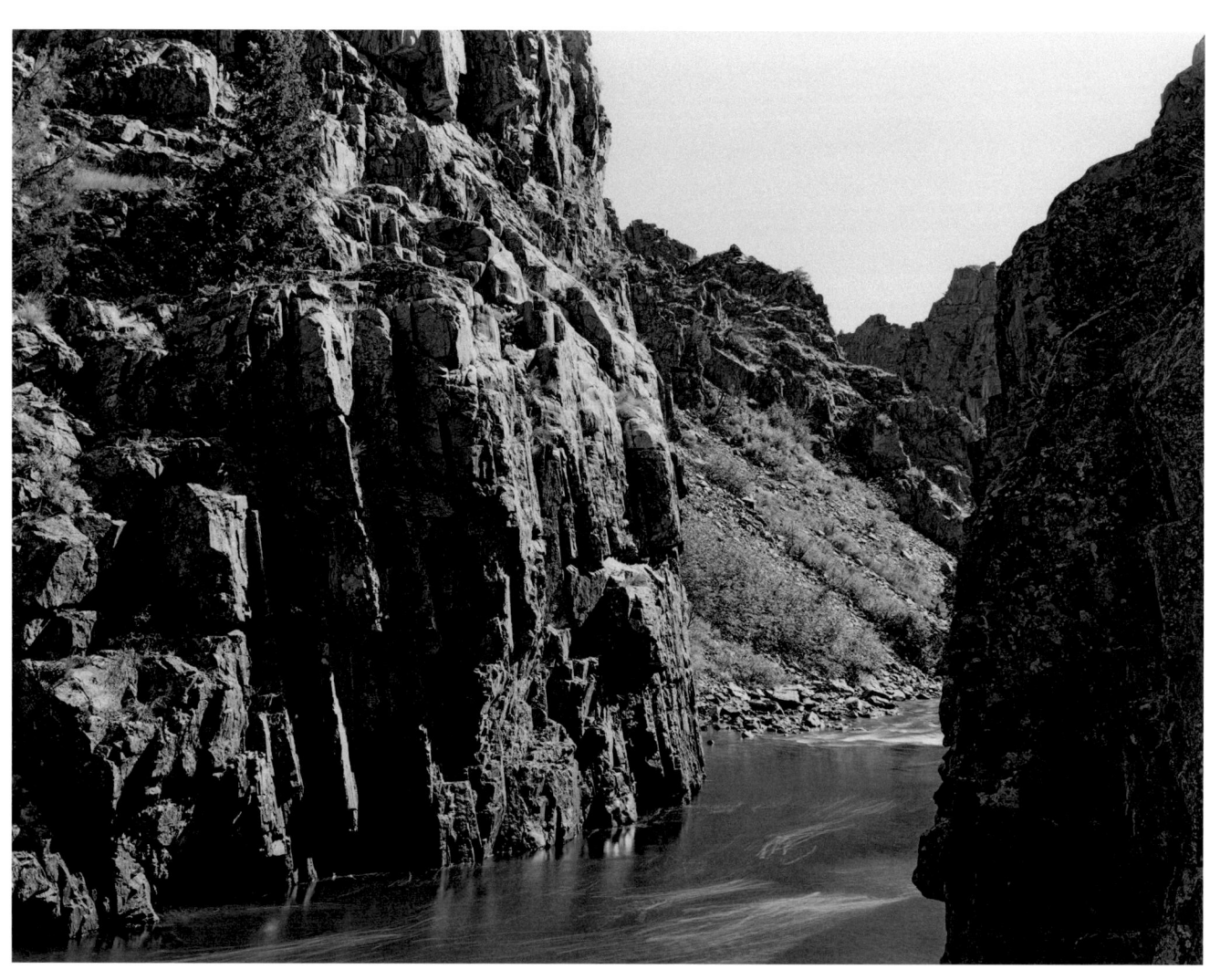

William Wylie
Narrows in Upper Canyon, Cache la Poudre River, Colorado, 1997
Sheldon Museum of Art, the Home Ground Collection

Narrows

Robert Macfarlane Geography as Generosity

Eighteen months before he crossed the river for the final time, Barry Lopez traveled from his home on the banks of the McKenzie to see me in Portland, Oregon, where I was passing through on my first trip to the American west coast. Barry and I had never met in person, though we'd corresponded by letter and email for several years. I was acutely nervous in the hours before our encounter, for Barry's influence on my life over the preceding two decades had been that of a north star: distant, blazing, and guiding. In my early twenties, while traveling in the Canadian Rockies, I'd read his masterwork *Arctic Dreams: Imagination and Desire in a Northern Landscape*, published in 1986, and it had changed the course of my life. That book—with its glittering, mica-like prose poetry, its luminous moral vision, and its vast freight of research and experience—had blown open my sense of what nonfiction could be and might accomplish and had confirmed in me my wish to become a writer about nature, landscape, place, and people.

Twenty years on, I finally had the chance to meet the person who had opened a life's path for me, as he had for so many others. I creaked down the stairs to the hotel lobby where Barry was waiting for me, heart-thuddingly anxious about disappointing him in some way I could neither foretell nor forestall. He rose with some difficulty—for his illness was at this point considerably advanced—greeted me with warmth and courtesy, bid me sit next to him, and then pointed to a big book already placed on the coffee table in front of us. It was a world atlas. He opened it. "I brought this," he said, turning to the section on Europe. "I thought you might show me some of the journeys you've made over the past few years and point out some of the landscapes you've described for me in your books." Set immediately at ease, I leaned forward, and for the next half hour or so we passed the atlas back and forth, finger-tracing paths of journeys taken, places known, recalling encounters with wise people, wild creatures, and fierce weather.

It was, I reflected later, a simple and beautiful thing for Barry to have done: geography as generosity. It allowed us quickly to find common ground—and encouraged each of us to speak to the other of our home grounds. For me these were the fenlands of Cambridgeshire and the Scottish Highlands, especially the Cairngorm massif in northeast Scotland. Barry's home grounds were the McKenzie River on the west slope of the Cascades, where he'd lived for half a century; the American and Canadian Arctic in which he had spent so much time as a watcher, walker, and writer; and the creeks and fields of the San Fernando Valley, where as a child he had learned to fly homing pigeons: "I would turn slowly under them in circles of glee," he later recalled in "A Voice," the introduction to *About This Life*, an image in which, counterintuitively, the tumbling pigeons become the fixed points around which that young life orbited in wonder.

A keynote—a grace note, really—of Barry's vast and varied body of work concerns the need to speak with precision about the places you inhabit and that inhabit you. To be able to disaggregate and denote the elements of your home ground is not to practice an Adamic, possessive form of naming, but rather to sharpen perception—and to begin to honor the immense complexities, human and more-than-human, of a given landscape and its communities. Good place-language, well used, opens onto mystery, grows knowledge, and summons wonder. And in the absence of an exact and detail-giving lexis, the living world can blur into a generalized wash of green, becoming an easily disposable backdrop. Certainly, the nuances observed by specialized vocabularies of place-perception are evaporating from common usage, burnt off by capital, apathy, and virtualization. The terrain beyond the city fringe has become progressively more understood in terms of large generic units (*field*, *hill*, *valley*, *wood*) and as such, more exploitable. Landscape has become blandscape, ripe for rezoning. We are increasingly blasé about place, in the sense that Georg Simmel used the term in his 1903 essay "The Metropolis and Mental Life," to mean "indifferent to the distinction between things."

In the early 2000s, Barry and his wife, the writer Debra Gwartney, began work on a project intended to celebrate and restore "the distinction between things." It was called *Home Ground: A Guide to the American Landscape* and might be described as a place-dictionary that answers the cry given by the Scottish poet Norman MacCaig in 1983: "Scholars, I plead with you / Where are your dictionaries of the wind, the grasses?" *Home Ground* retrieves, defines, organizes, and illuminates more than eight hundred words and phrases specific to aspects of American topography through the voices of forty-five American writers invited by Lopez and Gwartney. I say "defines," but that is not quite the right verb, at least not in its strict lexicographic sense. For *Home Ground* does not so much define as evoke. "That rivers and streams seldom flow (naturally) in straight lines is a gift of beauty. Otherwise we would not have canyons that bear the shape of moving water," begins Ellen Meloy's elegant entry for *gooseneck*, a term meaning those "meanders so tight in succession that their bows nearly meet one another." Lopez tells us a *shinnery* is "[a] type of low brush thicket . . . difficult to impossible to cross on foot or horseback" that takes its name from the shin oak (*Quercus havardii*). Here, human affordance is measured, as well as constituent flora. *Cowbelly*, perhaps my favorite of all the entries in *Home Ground*, refers to the velvet-soft river mud which forms "along the banks of slow-moving creeks, where the current slackens completely, that the very finest particles of sediment settle out of the water. . . . At the boundary where water becomes silt, the bottom is so plush the sinking foot [of the barefoot wader] barely registers the new medium, only a second change of temperature."

What a finely particular definition for a finely particular phenomenon! Here, as described by Conger Beasley, Jr., finesse exists within finesse: the generic "mud" is refined to a subcategory of itself, which is sensed haptically as an almost imperceptible change of temperature (rather than texture), felt by the bare stepping foot of the river-walker. One's grounding by the world becomes the means of knowing and distinguishing one's standing in the world.

The aim of *Home Ground* was, indeed, explicitly ethical rather than only taxonomic-descriptive. It shared with everything Barry wrote—and more broadly with the lived practice of his being-in-the-world as mentor, friend, ally, and teller—a belief that having such language available to us is vital because it encourages the kinds of allegiance and intimacy with one's places that might also go by the name of love, and out of which might arise care, grace, and good sense. I think of *Home Ground*, really, as less of a dictionary or onomasticon and more of a uniquely structured prose poem, exquisite in its precision and its metaphors and hopeful in its vision. It advances a way of seeing, as Barry put it in the introduction, that might "keep us from slipping off into abstract space."

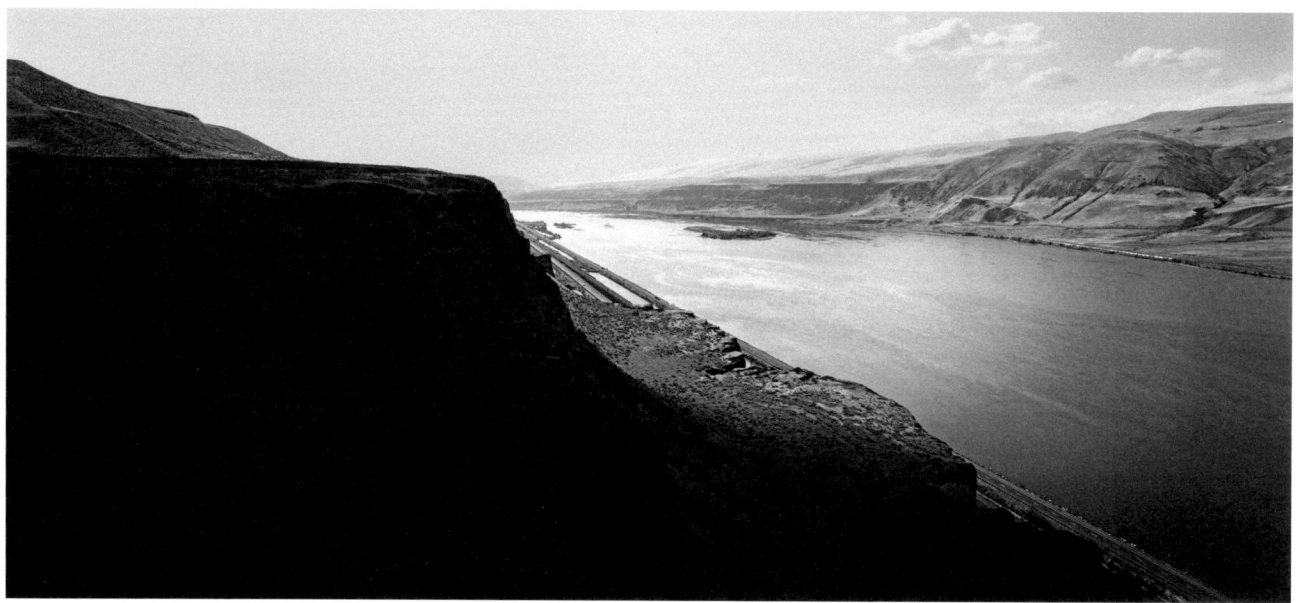

Terry Toedtemeier
View from the Rimrock below
Fairbanks Gap, One Mile West
of Celilo Drawbridge, Columbia
River Gorge, Oregon, 1987
Sheldon Museum of Art, the
Home Ground Collection

Gorge

I don't know whether Barry ever corresponded with the great geographer of the American vernacular landscape, J.B. Jackson, whose essays and lectures were so influential in dignifying and directing scholarly attention onto gas stations, lawns, woodlots, road-layouts, ballparks, and other everyday human structures as part of "the full imprint of human societies on the landscape," in Jackson's phrase. Jackson was a vocal critic of the exclusionary wilderness aesthetic as it existed in much mainstream North American conservation and (dread phrase) "nature writing." He and Barry shared a dislike of any way of seeing that sought dogmatically to exclude human presence from place. Both regarded landscape—to quote from Jackson—as "a complex and moving work of art, the transcript of a significant collective experience." Both felt that to use language well in speaking of place was to use it particularly: precision of utterance as both a form of lyricism and a species of attention.

They differed in two crucial ways, however. Barry recognized the land to be "home ground" to a community of life which extended far beyond the human species, and Barry also increasingly acknowledged the capacity of humans to damage and destroy the land's ability to be homely to that broader biota. It is worth recalling here that our word

14

"ecology" comes from the Greek *oikos*, meaning "household," "dwelling." Ecology is literally "the study of home." Human activity, immensely amplified by technology, is rapidly rendering the entire planet uncanny, *unheimlich*, unhomely. Aldo Leopold's famous line about the penalty of an ecological education being that one "lives alone in a world of wounds" came to ring truer and truer in Barry's work as it proceeded.

One means of measuring the distance that Barry traveled—from wonder and anxiety to rage and despair at the radical "unhoming" of life on Earth—may lie in the contrast between his essay "The American Geographies," first published in 1988 and reprinted in *About This Life*, and his 2020 essay "American Geography," the foreword to *American Geography: Photographs of Land Use from 1840 to the Present*, drawn from the collection of the San Francisco Museum of Modern Art. Both are dazzling pieces of writing, but where the first argues richly for a particularized, pluralized geographical knowledge as a precaution against damage, the second, three decades on, unflinchingly addresses a shattered ecological present and a calamitous future. Trouble, in the first, is starting to make itself felt: "a less noticeable pattern of disruption: acidic lakes, skies empty of birds, fouled beaches, the poisonous slags of industry, the sun burning like a molten coin in ruined air." Trouble, in the second, is everywhere apparent; the question is only how best to stay with it.

Here is Barry in 1989:

> So when I traveled, when I rolled my sleeping bag out on the shores of the Beaufort Sea or in the high pastures of the Absaroka Range in Wyoming, or at the bottom of the Grand Canyon, I absorbed those particular testaments to life, the indigenous color and songbird song, the smell of sun-bleached rock, damp earth, and wild honey, with some crude appreciation of the singular magnificence of each of those places. And the reassurance I felt expanded in the knowledge that there were, and would likely always be, people speaking out whenever they felt the dignity of the Earth imperiled in those places.

And here he is again in 2020:

> Crudely put, it is that we can no longer afford to carry on in a prolonged era of polite reflection and ineffective

resistance. An Era of Emergencies is bearing down on us. We must now consider, for example, how to organize the last industrial extractions of oil, fresh water, natural gas, timber, metallic ores, and fish in order to ensure our own survival; and we must consider, of course, what comes after that. We must reckon with the Sixth Extinction, which will remove, for example, many of our pollinators and one day, probably, many of us. We must invent overnight, figuratively speaking, another kind of civilization, one more cognizant of limits, less greedy, more compassionate, less bigoted, more inclusive, less exploitive.

"It seems he knew," Toby Jurovics said of this latter essay, "that there was no time left to be gentle." Only a few months later, wildfire—part of a combustive pattern in the American West intensified by global warming—ripped over the ridge to the north of the McKenzie River and tore down toward Barry and Debra's property, unhoming them for the last months of Barry's life and laying waste to the small outbuilding that housed more than five decades of his journals and correspondence.

The volume you hold in your hand is a field guide to both wonder and loss. Tonally speaking, we might say that it spans the range from "The American Geographies" to "American Geography." It contains images made by fifty of the most exceptional American landscape photographers of the past half-century and has its origin in Barry and Debra's wish, some fifteen years ago, to create a photographic exhibition that would stand as counterpart to, and extension of, *Home Ground*. It is now well known, I think, that Barry began his artistic life as a photographer as well as a writer, and that he remained deeply engaged with the art and its practitioners until his death. This volume stands as a means of celebrating and extending that long collaboration between page and image in his work.

I wish, of course, that he were here to walk and talk us through these photographs. None stands merely as illustration of the term of landscape-lexis to which it is latched. Each inflects, provokes, or illuminates. Some evoke huge forces of geology and geomorphology, the timescales of which humble the human instant: Emmet Gowin's *alluvial fan*, for instance, or the jagged ridge-blade of Laura McPhee's *sawtooth*. Some bring us close to the vernacular geographical vision that Barry shared with J.B. Jackson: Gregory Conniff's *yard*, with its rough picket fence, or Mike Smith's *blue hole*, its

Mark Ruwedel
Lower Colorado Desert,
The Horse Intaglio, 2005
Sheldon Museum of Art, the
Home Ground Collection

Desert pavement

two bathers lazily, happily afloat. Many focus upon the presence of human interventions—aesthetic, industrial—even in contexts that might be characterized as wild or wilderness. Mark Ruwedel's *desert pavement*, for example, will light up the mind of anyone who has read Barry's essay "The Stone Horse," in *Crossing Open Ground*. Joann Brennan's *pool and riffle* shows a humanly created riverine diversion, deepening the water to aid native trout reproduction; Virginia Beahan's *solfatara* is at once a reminder of our planet's geothermal volatility and the anthropogenic shift in the streamflow of the Colorado River that has exposed these vents.

The seeming absence of humans in Michael Berman's *borderland*—which the artist identifies as the crossing in Cormac McCarthy's *All the Pretty Horses*—disguises a contested, perilous frontier landscape, where migrant

17

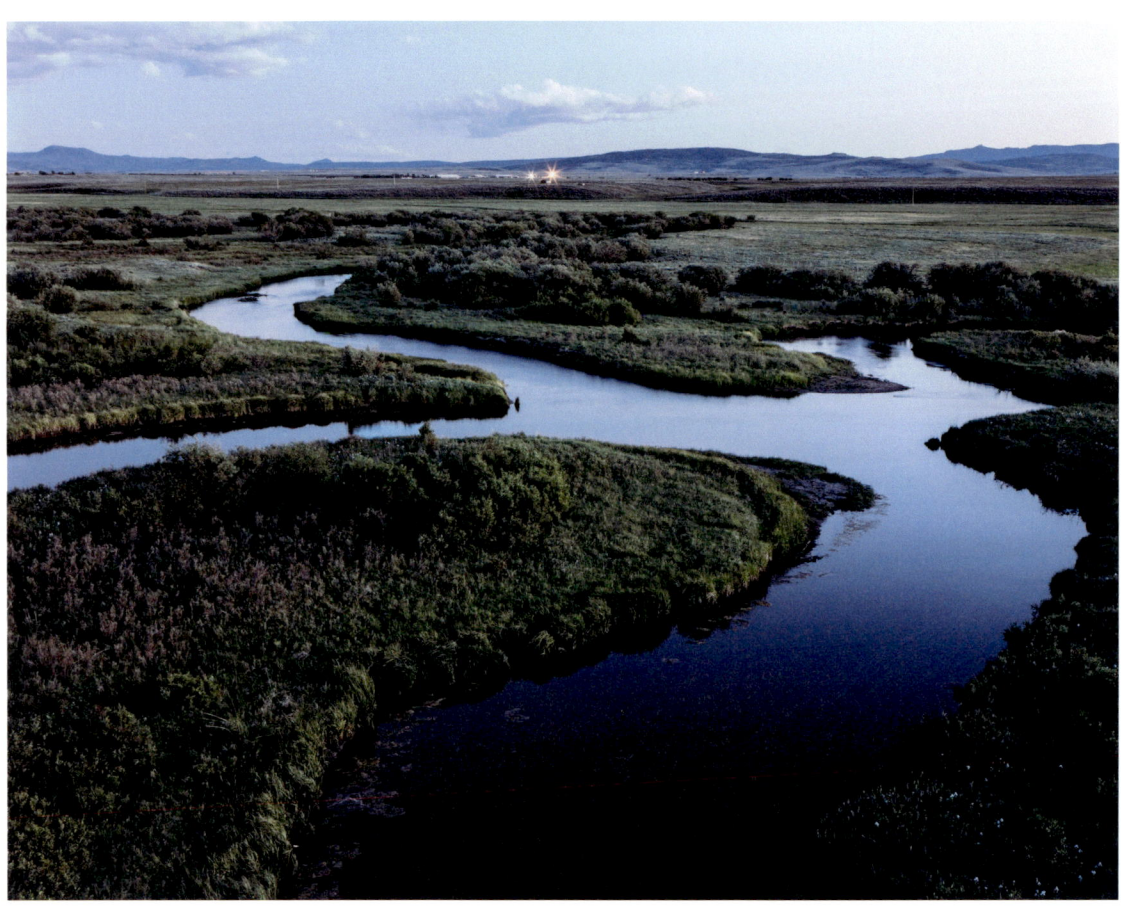

Jeff Rich
North Platte River Headwaters,
Jackson County, Colorado, 2018
Sheldon Museum of Art, the
Home Ground Collection

Headwaters

deaths too often occur. I relish the witty mischief of Rick Dingus's image showing *sandhills* viewed through visitor center windows in a state park in Texas—a reminder that our word "landscape" arrived into English from Dutch in the sixteenth century, carrying a viewerly or pictorial association with the then-emerging school of Dutch *landschap* painters. Andrew Borowiec's *Meigs County, Ohio*, chosen here to signify *wilderness*, shows a camper pulled up by the manicured bank of the Ohio River: it reminds me of a letter Jim Harrison once wrote me about his favorite "wild place" being the tree stump on which he'd left an empty beer bottle, out in his local woods. At the far end of the tonal range we find images like *clearcut*, *strip mine*, and *tailings pond*. Such landmarks are now as much part of the language of American geography as

18

mesas, canyons, and cirques, and it is important to be able to identify and speak of them with exactitude. Some of these images, then, offer modest tools for modest place-making. Others record landscapes that still resist conversion to standing reserve. Others bear witness to modification, interference, and damage on a variety of scales: entries in a desecration phrasebook. Taken in sum, they speak of landscape's ability to both pierce and ground the heart.

After Barry and I had finished our storytelling over the atlas that afternoon in Portland, we shared a public conversation upstairs in Powell's Books, and then we went for a beer together. We talked of Barry's plans for a last great trip: he wanted to drive from southeast to northwest, from Florida to Alaska, cutting a transect across the American landscape in its spectacular variety, moving from—as he put it—sanctuary to sanctuary, joining up places where people and creatures had gone to seek shelter and make home in precarious times. He never made that journey: illness and fire precluded it. Shortly before he began the long night drive back to his home at Finn Rock, he reached into his bag and took out a brightly colored headscarf, wrapped neatly around a small object. He unfolded the scarf to reveal a rock unlike any I'd seen before. It was a rough rhomboid, five-sided, black-brown in color, and its surfaces were eerily smooth to the touch. "This is for you," he said, placing the rock on my palm. It was, he explained, a ventifact—a stone weathered patiently into shape and finish by wind—that he had picked up high in the mountains of Antarctica years earlier while on a journey about which he had written in his last great work, *Horizon*. That stone sits on my writing desk in Cambridge, England. It is before me now as I finish this essay: an anchor point, a tethering post, the glimpse of a landscape, part of my home ground.

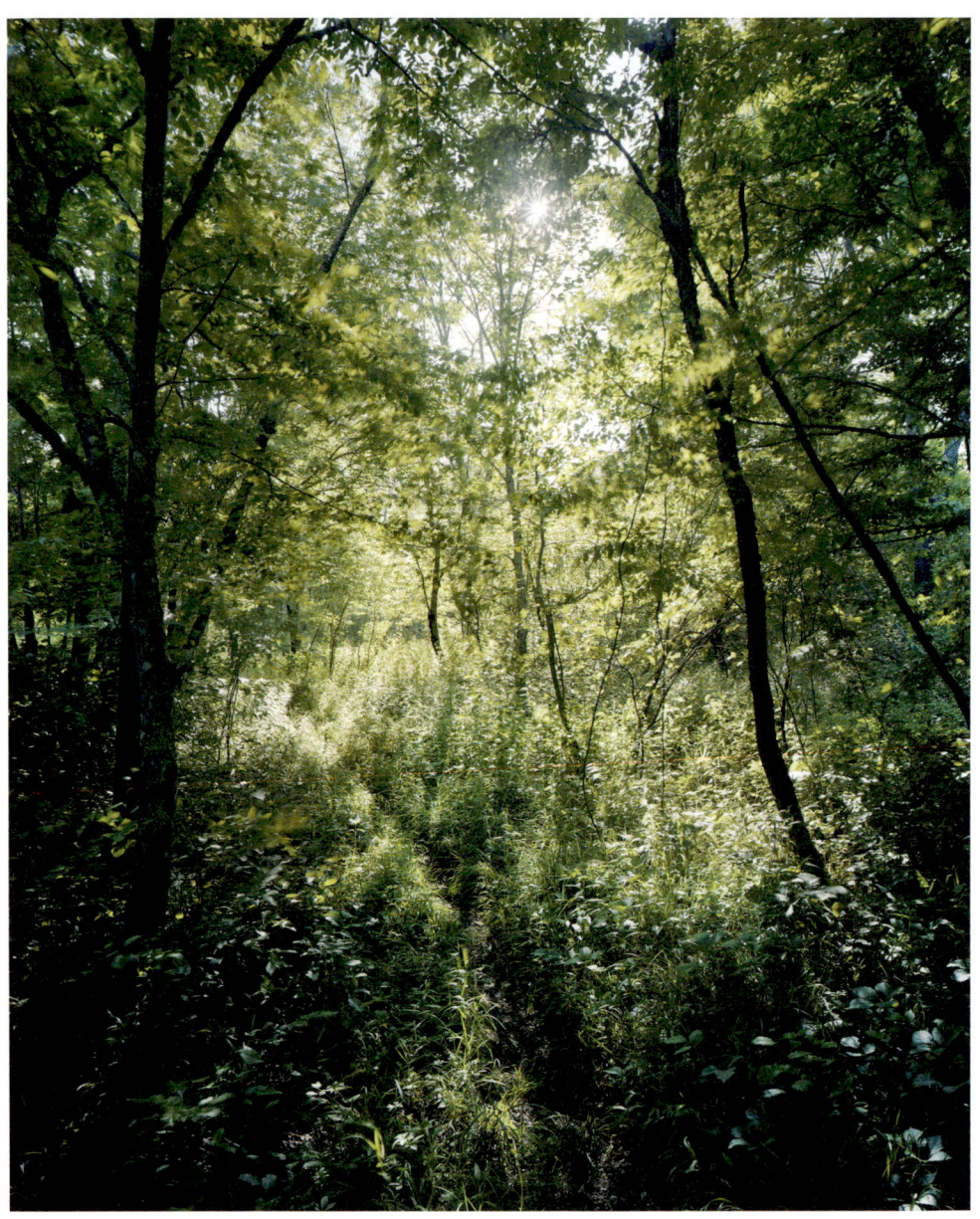

Barbara Bosworth
Along the St. George River, Maine, 2014
Sheldon Museum of Art, the Home Ground Collection

Forest

Debra Gwartney   Inventing Home Ground

Back in the early 2000s, Barry Lopez asked me about working together on an ambitious project that had been brewing in him for at least a decade. He had in mind a compendium of land and water terms distinct to North America, ranging from technical language such as *dendritic drainage* to regional colloquialisms like *thank you ma'am* and *desire path*. No such volume existed for a curious scholar or lover of the land (not to mention lover of language) to dip into, and that troubled him, this celebrated writer with an inimitable gift for acuity and precision in his own prose.

My first response was no. Though I worked as a journalist, which meant I'd parsed many a sticky issue, I had zero expertise in geography or geology. But as I thought over Barry's invitation, it seemed that someone like me, a person who would learn as I went along, inch-by-inch, word-by-word, might serve the project. Barry's reserve of knowledge and insight—he was indeed the book's visionary—and my willingness to scrounge through reference books and academic papers for a lay person's understanding of, say, *alluvial fan* and *terminal moraine*, turned out to be a collaboration that suited us both.

And so began our effort. First, we convinced ten highly qualified experts to serve on our advisory board, agreeing that not a single definition would make it into the book without approval from our esteemed group of geographers, geologists, and folklorists. We then went about identifying over 1000 terms that struck us as intriguing as well as useful (in the end, we whittled that down to 850—a far cry from exhaustive, but instead, as Barry often said, suggestive). He and I usually began work sessions in those early days by spreading a map of the United States on a table so we could pencil in regional terms—*campo* and *paraje* in the southwestern region of the country; *sassat* and *pancake ice* in Alaska; *'a'ā* and *punchbowl* in Hawaii; *cove forest* in the Smoky Mountains, to name a few. We made lists of contributors we hoped would take on terms from a given part of the country, and

Barry soon convinced forty-five accomplished writers to join the project. If the word *define* is to "state exactly the nature, scope, or meaning of," we urged the writers to consider an *evocation*, an *elicitation*, in the style of their own choosing instead. For instance, with a word like *domer*, which Ellen Meloy describes as resembling "a wet tortoise," she tells us that "[o]n the downstream side, a pourover drops abruptly into a squall of turbulence. It takes a quieter flow to produce a pillow, the cushion of water on the upstream side of a protruding rock." It's Meloy's attention to cadence and rhythm that delights, as does her word choice, that "squall" and that "pillow." She leans into the connotative rather than the denotative (as did the whole cadre of writers), and an obscure word such as *domer* is more alive for readers.

In keeping with this liveliness of language, Barry and I, along with the publisher, decided to add quotes from American literature—set in the page margins of the book—which prompted us to gather a committee of devoted readers whose mission was to seek out passages that included *Home Ground* terms. Here's a favorite of mine, accompanying *wash* and written by poet Joy Harjo: "I don't imagine the turquoise bracelet the dusky wash makes, or the red hills circling the dreaming eye of this sacred land. I don't imagine anything but the bracelet around my wrist, the red scarf around my neck as I urge my pretty horse home." Or lest we forget Melville's turn toward travel brochure when describing the whale: "Soon the fore part of him rose from the water; for an instant his whole marbleized body formed a high arch, like Virginia's Natural Bridge, and warningly waving his battered flukes in the air, the grand god revealed himself, sounded, and went out of sight."

As we went along with this project, this ingenious gazetteer invented by Barry, I realized that *Home Ground* was taking on the shape of America. That is, we were assembling a map (of sorts) of the settlement of this country by people whose first language was not English. The Dutch *kill* in upstate New York, the French *palouse* in the intermountain west, the Russian word *nilas*, which is a type of ice found in the far north. We were determined to find terms from Native American oral traditions, words and phrases that knit the backbone of what it meant to belong to a place. The arrival of European newcomers, the Dutch, the French, the Spanish, the Russian, and others, brought a gamut of languages to the country so that words indigenous peoples used to describe a particular stream of water, shape of a boulder,

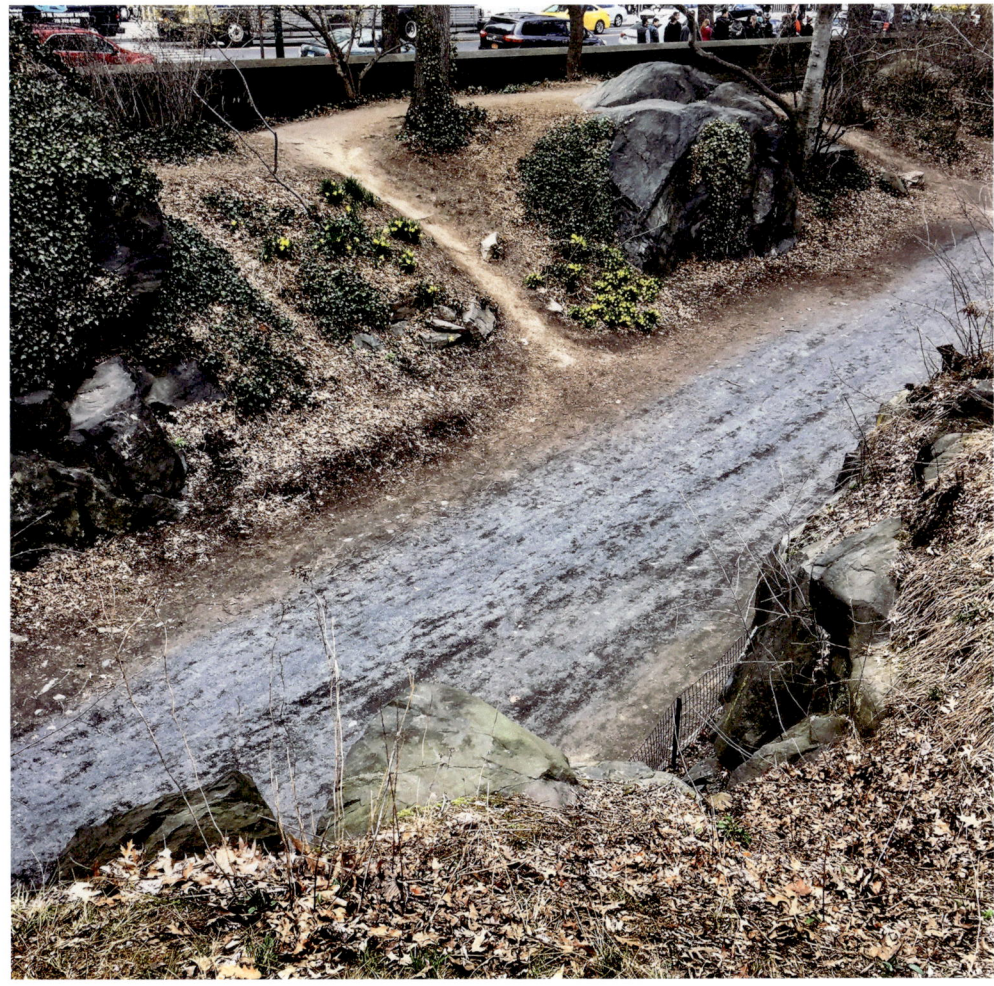

Gregory Conniff
Central Park, New York City,
2018
Sheldon Museum of Art, the
Home Ground Collection

Desire path

a rain-glistening plain was often subsumed. In the introduction to *Home Ground*, Barry poignantly called this forgotten language "so suited to the place being described, it fit against it like another kind of air."

Part of our mission, then, was to preserve terms that might otherwise disappear over time, as many already had. Barry also reminded us in the book's prologue that our project meant to push against the tarnish of capitalism. That is, commerce tends to rely on consumers to employ a common jargon, which makes selling that much easier. When it comes to place terms, we have the ubiquitous *park*, *hill*, *meadow*, *trail*, while regional precision fades into obsolescence. Over

23

the decades of industrialization and commerce, we've fallen into the habit of cultural sameness, a lack of distinction in our everyday lives. Our grocery stores, school buildings, the design of our homes—there's little difference from town to town. A strip mall in one neighborhood is identical to a strip mall in a neighborhood three states away, down to the colors of signs and the fading stripes in the parking lot. In environments like the ones we continue to build, terms such as *monadnock* and *kiss tank* and *drapery* and *yazoo* have become mere curiosities.

It was our dream that *Home Ground* might serve to remind readers of not only the richness but the actual power of precise North American terminology (in courts of law, in land use hearings, in teaching our children about where they live). There's tremendous value in saying exactly what you mean and describing where you are.

I remember the day Barry and I set about to picture our ideal reader. Of course, we knew the book would appeal to adult readers, but in our whimsy we imagined a curious eleven-year-old girl transported to various locations in the country that she could not otherwise picture except for the descriptions in *Home Ground*. She might read Lan Samantha Chang's definition for *Lover's Leap,* learning that along the Mississippi River (according to Mark Twain) there are at least fifty sites where "a troubled lover, or lovers, might contemplate a final act; [with] a beautiful, often exceptional view; and a quota of free fall with necessary dramatic effect." Our young reader might learn from Luis Alberto Urrea that "[a] narrow way; the narrows. A tight squeeze," is an *angostura,* a term he tells us "relates to the narrowest of mountain ravines or trails. . . . Anyone who has ridden a long-distance bus in Mexico, moreover, will never forget passing on a narrow curve at midnight." The child might be transfixed by Gretel Ehrlich's description of *candle ice,* named so "because in the process of decaying it forms in its interior clusters of vertical prisms resembling delicate, waxy tapers."

We could have had no finer goal than this one—providing readers of any age with highly accurate information, yes, but even more with the swell when a reader is washed with the lyricism of language. Language that, in this case, orients us in our home grounds. As Barry wrote in the introduction: "To hear the unembodied call of a place, that numinous voice, one has to wait for it to speak through the harmony of its features—the soughing of the wind across it, its upward reach against a clear night sky, its fragrance after a rain.

One must wait for the moment when the thing—the hill, the tarn, the lunette, the caliche flat, the bajada—ceases to be a thing and becomes something that knows we are there."

After the 2006 publication of *Home Ground*, Barry and I began exploring ideas for a visual version of the book. It was photography that Barry found most compelling and best aligned with the experience of *Home Ground*. An individual photographer's ability moves past the obvious, beyond the prosaic, stirring an emotional evocation from that which is being studied and chronicled. In recent years, Barry and his friend and colleague Toby Jurovics began to formulate a vision for such a show, which Toby continued to foster after Barry's death in December 2020. Which brings us to *From Here to the Horizon*. I'm grateful for the opportunity to help bring *Home Ground* back again and to complete what Barry and Toby started. The exhibit will, as Barry wrote about the book we made together, bring about "a sense of allegiance with our chosen places, and along with that a sense of affir-mation with our neighbors that the place we've chosen is beautiful, subtle, profound, worthy of our lives."

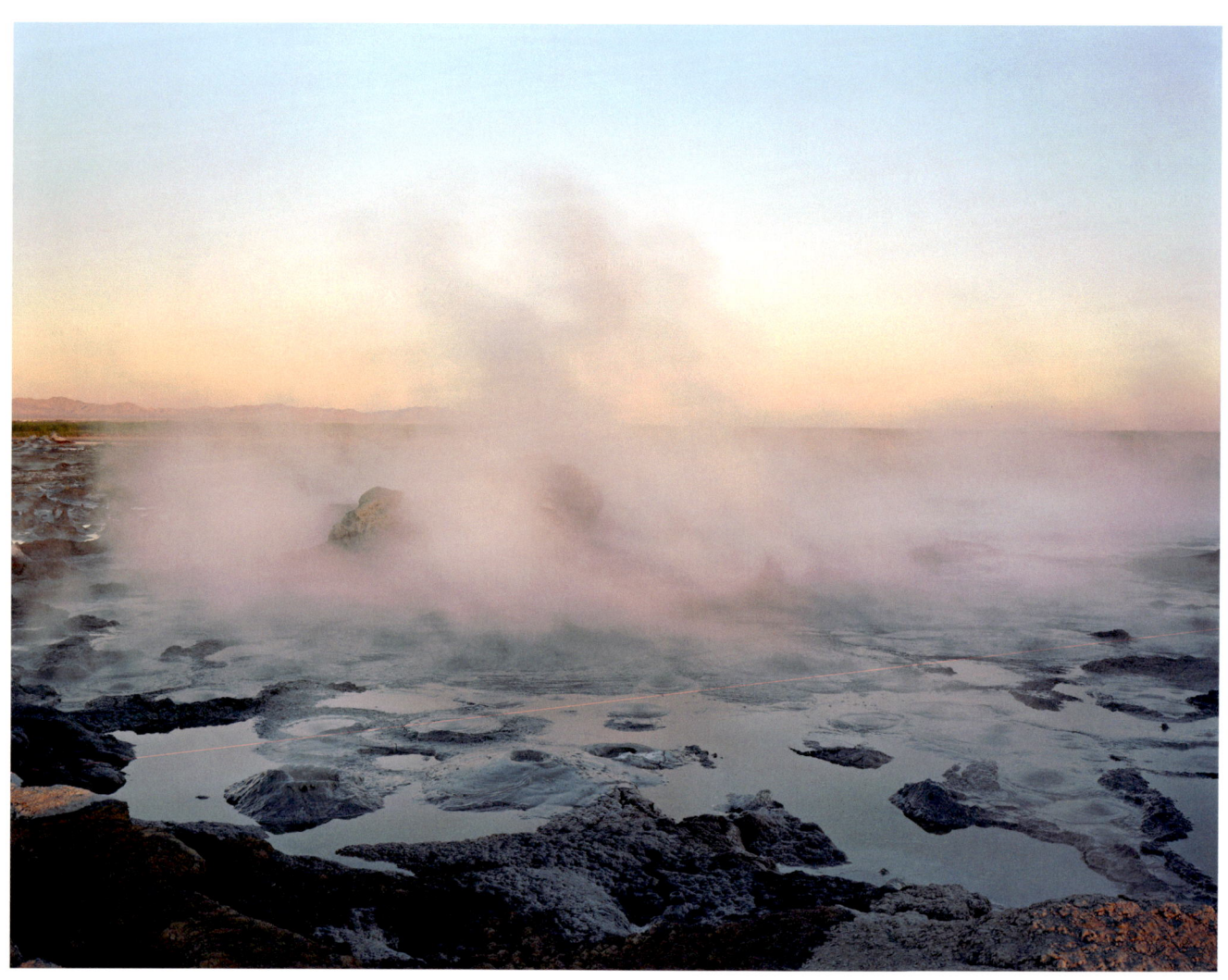

Virginia Beahan
*Geothermal Hot Springs Now Visible Due to Reduced Colorado
River Streamflow into the Salton Sea, on the San Andreas Fault
near Mullet Island, California,* 2014
Sheldon Museum of Art, the Home Ground Collection

Solfatara

The Home Ground Collection
in Honor of Barry Lopez

Barry Lopez's writing has been a major influence for me—I carried *Arctic Dreams* around for years, sharing passages and ideas from it with anyone who would listen. What impressed me so much about Barry's writing, and *Arctic Dreams* in particular, was the slow-moving attention to detail. I felt like he was with me, using his version of a view camera—or I was with him—as he studied and thought about and tried to make sense of the world.

—Virginia Beahan

The Home Ground Collection is the gift of fifty American photographers—colleagues and friends and admirers—assembled to honor the life and influence of Barry Lopez. It also marks the realization of his long-held desire to create a photographic companion to *Home Ground: A Guide to the American Landscape*, the "reader's dictionary" of our national geography that he compiled with Debra Gwartney in 2006. Each photograph in the collection was selected in relation to an entry in *Home Ground*, the following fifty plates corresponding to the checklist of the traveling exhibition. Some associations are specific, an image depicting the exact location or landform as described—Lukas Felzmann's *foothill*, Emmet Gowin's *alluvial fan*, or William Sutton's *comb ridge*. Others are evocative—Allen Hess's panorama of a *bend* in the Monongahela River places us in a *lookout* high above its banks, while we follow Peter de Lory on a hike through a *slot canyon* as he collects a trio of images. An *irrigation circle* photographed by Andrew Moore draws from the Ogallala *aquifer*, which straddles the *hundredth meridian*—two vital landmarks that are nevertheless difficult to visualize on the ground; likewise, Mary Peck asks us to imagine the *boreal forest* before it was cleared to make way for a tar sands refinery. These pairings are by no means definitive, and many images relate to a number of possible entries—

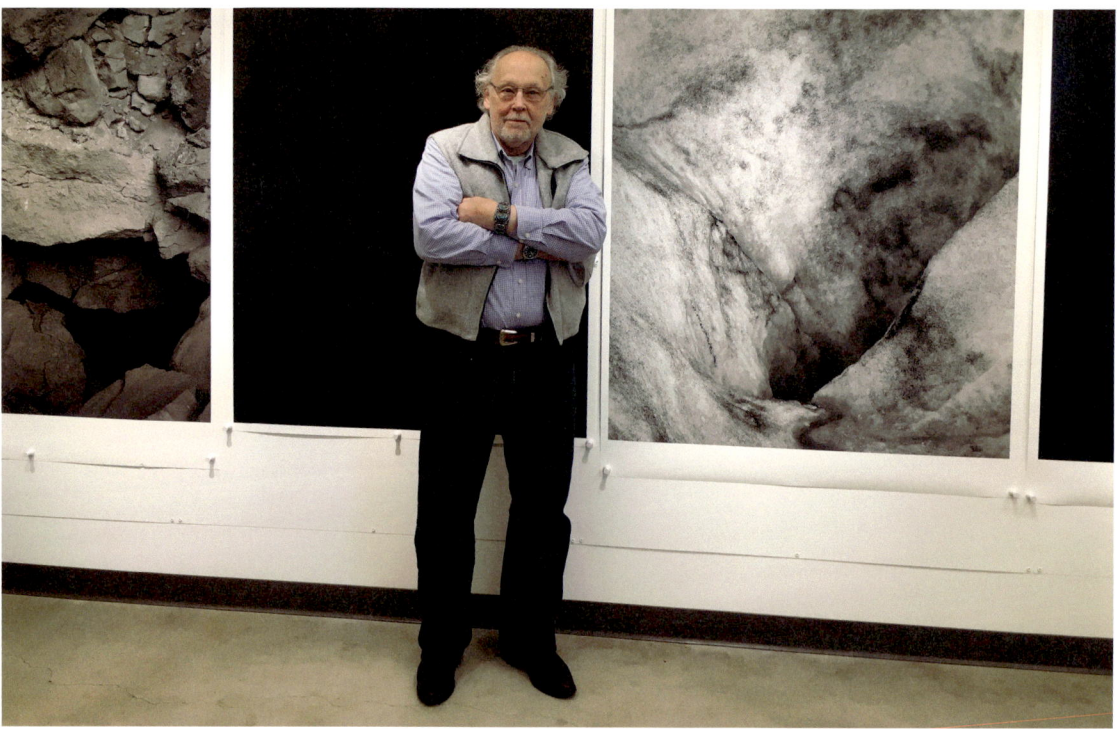

Barry Lopez, Eugene, Oregon, August 5, 2020, by Ron Jude

Thomas Joshua Cooper's *dry fall* could just as easily stand for a *derramadero*, *diversion dam*, or *plunge pool*. Similarly, much can be found in a single vista. Steve Fitch's animated jaguar overlooks the Tularosa Basin as well as the Oscura and San Andres Mountains, a Bureau of Land Management Wilderness Study Area, Hollman Air Force Base, White Sands National Monument, and the Trinity Site, where the first atomic bomb was detonated.

It is hard for those who admire language and landscape to read Barry's iconic 1986 book *Arctic Dreams: Imagination and Desire in a Northern Landscape* only once. Even returning to it after many years, one senses an accumulated familiarity with a place most of us are unlikely to visit yet nevertheless feel connected to through the care and clarity of his language. Likewise, the account of Skraeling Island in his memoir *Horizon* is so carefully detailed that, were one suddenly transported to its shores, it feels as if you would immediately recognize where you had landed and, taking a moment to get your bearings, know which direction to head next. In an essay he aptly titled "Learning to See," Barry recounted working as a landscape photographer for nearly fifteen years, as well as the moment he put his cameras down for the last time. Describing that event, while following a polar bear across the ice in the Beaufort Sea, he recognized the competing pull of his two pursuits and believed he could better attend to his responsibilities as a writer if his observations in the field weren't mediated by the camera. That said, Barry maintained a kinship with photographers—"a sort of running conversation"—and it is easy to understand how the bright, sharp attention to detail in his writing might be considered a form of photographic precision.

For their part, many photographers found an affinity with Barry's writing. As Virginia Beahan notes above, his use of language feels familiar to artists who are accustomed to studying every edge and corner of the ground glass or viewfinder before making an exposure. And, as in the best photographs, his accuracy and faithfulness carried more weight than a simple, forthright report: "The other lesson Lopez taught me," explained Robert Macfarlane, "was that while writing about landscape often begins in the aesthetic, it must always tend toward the ethical. Lopez's intense attentiveness was, I later came to realize, a form of moral gaze, born of his belief that if we attend more closely to something then we are less likely to act selfishly towards it. To exercise a care of attention toward a place—as toward a person—is to achieve a sympathetic intimacy with it." This care of attention laid the foundation for *Home Ground*, and again for this collection. To Barry, the land was never simply the stage or background for human activity but reflected who we are, our histories and desires and aspirations, as if woven together in a loom.

Beyond standing as a marker of the admiration and affection of Barry's peers, like a cairn of stacked stones to guide us through the landscape, it is hoped that *From Here to the Horizon* will spark the imagination of every reader—for places we remember, or hope to one day visit, or may never see yet carry with us thanks to a carefully written verse or a well-made photograph.

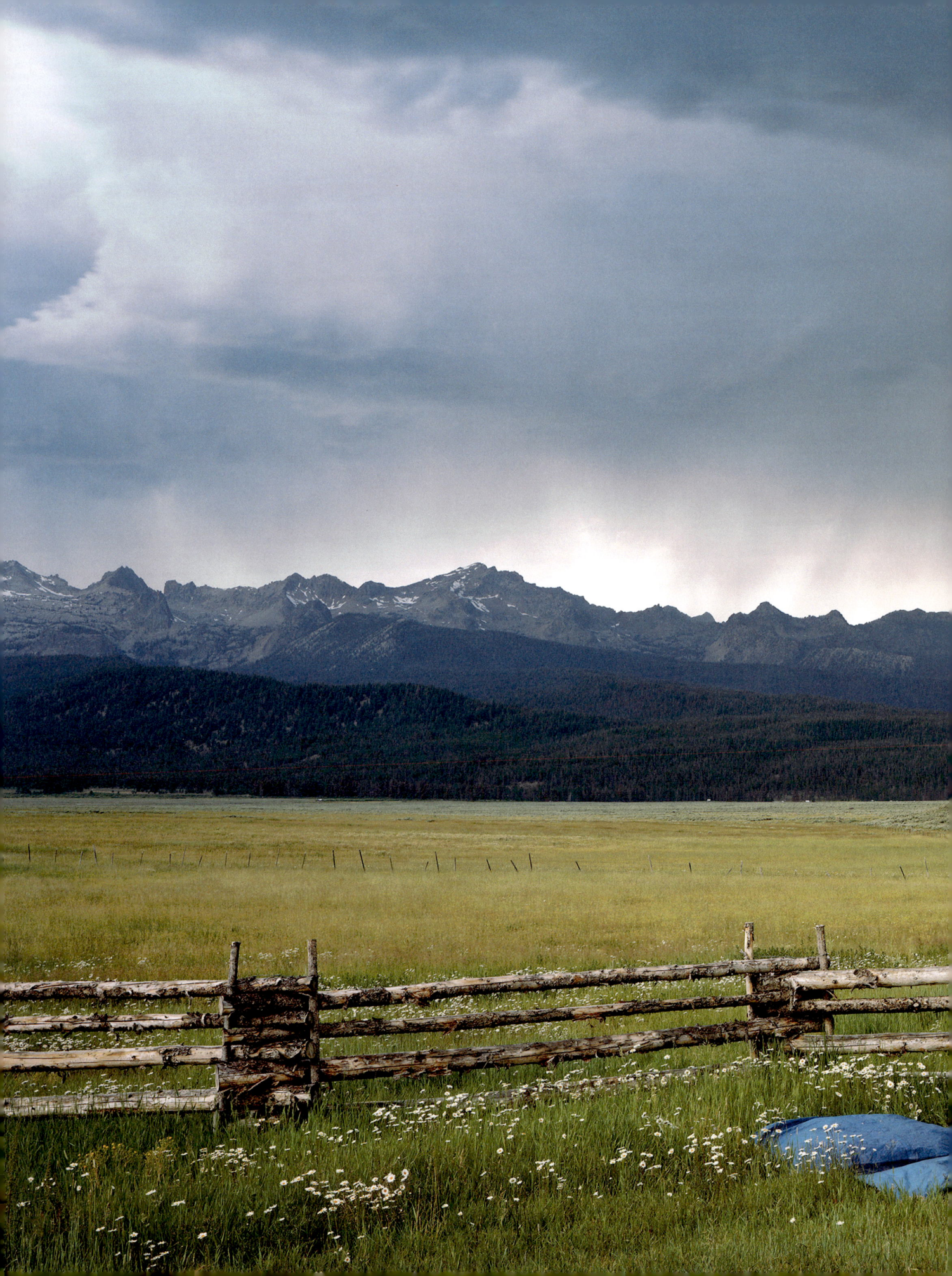

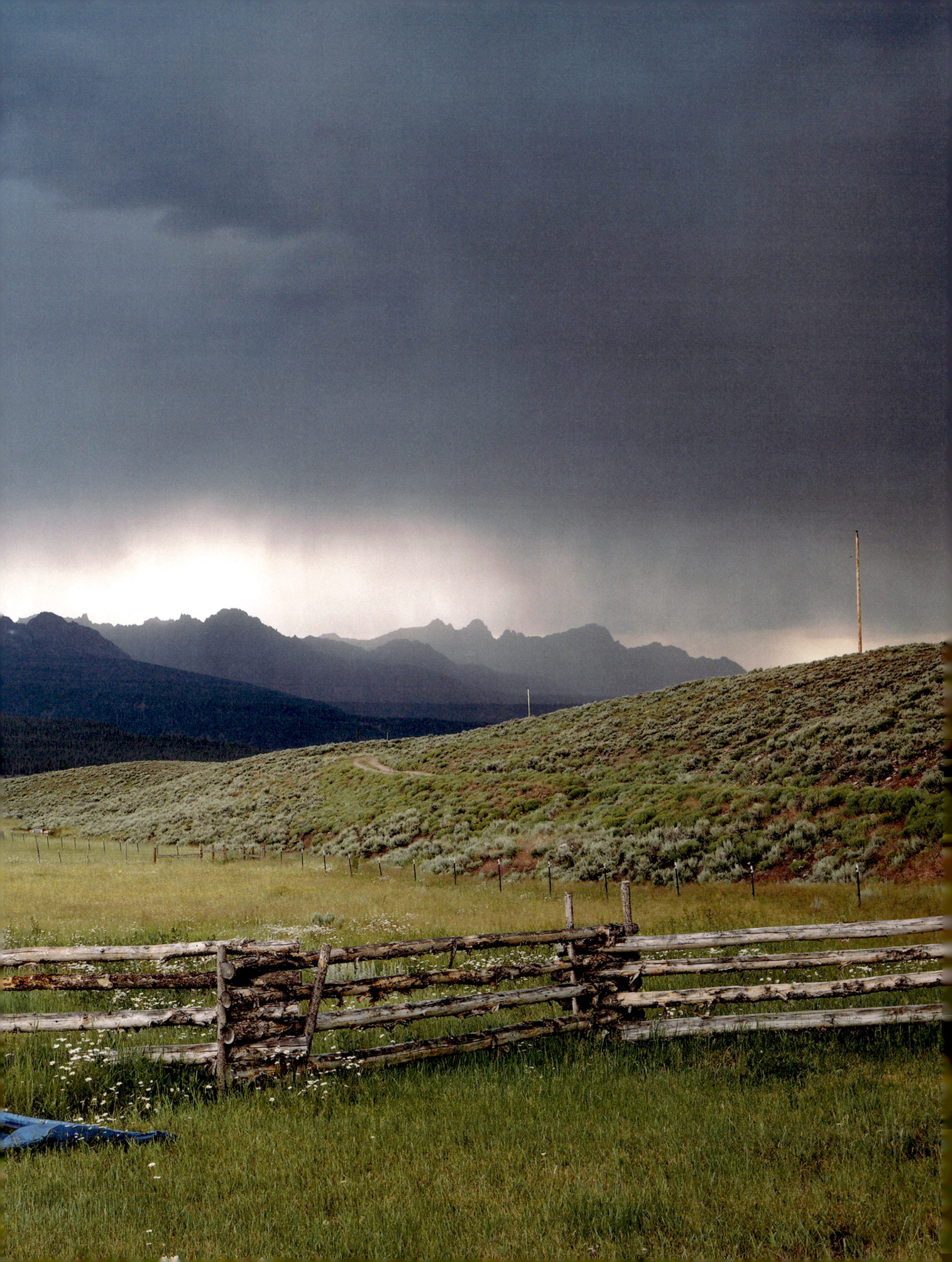

Old-growth forest   Forest as elder, where trees coexist in the full spectrum of their development—from seedling to sapling to ancient, to snag and generative nurse log: old-growth forest features include thick duff, trees hoary with age, and certain indicator species that rely on the settled richness of variety in plant, insect, lichen, and other life forms. It seems to take about two centuries for these features to develop, by which time a forest crosses a threshold between a monoculture of trees of similar age—often the result of catastrophic fire or clearcut—to a multiage population of trees, with attendant opportunities for broad range in plant and animal populations. What old age gives the individual person, old growth conditions give a forest: a life-library of survival wisdom, flexibility, initiative, and a sustaining life process. Formerly called virgin forest, as untouched wilderness, old-growth forest has become controversial and precious. Besides the old-growth forests dominated by Douglas fir in the Pacific Northwest, old growth includes local stands of redwood in California, ponderosa pine east of the Cascade Mountains, eastern hemlock in the Great Smoky Mountains, as well as cedar, cypress, tulip tree, oak, and other species, often in tiny forest remnants. —Kim Stafford

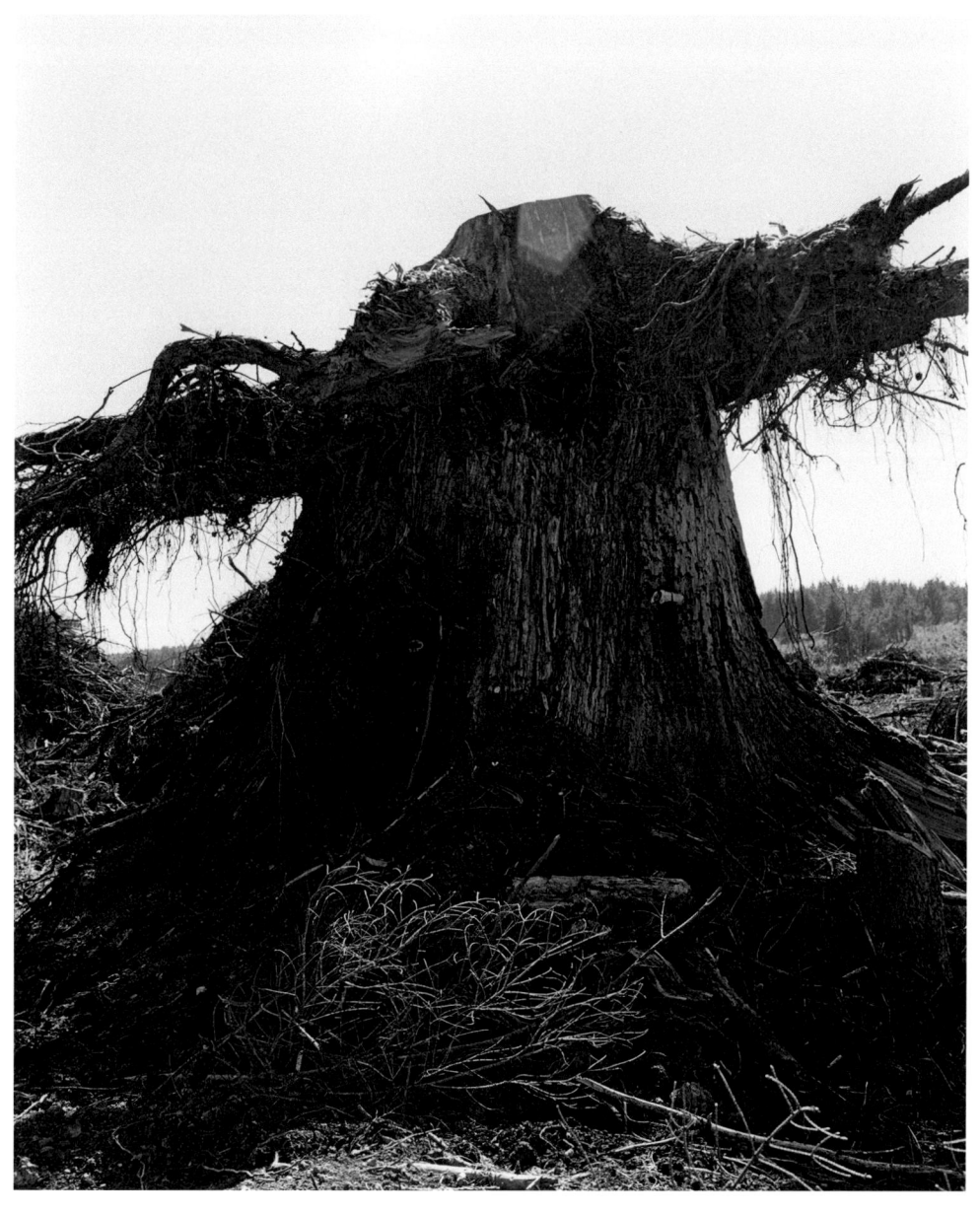

1. Robert Adams   Born Orange, NJ, 1937 – lives Astoria, OR
Clearcut. Second-growth Stump on Top of Old-growth
Stump. Coos County, Oregon, 2013

Oasis The word oasis is apparently of Egyptian origin and refers to a place in the desert where water is present. An oasis means life and fertility: permanent plant growth and the possibility for human settlement, drinking water, and enough moisture to grow plants and trees. An oasis can vary in size, from an ooze in cracked mud to a gurgling spring, to a pond or spring system so large it can hold whole cities. Natural oases occur in artesian basins or in deflation hollows, where dunes and sediments have been removed by wind, thus exposing an area that is at groundwater level. Nearly one hundred places in the United States are named Oasis, including the town of Oasis, California, the Oasis Reservoir in Colorado, Oasis Pond in Montana, and Oasis Lake in Texas. Another sort of oasis can be found in polar deserts—an ice-free area in an icebound landscape. Pearyland at the top of Greenland is one. Historically, the word oasis has been used to refer to the dark spots occurring on Mars. But most often an oasis is an island of aquatic relief. It is the place where lives are saved, and figuratively speaking, refers to any calm center. The piece of foam that holds flower stems in a floral arrangement is called an oasis; it too, represents an island of security, but one that sits just under the water's surface. As a topographic feature, an oasis is life; it is a gathering point, a sanctuary, and a feeding station. It is the desert's umbilical.
—Gretel Ehrlich

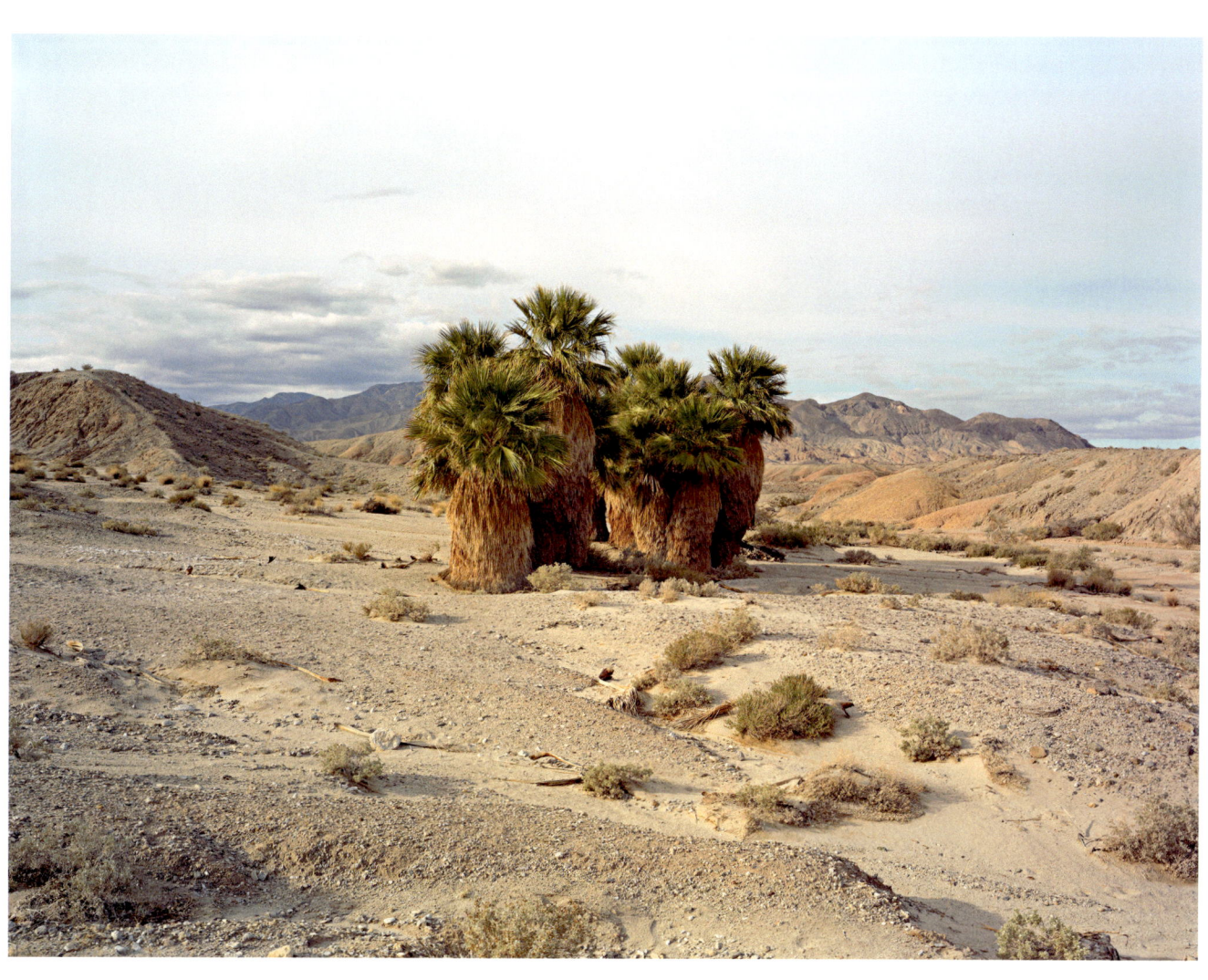

2. Virginia Beahan   Born Philadelphia, PA, 1946 – lives Lyme Center, NH
17 Palms Oasis, Anza-Borrego Desert State Park, California, 2013

Mangrove swamp   To poet Elizabeth Bishop, mangroves made up the "celestial landscape" of Florida, with herons in "tiers and tiers of immaculate reflection" shining whitely among the leaves. She compared the roots of one mangrove, a red mangrove, *Rhizophora mangle*, to Gothic arches because of its distinctive bower of aerial roots and numerous fingerlike breather roots—pneumatophores—rising from the mud. Though mangroves flourish worldwide in tropical and subtropical areas, this particular one, the red, can be found only in Florida, while the white and black are found in Florida and elsewhere. Possessing all three of these salt-loving, tropical-zone trees, Florida has luxuriant mangrove "forests." The red is the great colonizer, its foot-long seedlings dropping and rooting in the protective tangle of detritus below, or drifting off in storm-season tides to implant themselves elsewhere. Mangroves are essential to many water birds for rookeries and rest—the brown pelican nests almost exclusively on mangrove islands—and the watery, airy mazes the trees provide are favored by lobster, tarpon, and manatee alike. A peculiar environment, the mangrove swamp: displeasing to man in its tangled impenetrability, but celestial to a great and lovely multitude that is not man. —Joy Williams

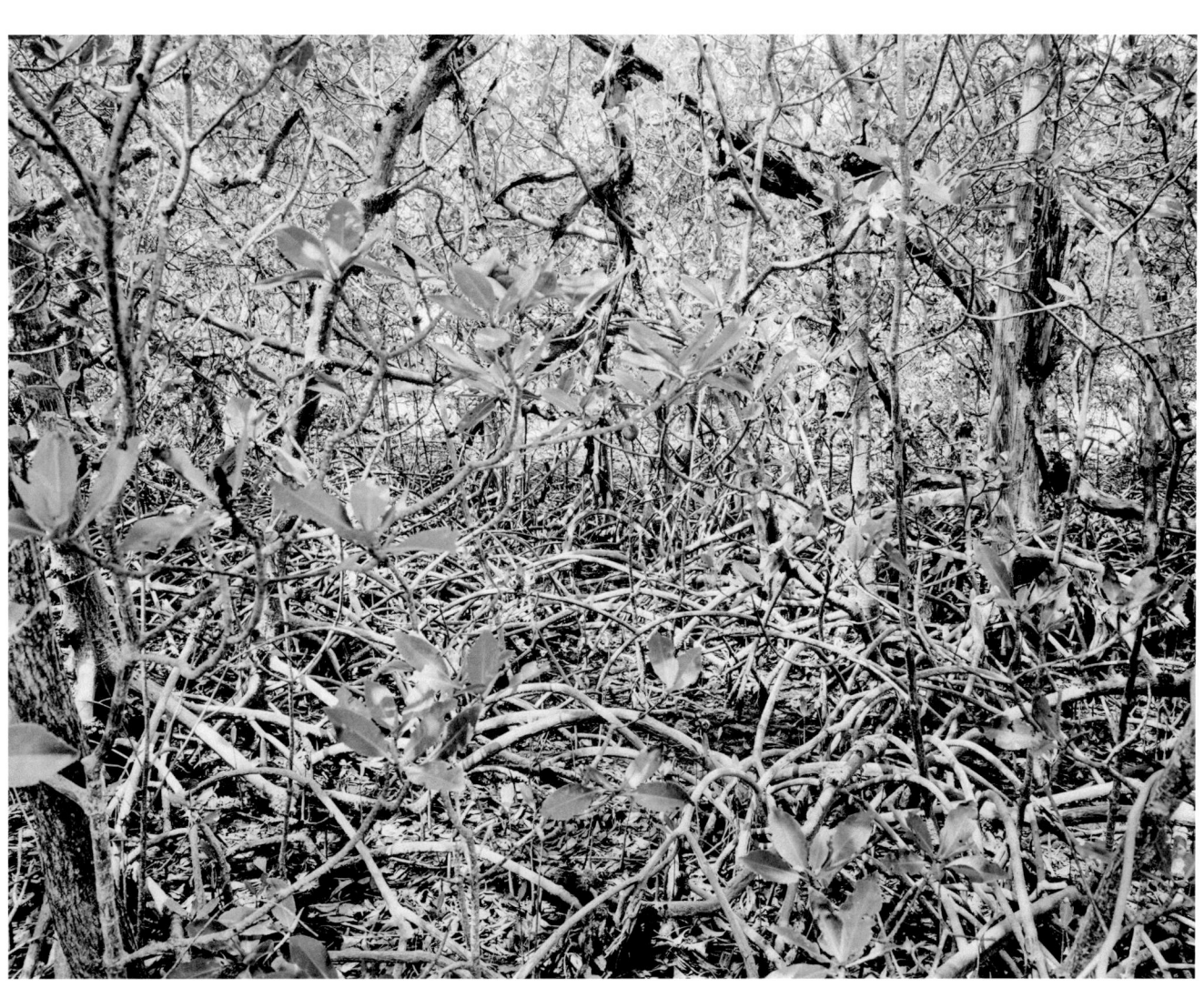

3. Marion Belanger   Born Willimantic, CT, 1957 – lives Guilford, CT
Mangroves, Everglades City, Florida, 2002

Borderland   A land or district on or near the border between two countries or districts is borderland, conveying the idea of a fringe or intermediary state or region. In the Southwest, the borderland is the stretch between Mexico and the United States, and the term carries with it the idea of a mixing and confluence of cultures. It also includes the idea of disparate economic systems that produce poverty, along with cultural interactions rich in ambiguities and tensions. Chicana poet and activist Gloria Anzaldúa describes the U.S.-Mexico borderland as *"una herida abierta"*—an open wound. Borderland is thus no longer a geographical term but a geopolitical one. —Arthur Sze

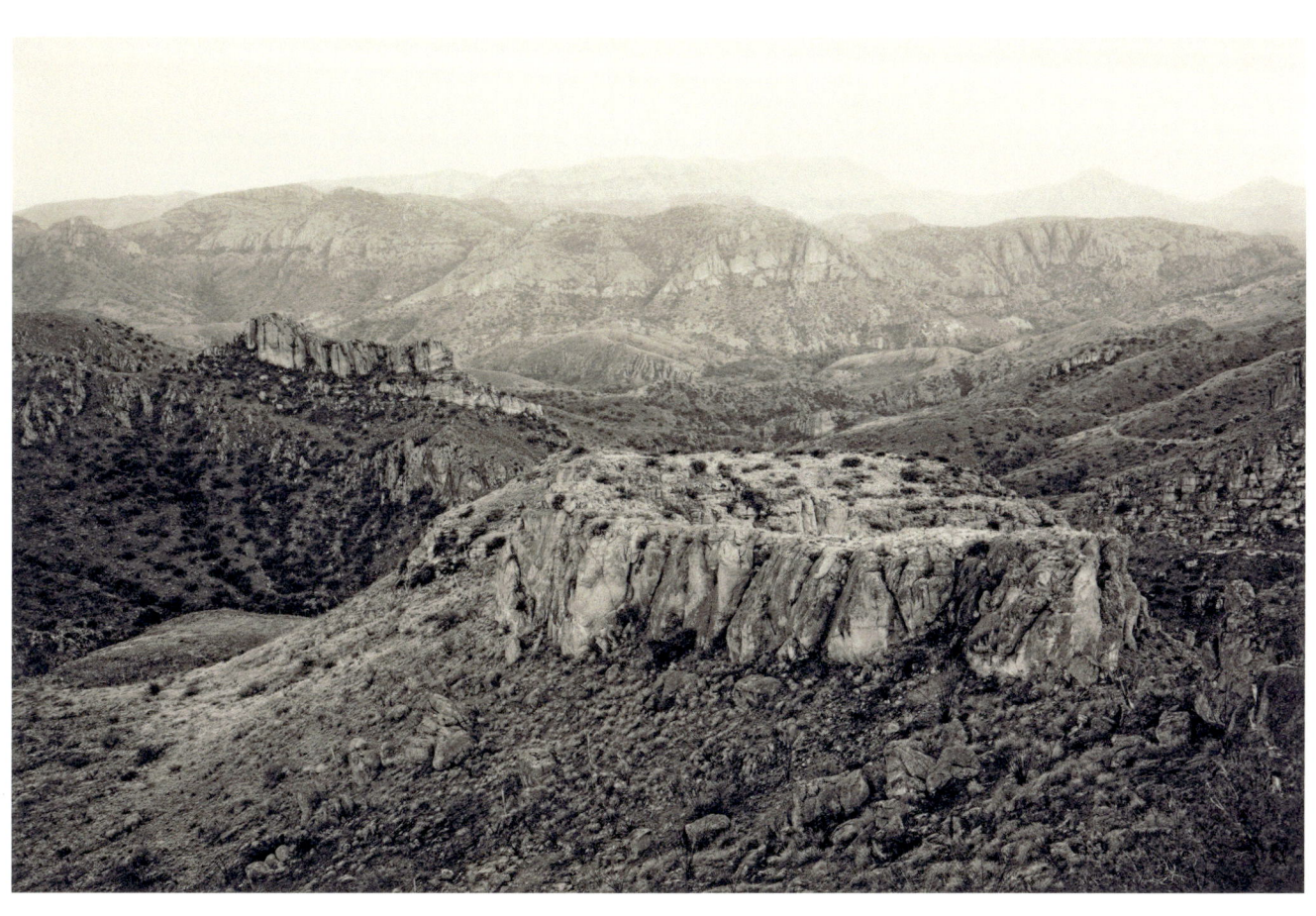

4. Michael Berman Born New York, NY, 1956 – lives Silver City, NM
Cajón Bonito, Sierra San Luis, Chihuahua, Mexico, 2020

Wilderness   Wilderness is a cultural, not an ecological, concept. While its meaning and the values that attach to it have shifted through the ages, it stands essentially for the land and space where culture is not, or at least where the impacts of human culture are minimal: the desert wilderness of the Old Testament; the Adirondack wilderness of the Hudson River painters; the comparatively prosaic concepts of backcountry, bush, or the "high lonesome"; and the administrative designation conceived by Aldo Leopold as "a continuous stretch of country preserved in its natural state . . . big enough to absorb a two weeks' pack trip, and kept devoid of . . . works of man." The most powerful of all definitions of wilderness is to be found in the 1964 Wilderness Act: "A wilderness, in contrast with those areas where man and his own works dominate the landscape, is hereby recognized as an area where the earth and its community of life are untrammeled by man, where man himself is a visitor who does not remain." The National Wilderness Preservation System, which the act established, now includes over 105 million acres of federal land, more than half of which is in Alaska. Irony necessarily abides in so protean a term: land that westering white Americans in the nineteenth century judged to be wilderness was home ground from the point of view of native tribes, and the birth of the wilderness preservation movement in the twentieth century occurred only after the lands on which it focused had been substantially tamed by the removal of the natives who inhabited them. Today wilderness remains one of the most evocative concepts in American culture. It might be said to describe any place on land (or sea) where the powers of nature are paramount and where the call of the wild might be heard. Ed Abbey, among many others, had meditated on its meaning: "Wilderness. The word itself is music. Wilderness, wilderness. . . . We scarcely know what we mean by the term, though the sound of it draws all whose nerves and emotions have not yet been irreparably stunned, deadened, numbed by the caterwauling of commerce, the sweating scramble for profit and domination." —William deBuys

40

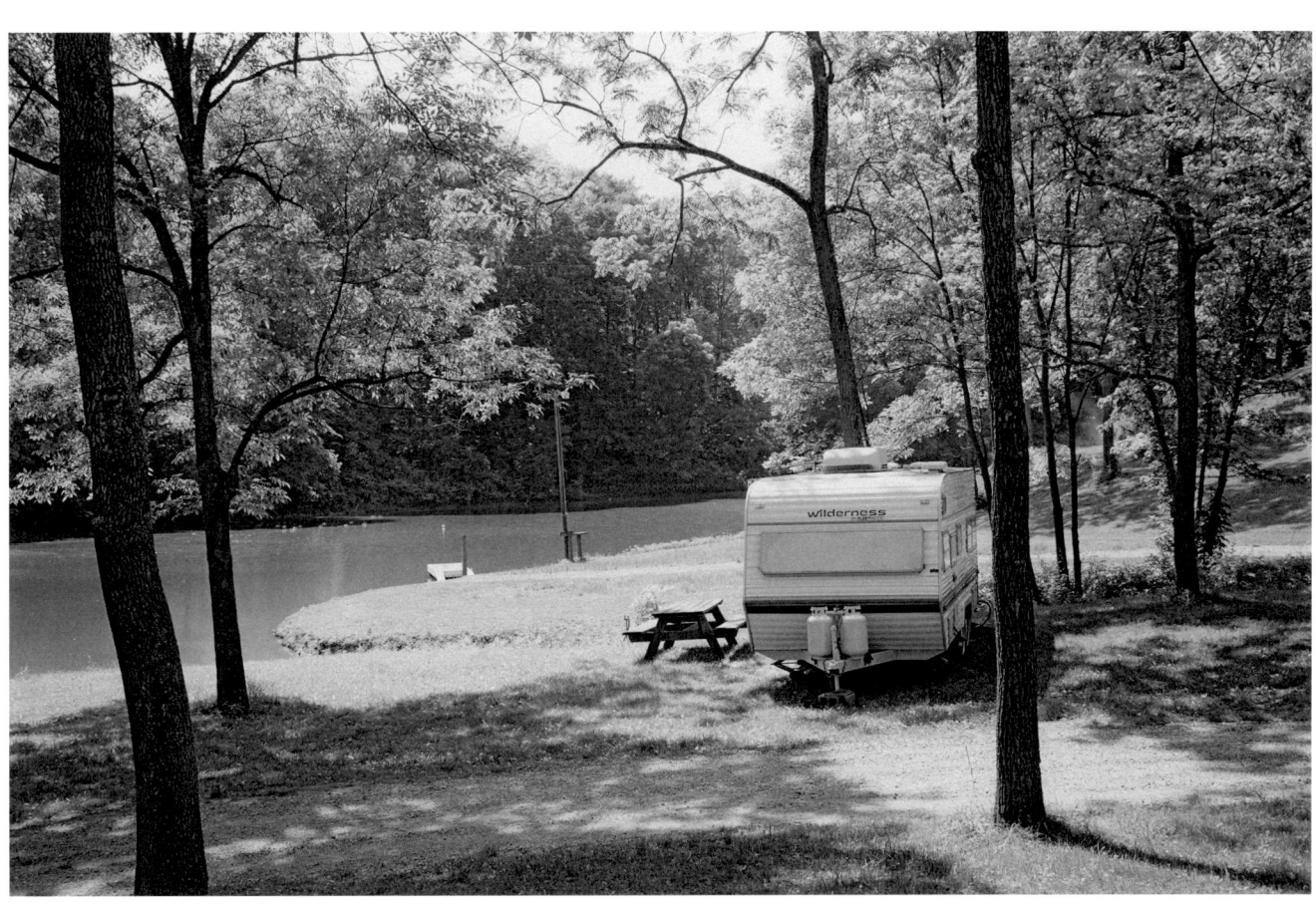

5. Andrew Borowiec   Born New York, NY, 1956 – lives Akron, OH and New York, NY
Meigs County, Ohio, 1998

Meadow   Land covered with grasses, or a grassy field, or other discernable area of grassland either mown for hay or used as pasture is known as a meadow. Also, though rarely, the hay that is mown from this area. The term is used either to denote a "natural" (uncultivated) meadow or one planted to enhance the presence of particular flowers or to discourage the invasion of others. This distinction between an uncultivated and cultivated meadow usually depends on the context in which the word is used. Thus, a meadow can be wild or landscaped, but in general a healthy meadow has fifty percent of its surface in some form of grass. (Subalpine meadows, however, are dominated by herbaceous plants). In North American usage, meadow refers most often, though not exclusively, to a tract of uncultivated grassland, often along a river or in a marshy region, as described by James Galvin in *The Meadow*: "There is an island on the island which is a meadow, offered up among the ridges, wearing a necklace of waterways, concentrically nested inside the darker green of pines, and then the gray-green of sage and the yellow-green of prairie grass." Though rare, meadow can mean—chiefly in Newfoundland—an area of sea ice where seals come out of the water in large numbers, thus also seal meadow. Meadow is often a modifier or part of a compound noun, as in meadow flower, meadowlark, meadow mouse. This modifying habit is especially notable in the names of plants, denoting species that thrive in meadows, such as meadow barley, meadow buttercup, meadow campion, meadow clover, and meadow crocus. Sometimes the linkage creates an entirely new and figurative meaning, as in meadow silver, an obsolete term for a cash payment made in lieu of the feudal service of mowing. Meadow thatch is another such term, meaning the coarse grass or rush used for roofing a cottage. There is as well the term salt meadow, which is a grassy area subject to flooding or overflow by salt water. The etymology of meadow is directly related to mead, the alcoholic beverage made by fermenting honey and water. And mead, in turn, may have been a noun-form of the adjective meaning "sweet" in many old forms of languages as diverse as Frisian, Dutch, Icelandic, Swedish, Gothic, Sanskrit, Irish, Breton, and Church Slavonic.
—Patricia Hampl

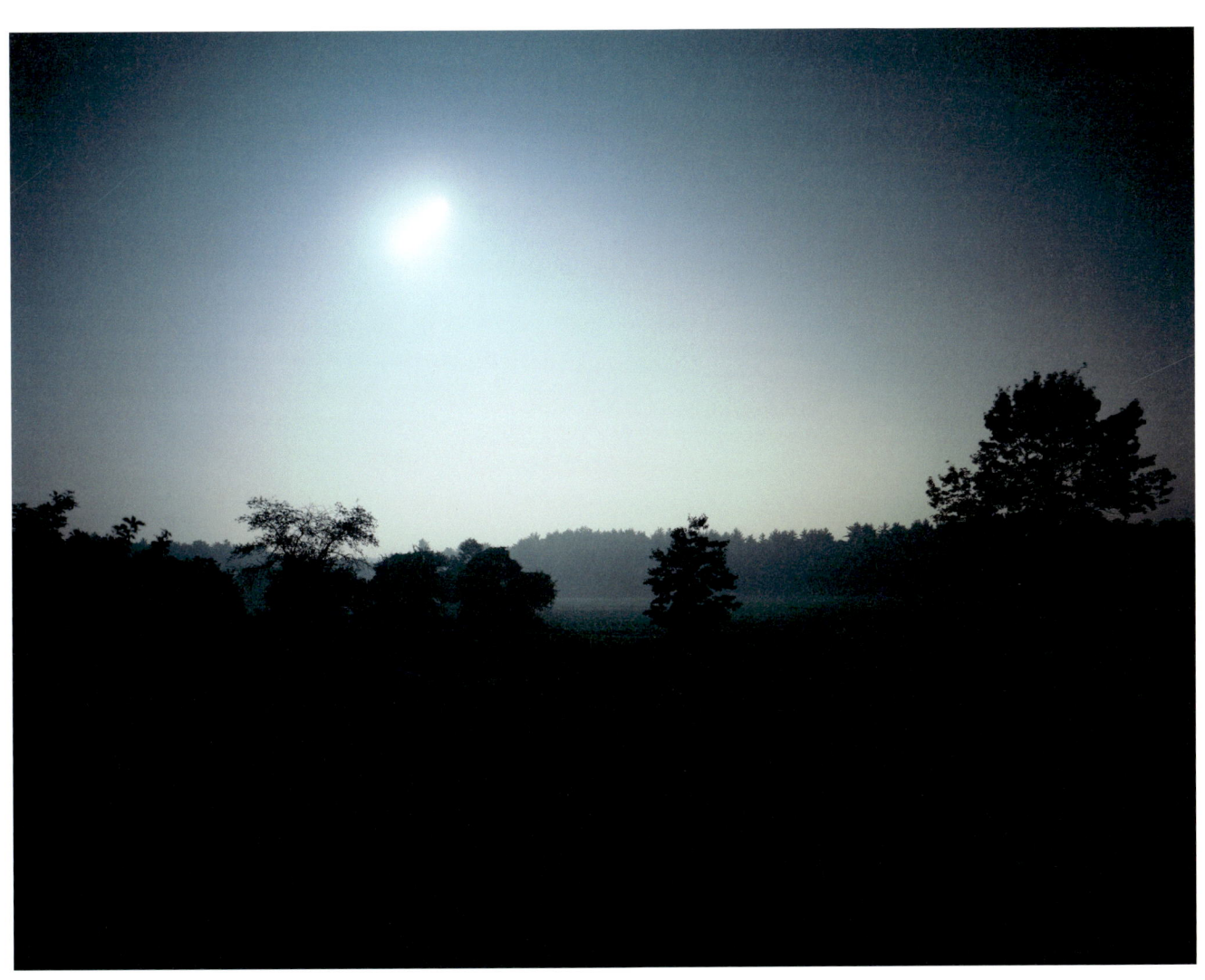

6. Barbara Bosworth   Born Novelty, OH, 1953 – lives Stow, MA
*Moon Rising, the Night the Bird was Singing, Carlisle,
Massachusetts*, 2006

Pool and riffle   Few things assert the dynamism of nature better than the development of pools and riffles in a stream. Even if a channel is straight and the bed uniform, flowing water will generate turbulence. Depending on the resistance of the streambed, this turbulence may scour pools in certain places, which alternate with shallow bars called riffles or drops, where the excavated material is deposited. Generally the distance from one pool to the next is five to seven times the width of the stream, and successive pools will tend to develop on opposite sides of the channel, precursors to the formation of meanders. Very steep streams have step-pool sequences with similar cyclicity. Experienced anglers tend to be attentive to the pattern of pools and riffles, as fish like to wait in the slow water of a pool while watching for food to arrive from the faster flow of an upstream riffle. —William deBuys

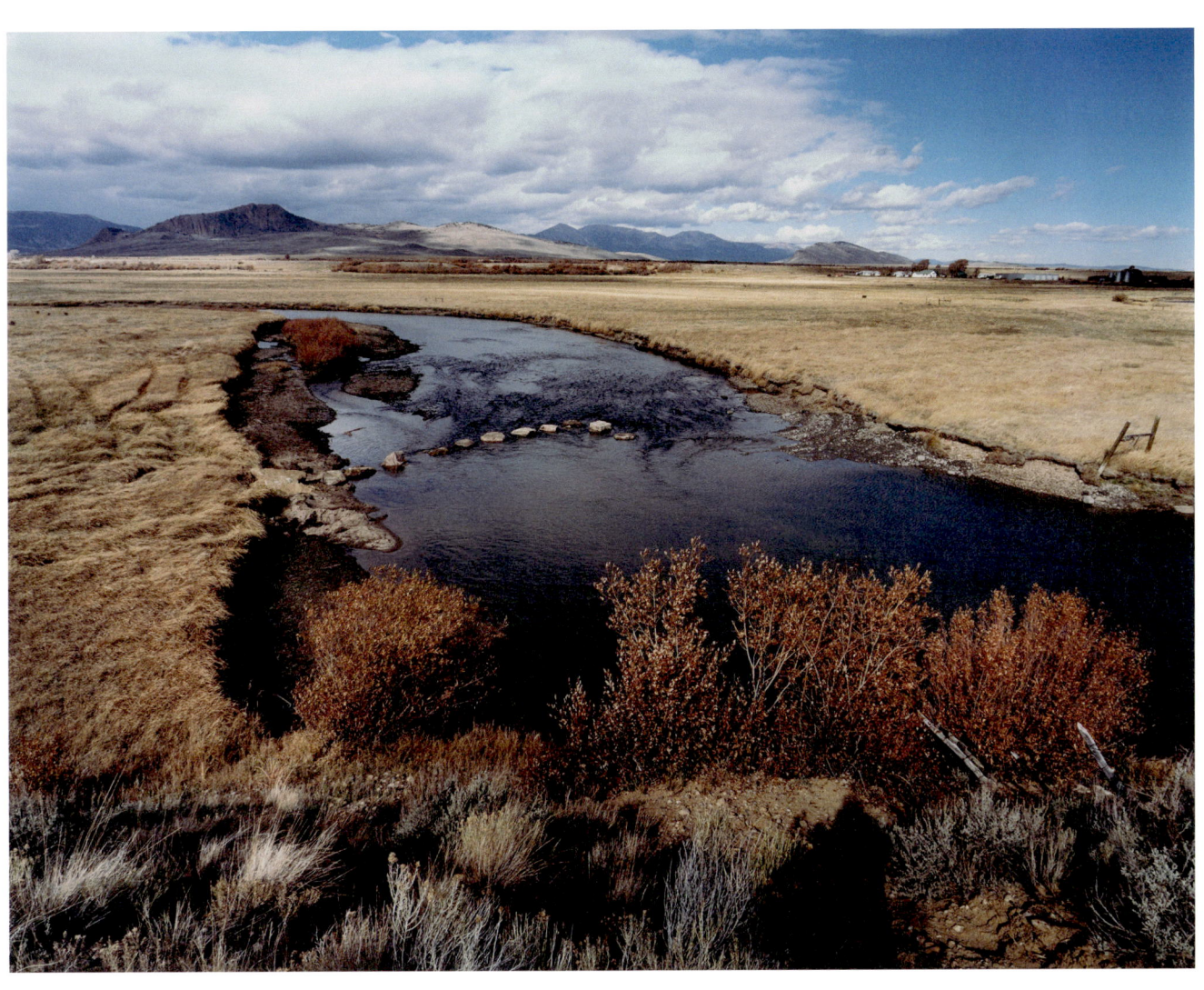

7. Joann Brennan   Born Philadelphia, PA, 1962 – lives Denver, CO
North Platte River Reclamation, Walden, Colorado, 2000

Badlands   Badlands are regions dissected into steep hills and deep gullies by the action of wind, rain, and flash floods. The name was originally applied to a semiarid area in South Dakota east of the Black Hills, called *les mauvaises terres à traverser* by the French because it was so difficult to cross; the term is now generally applied to similar lands throughout the continent. In *All the Strange Hours*, Loren Eiseley writes: "I will never forget my first day of registration at the University of Pennsylvania. I had come directly from the Mauvaises terres, the Tertiary badlands of western Nebraska, into a great city of banging, jangling trolleys, out of a silence as dreadful as that of the moon." The friable topography of the Badlands, composed primarily of shales, clays, and sandstones, has been sculpted into a maze of barren ravines and tunnels, and grassy-topped tables. (The sparse vegetation is deceptive; while puny on the slopes, it can be comparatively lush on the flat tops.) The average slope angle in the heart of this desiccated world often exceeds thirty-five degrees—steep enough to drive rain from seasonal summer thunderstorms downhill with scouring force, leaving the sides of the tables looking barren and peeled. The Lakota Sioux name for the Dakota Badlands is *Mako Sica*, meaning "eroded land," a region they were wary of. During the Ghost Dance conflicts of the late 1800s, diehard Lakota warriors assembled on remote tables in the depths of the Badlands, out of sight of white authorities who feared the dancing would foment an outbreak of violence. —Conger Beasley, Jr.

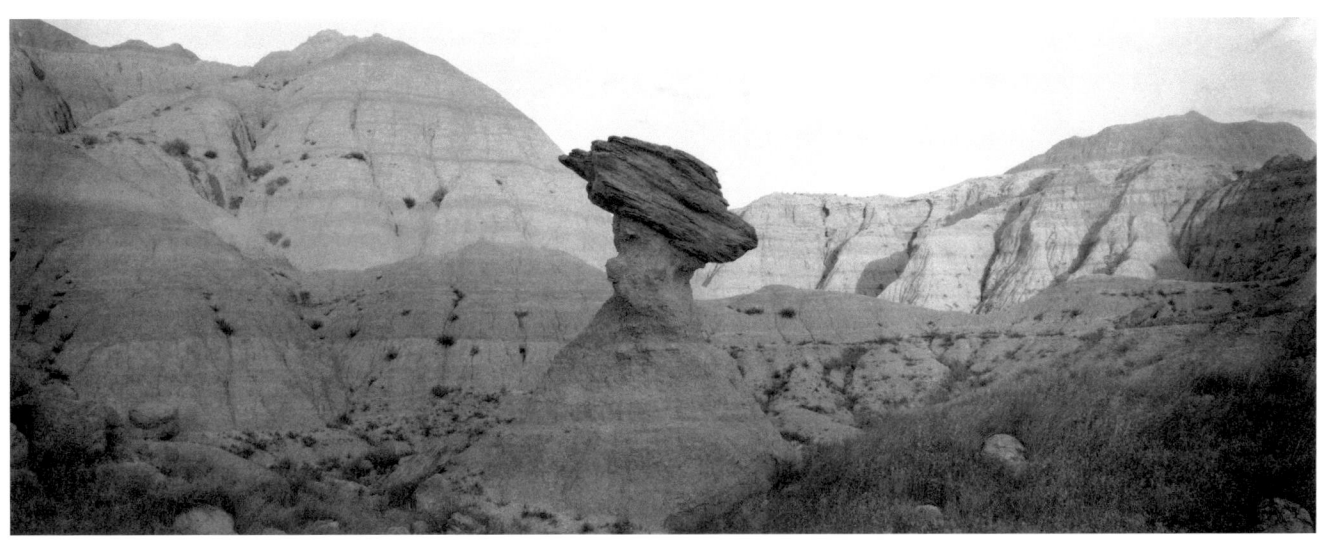

8. Lois Conner   Born Rockville Centre, NY, 1951 – lives New York, NY
Badlands National Park, South Dakota, 1996

Yard   You can hear in yard its resemblance to garden and girdle. All three words arise from a root meaning "to enclose, surround." The most familiar sort of yard is the plot of ground surrounding a house, often planted in grass, flowers, and bushes—hence the ubiquitous yard sales and laborious yard work. Nearly as familiar, and probably older, is the use of yard to describe a plot of ground that is itself enclosed by a fence or wall and devoted to a specific purpose, as in a farmyard, churchyard, or shipyard. When loggers haul felled trees to a landing, they are said to be yarding. By analogy to the pen where poultry and livestock are kept, yard also means a place where deer or moose gather to feed in winter.
—Scott Russell Sanders

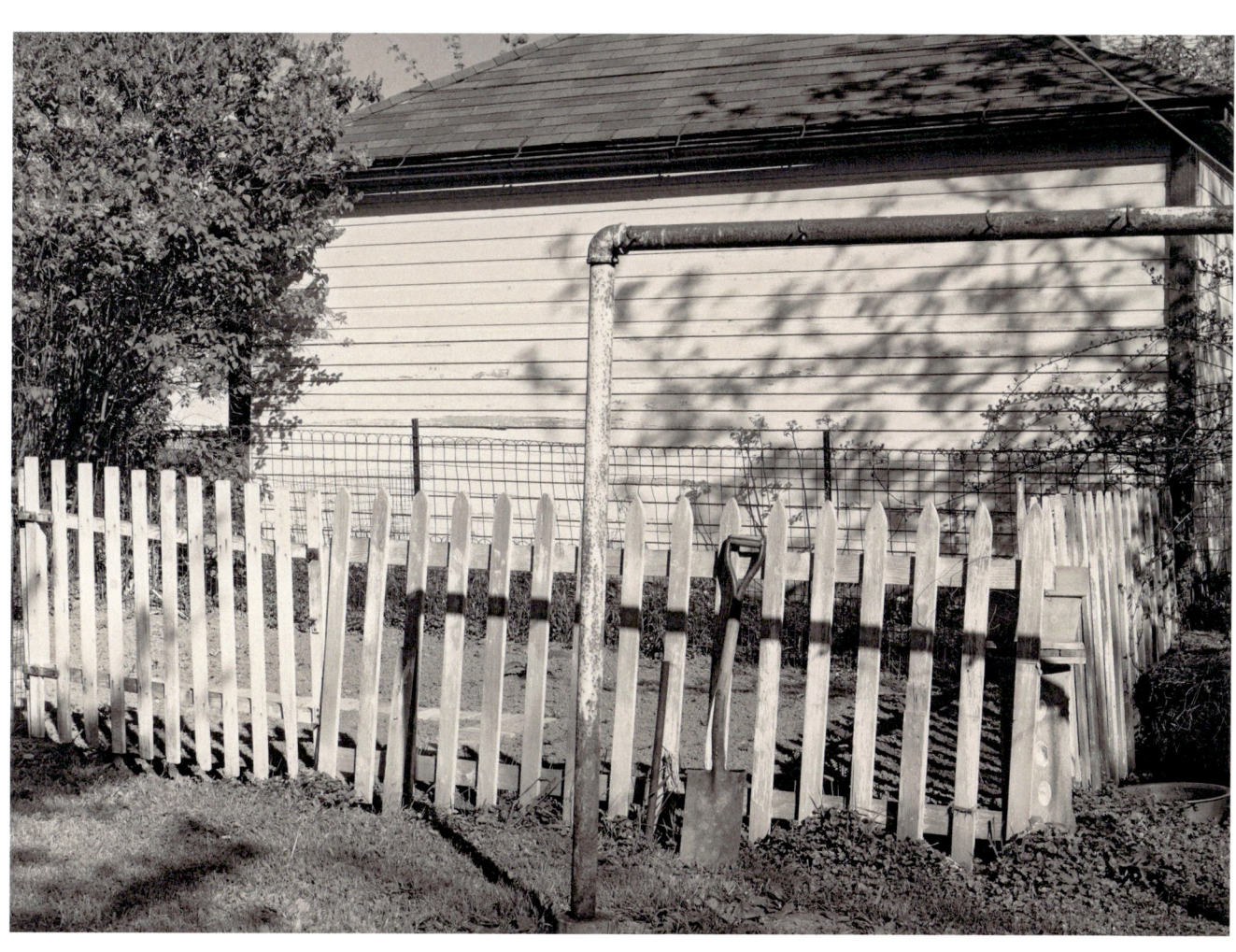

9. Gregory Conniff   Born Jersey City, NJ, 1944 – lives Madison, WI
Madison, Wisconsin, 1979

Pāhoehoe Galway Kinnell captures the marked differences in the con-
gealed flows of the two types of lava erupted by Hawaiian
volcanoes in his poem "Lava": smooth, ropy pāhoehoe is "a
clear brazened surface/one can cross barefooted," while jagged 'a'ā resembles "a mass of rubble still/ tumbling." These
terms are now standard for Western geologists describing
the highly fluid basalt erupted by shield volcanoes (though
Icelanders have their own names: *helluhraun* for pāhoehoe
and *apalhraun* for 'a'ā). As it cools, a slow-moving pāhoehoe
flow may solidify into fantastic forms: geologists speak of
entrail, as well as filamented, corded, sharkskin, slab, and
shelly pāhoehoe. What Hawai'i residents call blue rock is an
unusually dense basalt sometimes encountered when cutting roads through old lava. —Pamela Frierson

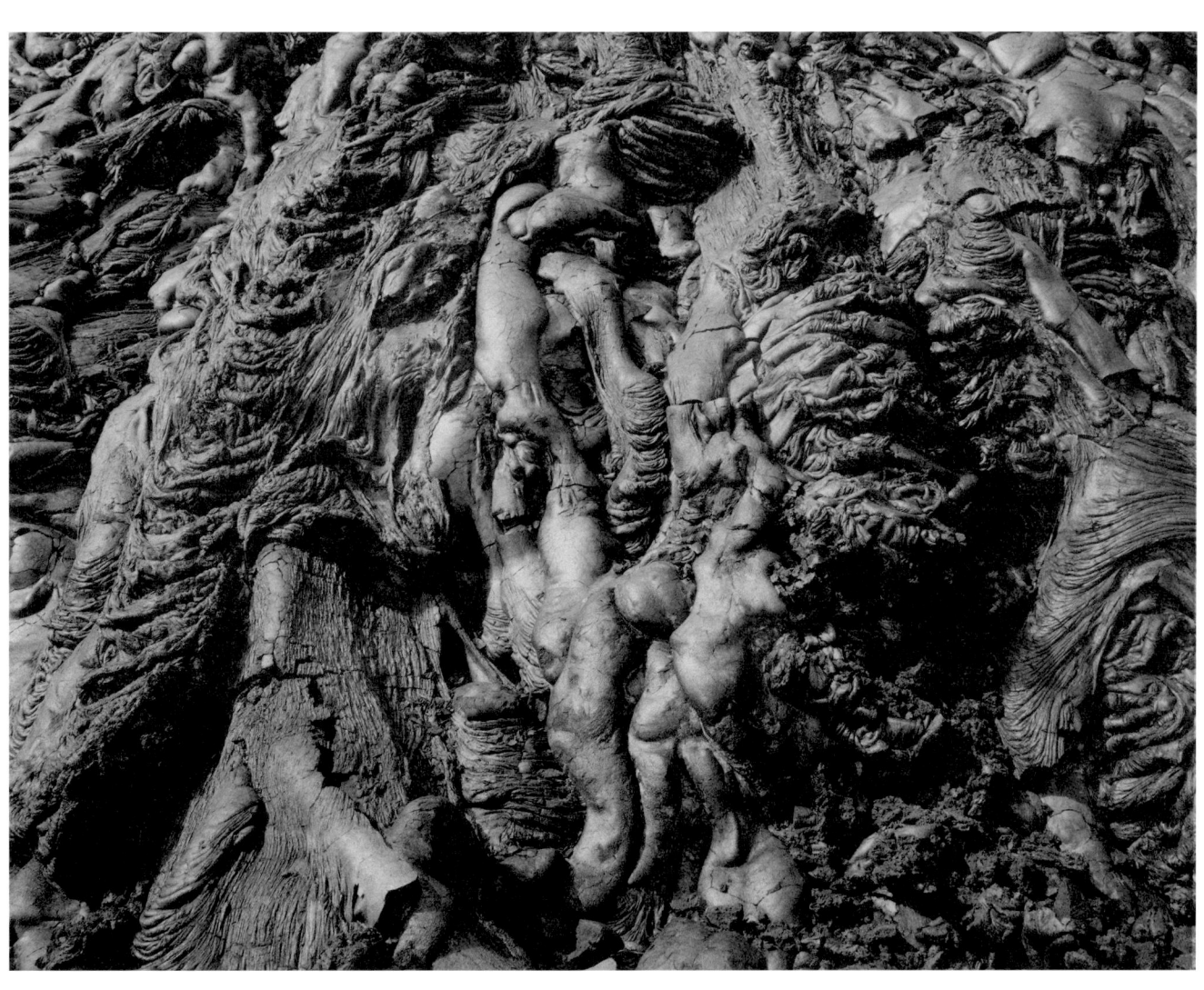

10. Linda Connor   Born New York, NY, 1944 – lives San Francisco, CA
Lava, Hawaii, 1979

Cauldron   A particularly chaotic type of gaping river hole, a cauldron is characterized by "big, squirrelly, boily water," in the words of one river runner. River cauldrons form where rocks, which have accumulated on the riverbed at a spot where the river suddenly drops, scour out a bowl-shaped depression. The surface of the river churns and explodes here like soup boiling over in a pot. Sulphur Cauldron, on the upper Yellowstone River in northwestern Wyoming, is one of many famed river cauldrons. Cauldrons are also a seacoast feature. When ocean swells and breakers surge into constricted openings in the seaward face of the land, they sometimes produce ferocious hydraulics—violent whirlpools, geysers, and suddenly collapsing haystacks of white water. —Terry Tempest Williams

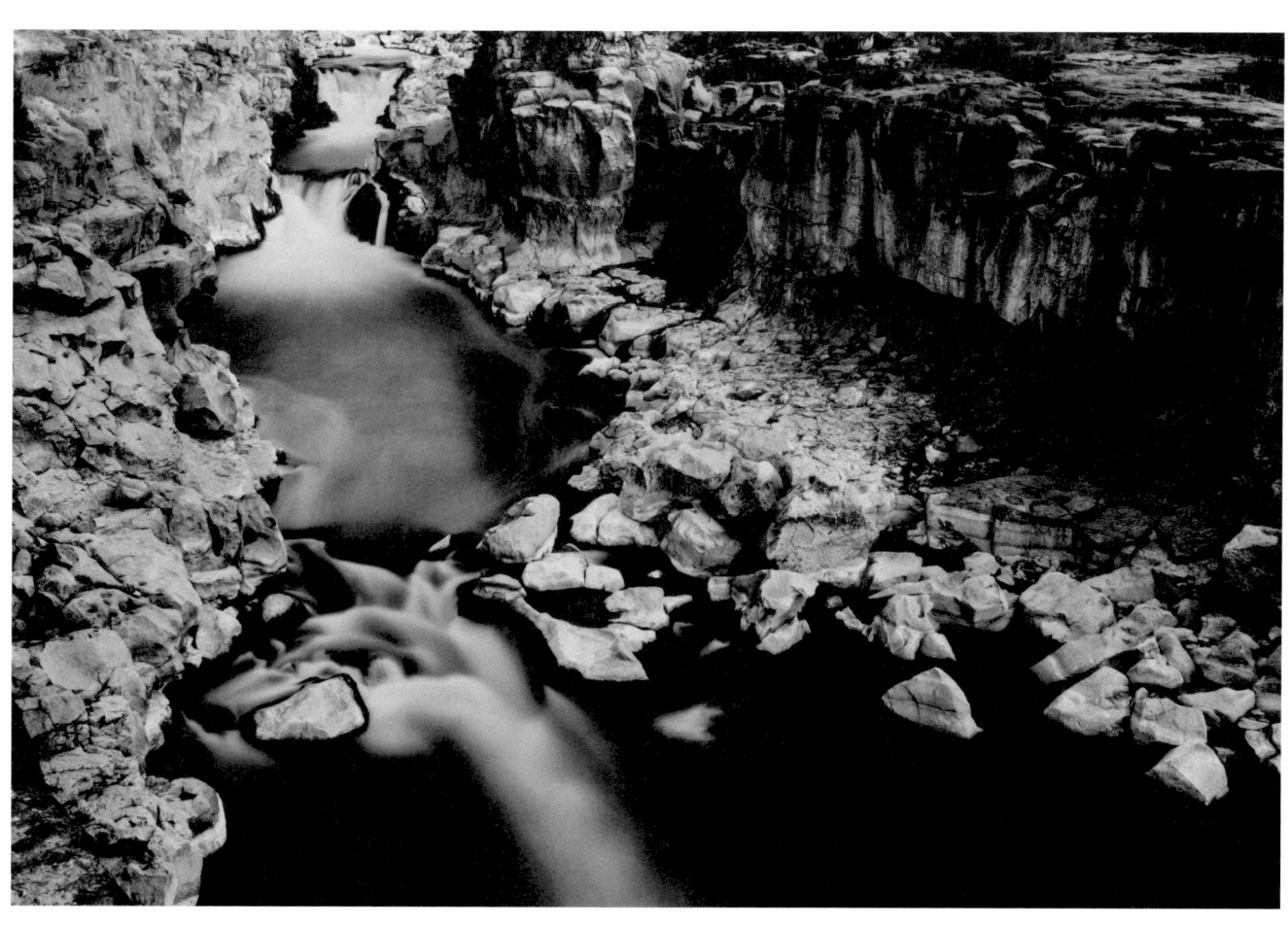

11. Thomas Joshua Cooper   Born San Francisco, CA, 1946 – lives Glasgow, Scotland
*The Snake River / Cauldron Linn, No. 2 / Jerome County,
Idaho*, 2003–2004

Glory hole   The term glory hole can refer to a cylindrical feature in a reservoir, built right in front of the dam, designed to keep the dam from being overtopped—that is, if the water gets too high, it flows into the glory hole and is transported under the dam and downstream. However, glory hole is most often used as a mining term. Originally conjured during the gold rush to describe the process employed by those miners who could not afford conventional and more sophisticated extraction methods, the glory hole was the single shaft dug straight down in hopes of happening upon a gold seam. The Glory Hole near Central City, Colorado, for instance, was once part of the most productive gold mining area in the world. In modern mining, the term has come to signify the belowground cavern—whether natural or man-made—from which material is mined. This contemporary sense, ironically, harks back to another colloquial use of the term to mean any small room or cupboard, or, in the instance of Jack London's novel *Michael, Brother of Jerry*, the hidden locker at the stern of a ship. Connotatively, the expression indicates both the means to, and the chamber of, secret and sequestered booty. —Antonya Nelson

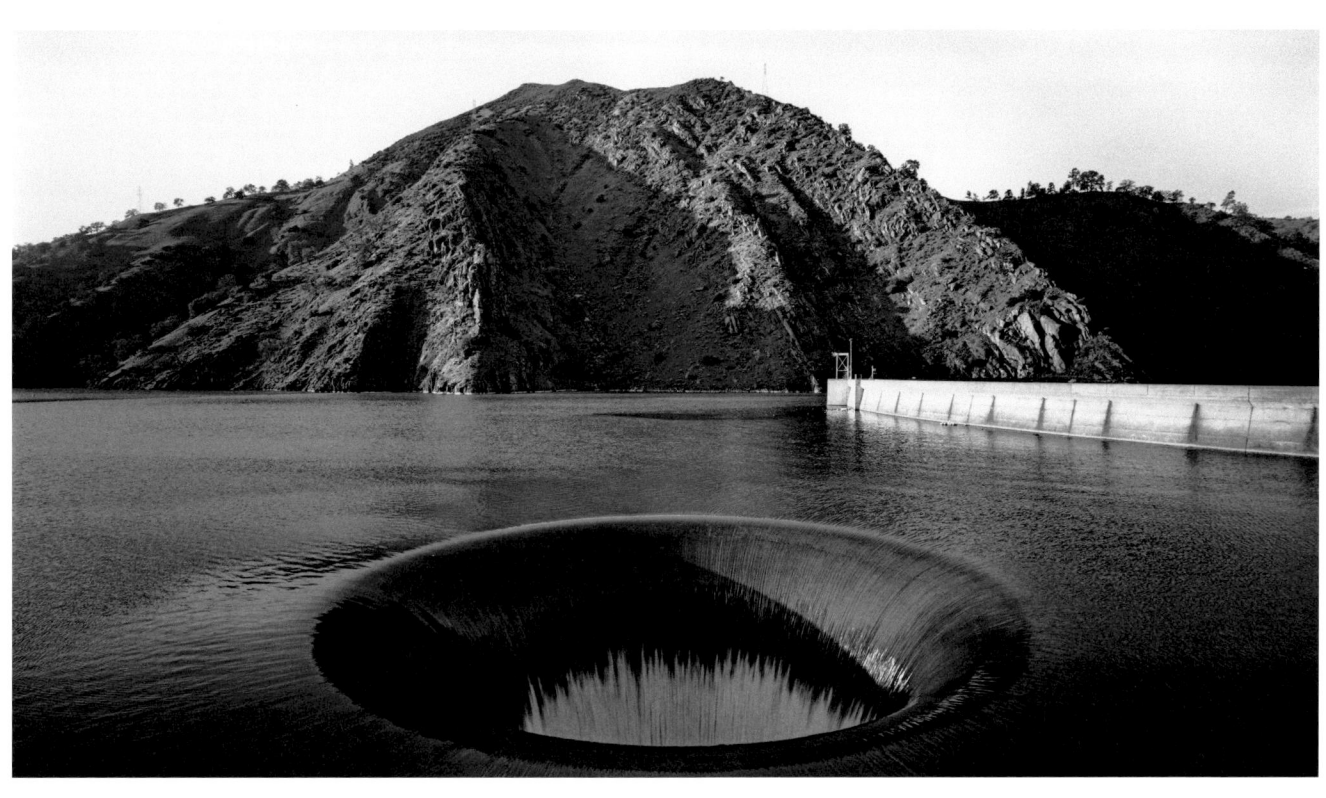

12. Robert Dawson   Born Sacramento, CA, 1950 – lives San Francisco, CA
Spillway, Lake Berryessa, California, 1986

Slot canyon   Slot, or slit, canyons are rare formations, the result of the combined forces of wind and water on sandstone. The narrow crevice sliced through a mesa by rushing water evolves from a hairline crack into a series of convoluted hollows, in some instances stacked many stories high. Little light enters, but its quality, as filtered, refracted, reflected, and observed from below, illuminates incandescent striations of the sandstone as it has been etched over centuries by the flow of subterranean rivers. In 1931, a twelve-year-old girl was herding sheep in what is now the Navajo Indian Reservation in the Four Corners region when she discovered the country's best-known slot canyon. It's most often called Antelope Canyon, but is also referred to as Corkscrew, Upper Antelope, Wind Cave, or the Crack. A slot canyon that looks as if it has been cut out of sandstone with a saw is called a saw-cut canyon. Most U.S. examples of this feature are found in Arizona's Glen Canyon, and include Labyrinth Canyon, which is about three miles of a twisting, turning passage that's no more than two or three feet wide at the bottom and hundreds of feet high. —Antonya Nelson

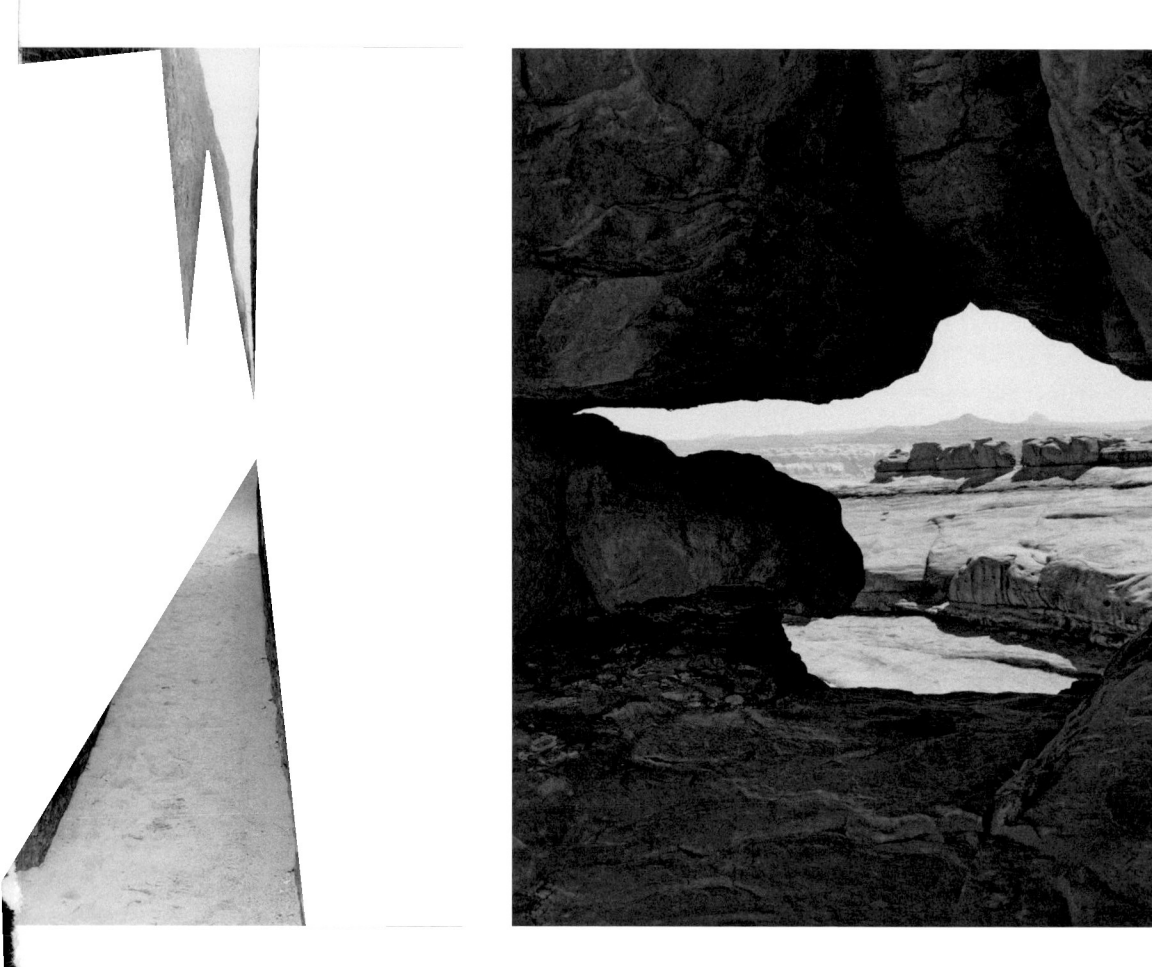

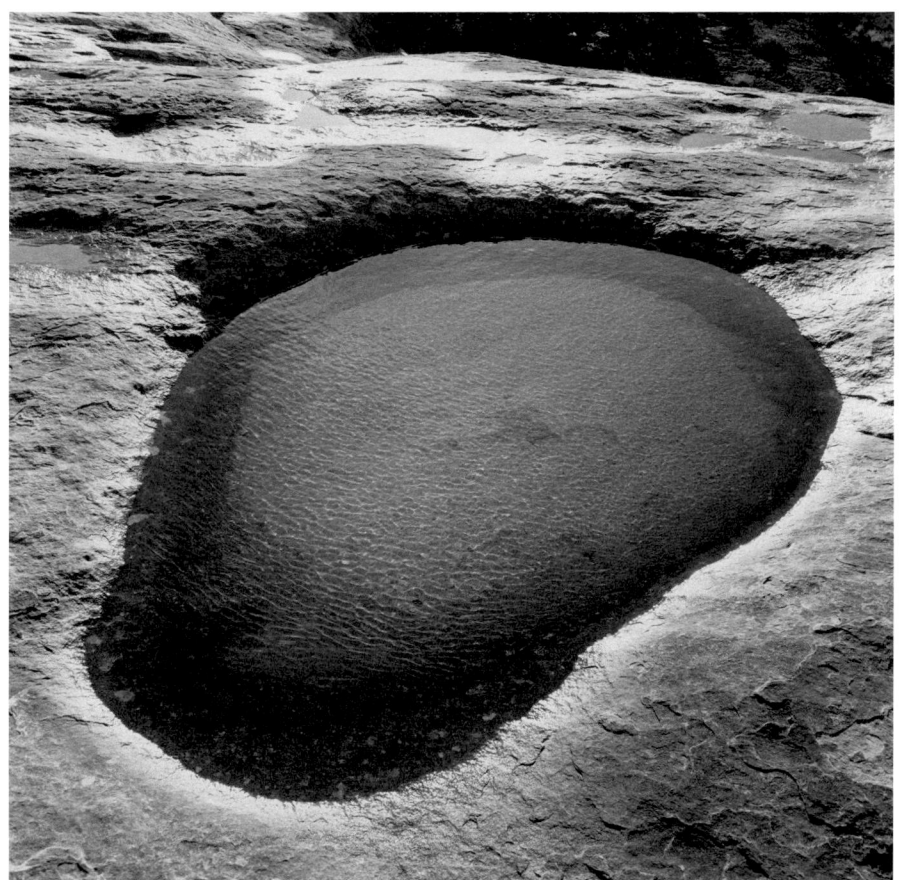

13. Peter de Lory   Born Fall River, MA, 1948 – lives Seattle, WA
Canyonlands Saunter: Slick Rock Pool; The Narrows;
Peek-a-Boo Canyon, Canyonlands National Park, Utah, 1997

Horizon   The horizon or sensible horizon is, first of all, the visible place where earth, or sea, and sky appear to meet. At a hundred feet above sea level, the horizon is approximately fourteen miles away. The word has other technical meanings. A true, astronomical, or celestial horizon in astronomy is the circle on the celestial sphere whose plane is at right angles to the visible horizon. In geology, the horizon is the plane of a stratified surface containing a particular series of fossils. In soil science, it is a layer of soil in a cross section of land. In literature it is, of course, often a symbol for opportunity, especially if it is out of reach. Here is Zora Neale Hurston in *Their Eyes Were Watching God*: "Ships at a distance have every man's wish on board. For some they come in with their tide. For others they sail forever on the horizon, never out of sight, never landing until the Watcher turns his eyes away in resignation." In the plural horizons can be sequences of days, as in this seascape from Wallace Stevens's "The Idea of Order at Key West": "Theatrical distances, bronze shadows heaped/On high horizons, mountainous atmospheres/Of sea and sky." —Robert Hass

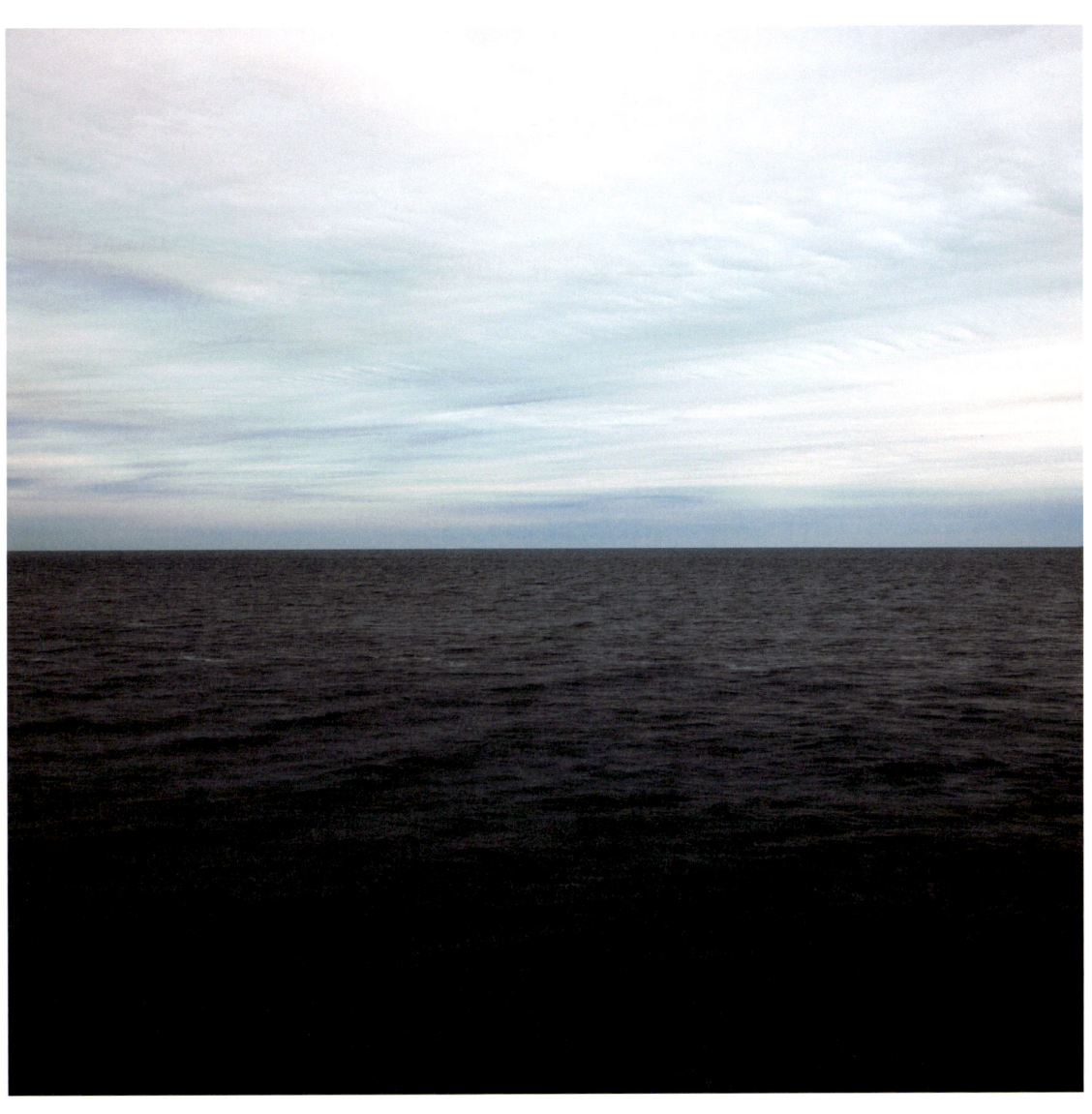

14. Lucinda Devlin   Born Ann Arbor, MI, 1947 – lives Belmont, NC
Lake Huron, 5-10-2011 8:43 pm, 2011

Sandhill Landlocked and located far from existing coastlines, some sandhills are the remains of dune fields and beaches once amassed along the shores of ancient oceans; others are the windblown products of erosion. Like present-day coastal dunes, sandhills are eolian landforms, shaped by winds acting on plentiful supplies of sand. Their various locations—southwest from the Texas Panhandle; miles inland from the Carolina and Georgia coasts; in the heartland of Nebraska—are a geological timepiece, marking these notably dry regions as former marine and riverine habitats. The Carolina Sandhills, for instance, indicate that the Atlantic Ocean was once much higher than today, its waves anciently crashing near the present-day Piedmont fall line. The extensive 24,000-square-mile sandhill region of Nebraska has a more complex history: blown sand from ancient river deposits eroded from the sandstones of the Rocky Mountains, which were, in turn, the former seabed of an ancient inland sea that vanished as the North American continent and mountains were uplifted. In time the sandstone of the newly formed mountains began to erode; the resulting sand (along with silt and gravel) was transported across the plains by braided rivers, blanketing the plains east of the mountains. Then, over the last several million years, new rivers dissected the mass of sand, carrying some away, and exposing some to wind. Through differential wind-generated erosion, the finest particles were blown eastward to form loess deposits in Iowa; the heavier sand-sized particles remained behind and were moved only a short distance, forming the Nebraska Sandhills. Vast and undulating, ranging up to six hundred feet high, sandhills are majestic, serene, and elemental places. For many of the Plains Indians, they were sacred, the final home for departed spirits. The term has been applied to towns (Sandhill, Texas); entertainment facilities (Sandhills Drive-In Theater, Box Butte, Nebraska); a magnificent bird (the sandhill crane); and historically, to inhabitants of the pinelands of South Carolina and Georgia, who were known as sand-hillers.
—Emily Hiestand

60

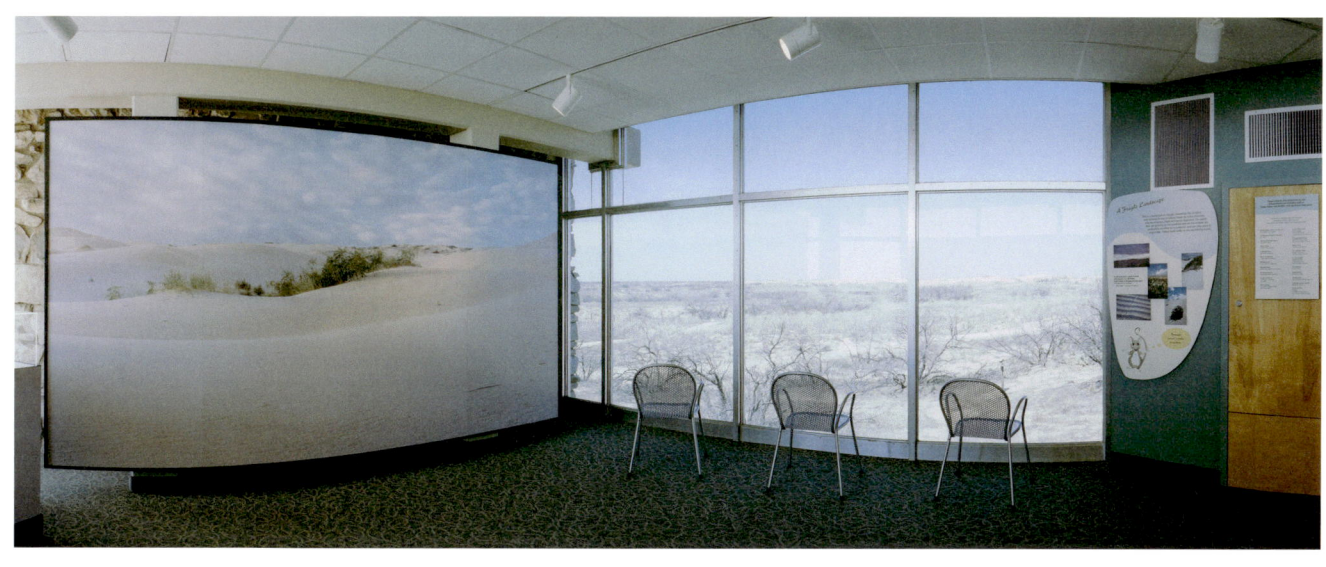

15. Rick Dingus   Born Appleton City, MO, 1951 – lives Bend, OR
Visitor Center, Monahans Sandhills State Park, Texas, 2004

Meander   The river Menderes, which rises in what is today western Turkey and was known among the ancient Greeks as the Maiandros of Phrygia, flows to the Aegean with such seeming reluctance that it continually doubles back on itself, wreathing its floodplain in loop after serpentine loop of wandering channel. The name of the river, descended to modern English from Greek, gives us meander, which is our best verb for expressing randomness in thought and movement. The coinage is not without its irony, however, for the meandering of a river is only superficially random. If one thinks of a river or stream as energy moving through terrain, one can begin to see the ordered sinuosity of a meandering channel as the expression of how that energy is spent by the river and absorbed by the land. A river does two kinds of work: it transports its volume of water downhill, and it also transports some amount of earthen freight consisting of silt suspended in water (suspended load) and rocks and gravel tumbling along the riverbed (bed load). If by virtue of velocity or volume a river has more energy than it needs to accomplish its work, it will spend that extra energy to reshape its course. Sometimes a river will incise its channel, ultimately lowering its bed, which is a way of diminishing the gradient at which it moves downhill; this in turn diminishes its velocity and the energy it has to spend. In other instances a river will extend its channel laterally by carving a series of curves or meanders. Here the river diminishes its gradient by lengthening the distance over which it descends a given amount of elevation. Meander formation is especially characteristic of rivers that flow through soft material and lack the erosive tools (i.e., bed load) to incise their channels. The Mississippi, twining from Cairo, Illinois, to New Orleans, is a classic meanderer, while the canyon-carving Colorado River is the Mississippi's incisive opposite. The physics of meandering are consistent across all scales of flowing water, from great streams like the Mississippi to rivulets of meltwater on the surface of a glacier. Notably, the distance from the apex of one meander to the next, known as the wavelength of the meander, tends to be seven to fifteen times the width of the channel. Also noteworthy is the fact that meandering is not restricted to terrestrial waters and distractible humans. Ocean currents like the Gulf Stream meander, as do the jet stream and other currents of air. —William deBuys

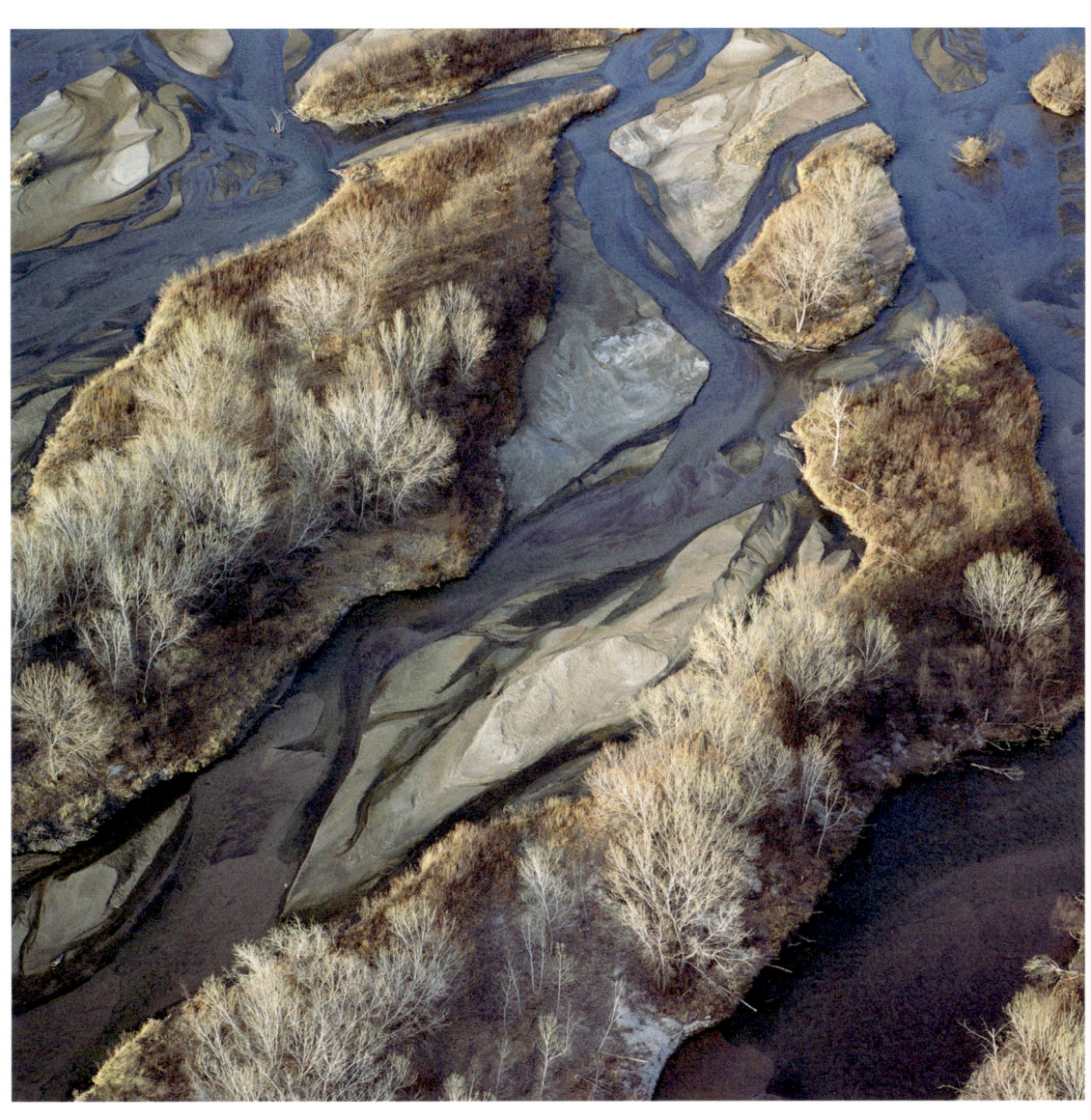

16. Terry Evans Born Kansas City, MO, 1944 – lives Chicago, IL
Platte River, Nebraska, 1990

Foothill The base of a mountain or a mountain range is usually ringed or lined by a series of low rises. These are called foothills. The western slope of California's Sierra Nevada offers a spectacular example of a complex and manifold system of foothills. Starting east of Sacramento it begins as soft, elevated undulations that develop into rounded but steeper and eventually sharper hills, morphing into one of the most sublime North American mountain ranges. A more gentle and extended range of foothills is the Piedmont area of the Middle Atlantic States, stretching from Maryland through the Carolinas. Compared with the ascendant and aristocratic peaks and ridges presiding above them, foothills are like steady commoners who occupy a middle ground between flatland and mountains. One feels at home in this proletarian landscape, consoled and reassured by its human scale. —Michael Collier

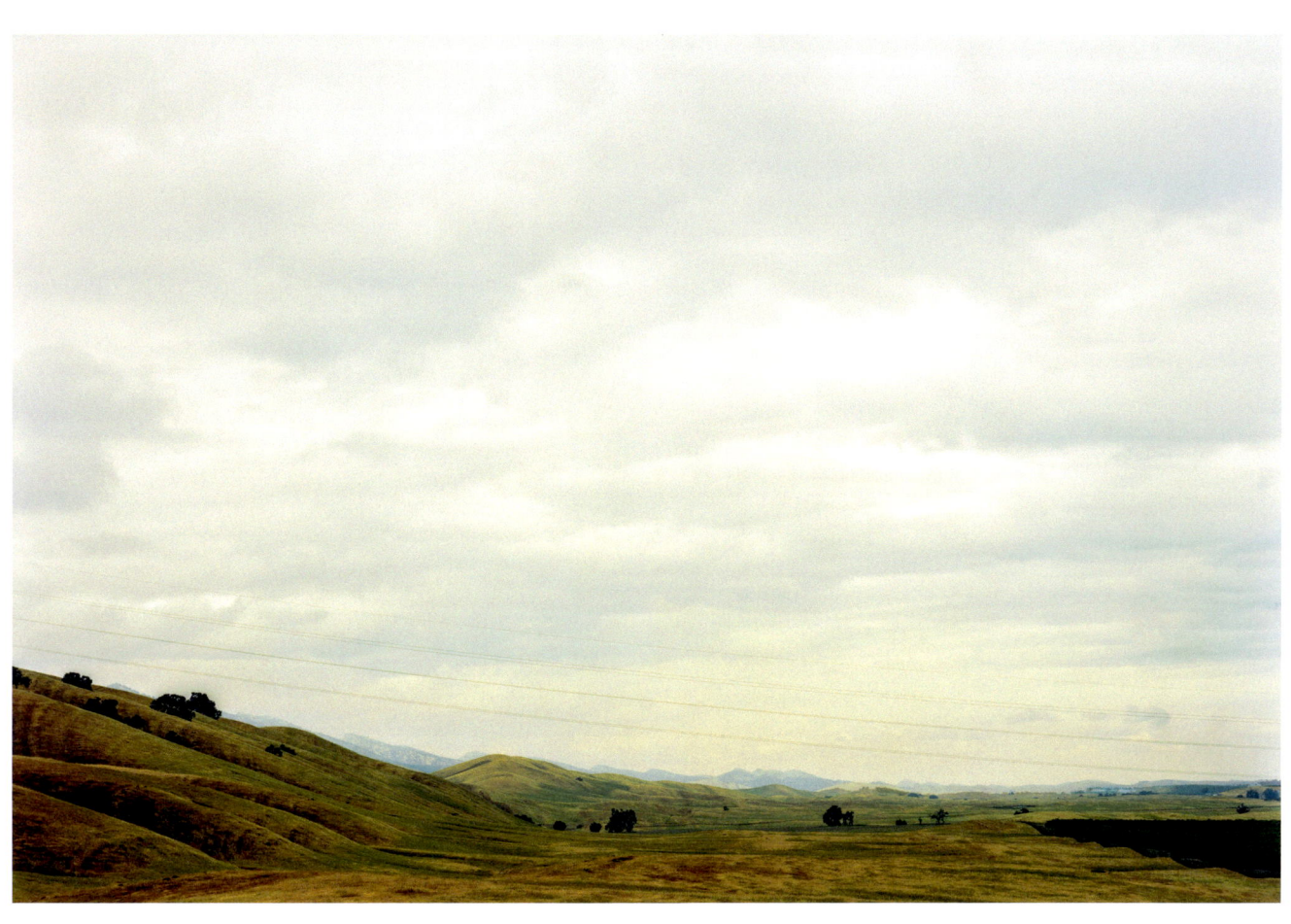

17. Lukas Felzmann   Born Zürich, Switzerland, 1959 – lives San Francisco, CA
The Western Edge of the Sacramento Valley, California,
2009

Basin A basin is a large hollow or depression in the earth, either erosional or structural in origin; it is also a region that is drained by a river and its tributaries. The Mississippi River and its tributaries drain a basin that covers approximately two-fifths of the coterminous United States. The term basin also applies to an area of inland drainage where rivers unable to reach the sea flow into lakes or evaporate in playas. The Great Basin, centered in western Utah and Nevada, is a prime example. A cold desert in the Basin and Range province, the Great Basin encompasses Death Valley, nuclear bomb test sites, and Yucca Mountain, a proposed nuclear-waste storage site. In his book *Basin and Range*, John McPhee describes the Great Basin as "an ocean of loose sediment with these mountain ranges standing in it as if they were members of a fleet without precedent." The term is also widely used for many of the land's bowl-shaped features, such as a ski basin in a single mountain. In her poem "The Matrix," Amy Lowell writes: "Brown-lily-pads lie heavy and supine/Within a granite basin, under one/The bronze-gold glimmer of a carp; and I/Reach out my hand and pluck a nectarine." —Donna Seaman

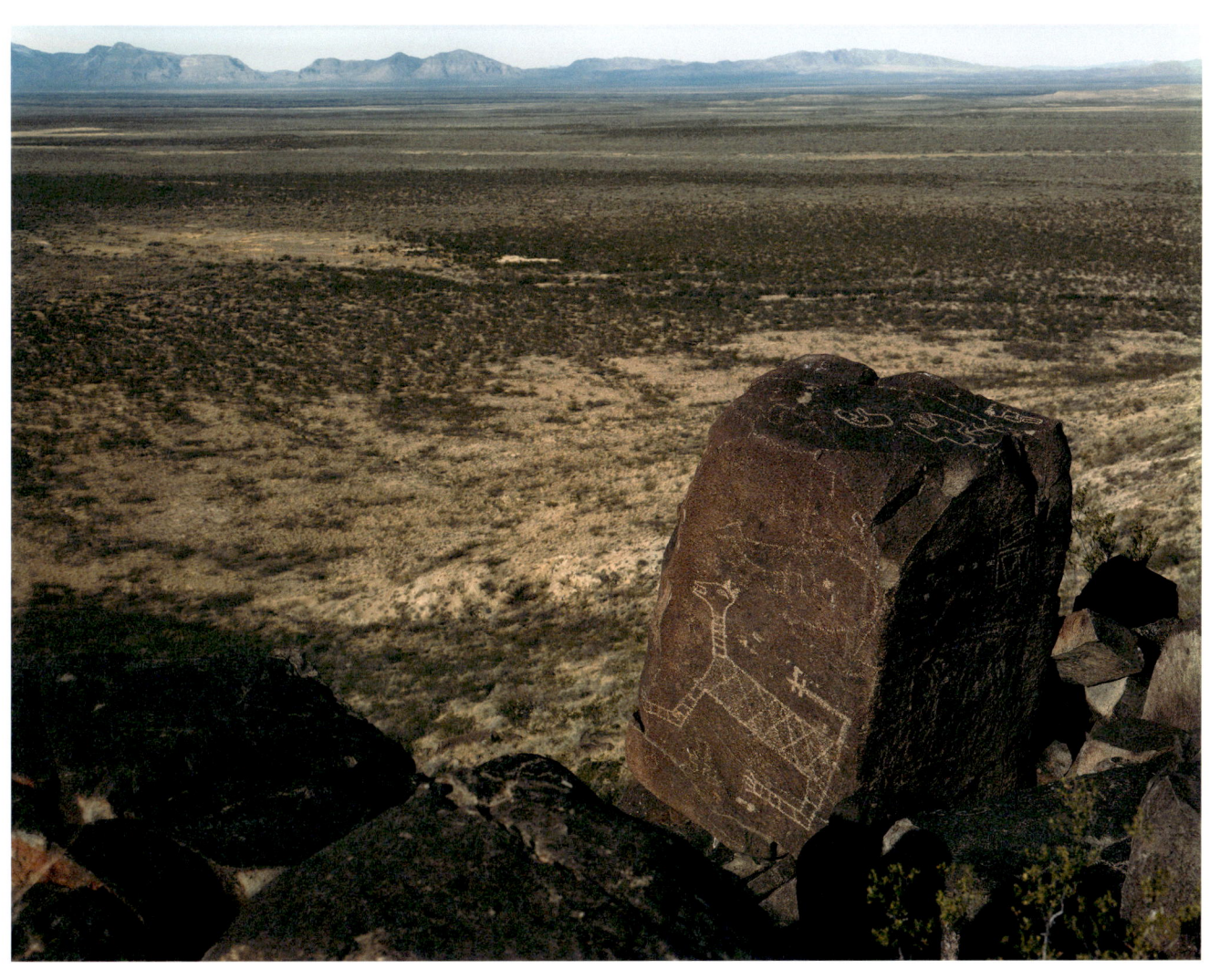

18. Steve Fitch   Born Tucson, AZ, 1949 – lives Santa Fe County, NM
Jaguar with a Rattlesnake Tail Petroglyph, Overlooking the
Tularosa Basin and Trinity Site, Three Rivers, New Mexico,
January 10, 1983, 1983

Lahar   Javanese for rapid mudflow associated with volcanic activity, a lahar is created when volcanic ash is converted into a mobile paste by water from torrential rain, snowmelt, or breaching of the walls of a crater lake. This fluid landslide may spread many miles from the source volcano when confined along preexisting valleys: the five-thousand-year-old Osceola Lahar of Puget Sound in Washington is up to five hundred feet thick and extends over two hundred square miles. When the Electron Lahar that swept from Mount Rainier about five hundred years ago was excavated in 1993, remnants of an old-growth forest were exposed. Associated with lahars are *nuées ardentes*, French for glowing clouds—highly mobile, turbulent, and sometimes incandescent clouds erupted from a volcano and containing large amounts of ash and other pyroclastics. Such a mixture, once it settles, is quite fluid, and it can move rapidly down even a gentle slope. When the mixture comes to rest, the hot glass fragments meld together, forming a welded tuff. It was an eruption of this kind from Mount Vesuvius that buried the city of Pompeii in A.D. 79. In 1985, more than twenty-three thousand people were killed by a lahar that swept through Armero, Colombia. Lahars are, in fact, often catastrophic and the cause of most volcanic fatalities, which is why the United States Geological Survey recently instituted a pilot project in Washington called the Mount Rainier Volcano Lahar Warning System. —Kim Barnes

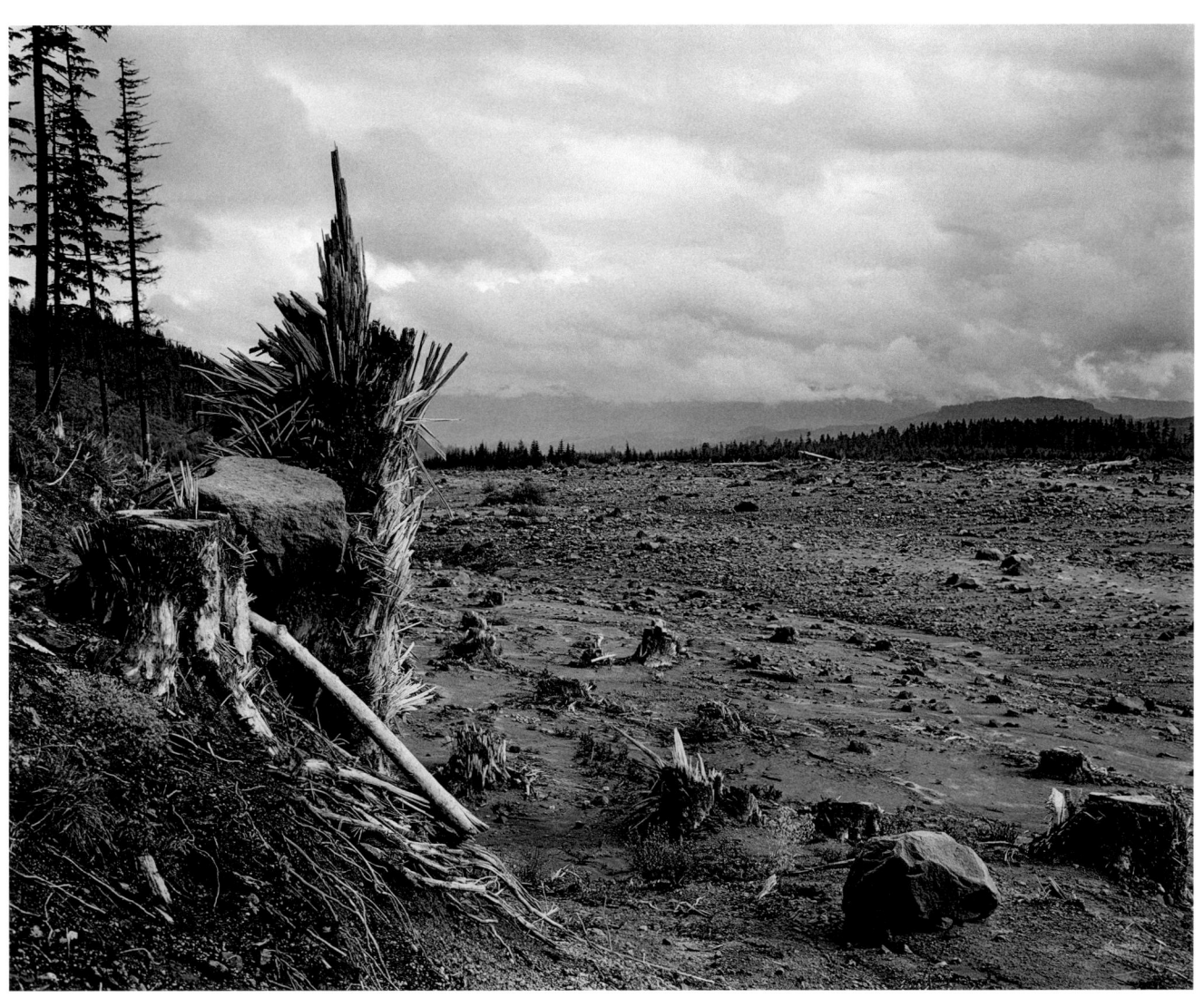

19. Frank Gohlke   Born Wichita Falls, TX, 1942 – lives Tucson, AZ
Looking Southeast across Lahar (mud flow), Six Miles
Southeast of Mount St. Helen's, Washington, 1983

Tapestry wall   Sheets of darker colors seem to hang like curtains on the faces of many canyon walls in arid environments. The towering, buff-colored sandstone cliffs of Canyon de Chelly in northeastern Arizona, for example, which are famously revealed in the photographs of Edward Curtis and others, seem draped with umber hangings. The patterns of color on such tapestry walls record the patterns of water spills and seeps that periodically irrigate the walls with snowmelt and storm runoff. When the water evaporates, it leaves behind microscopic deposits of the minerals it once contained. These minerals gradually oxidize, perhaps as a result of the metabolic activity of bacteria that colonize the rock, and the buildup of oxides, rusty to brown where iron is dominant, accounts for the contrasting colors of the tapestry. Vegetation can also produce the impression of a tapestry hanging on the sheer face of a cliff or canyon wall. Vesey's Paradise in the Grand Canyon, for example, is fed by a spring that pours from a seam high on the side of the lower canyon. A jungle of green seems to hang from the mouth of the spring, and, notwithstanding that much of this vegetation consists of nettle and poison ivy, such a profusion of green in a sere and sun-blasted environment gives an impression of a kind of Eden. —William deBuys

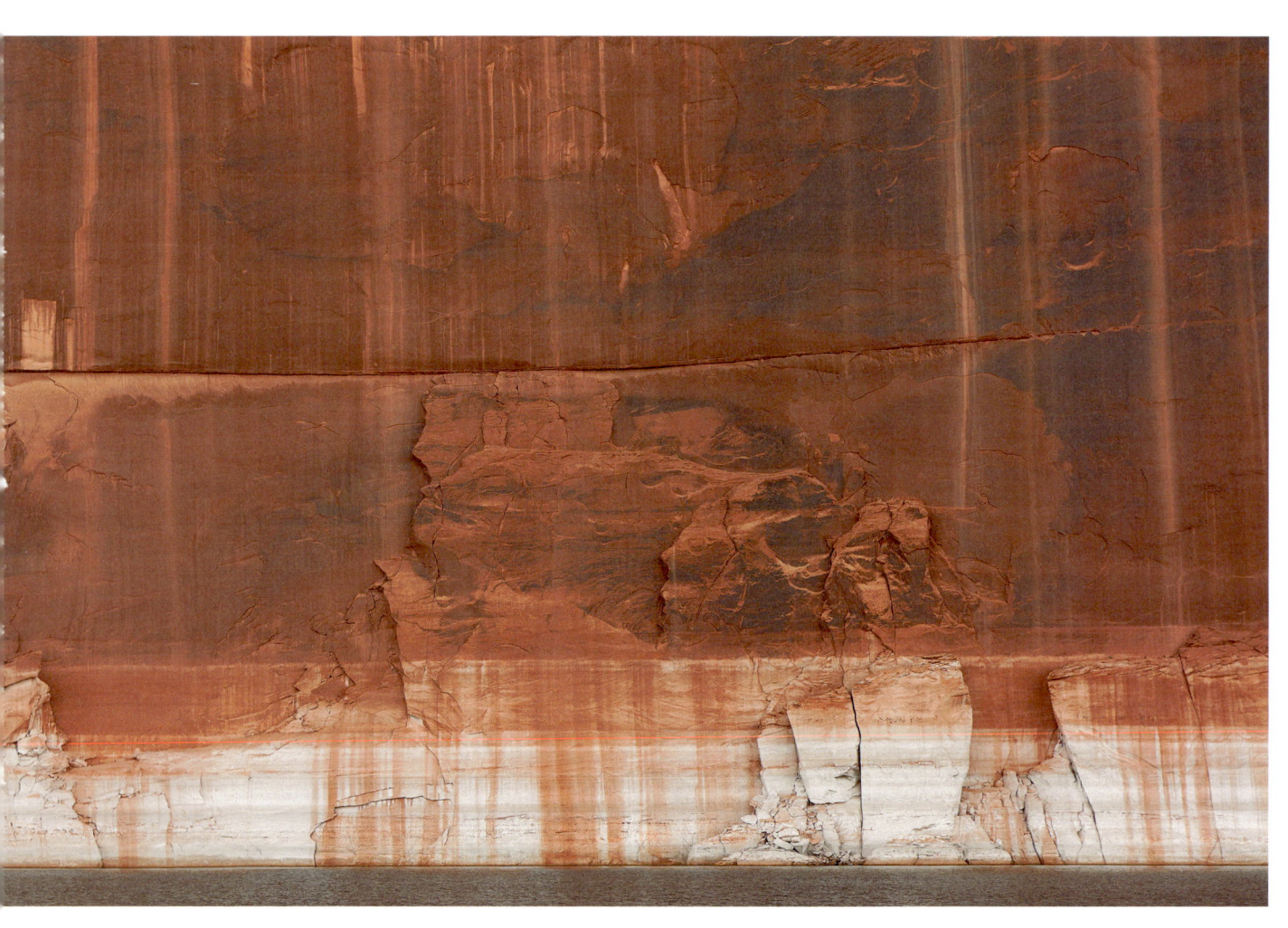

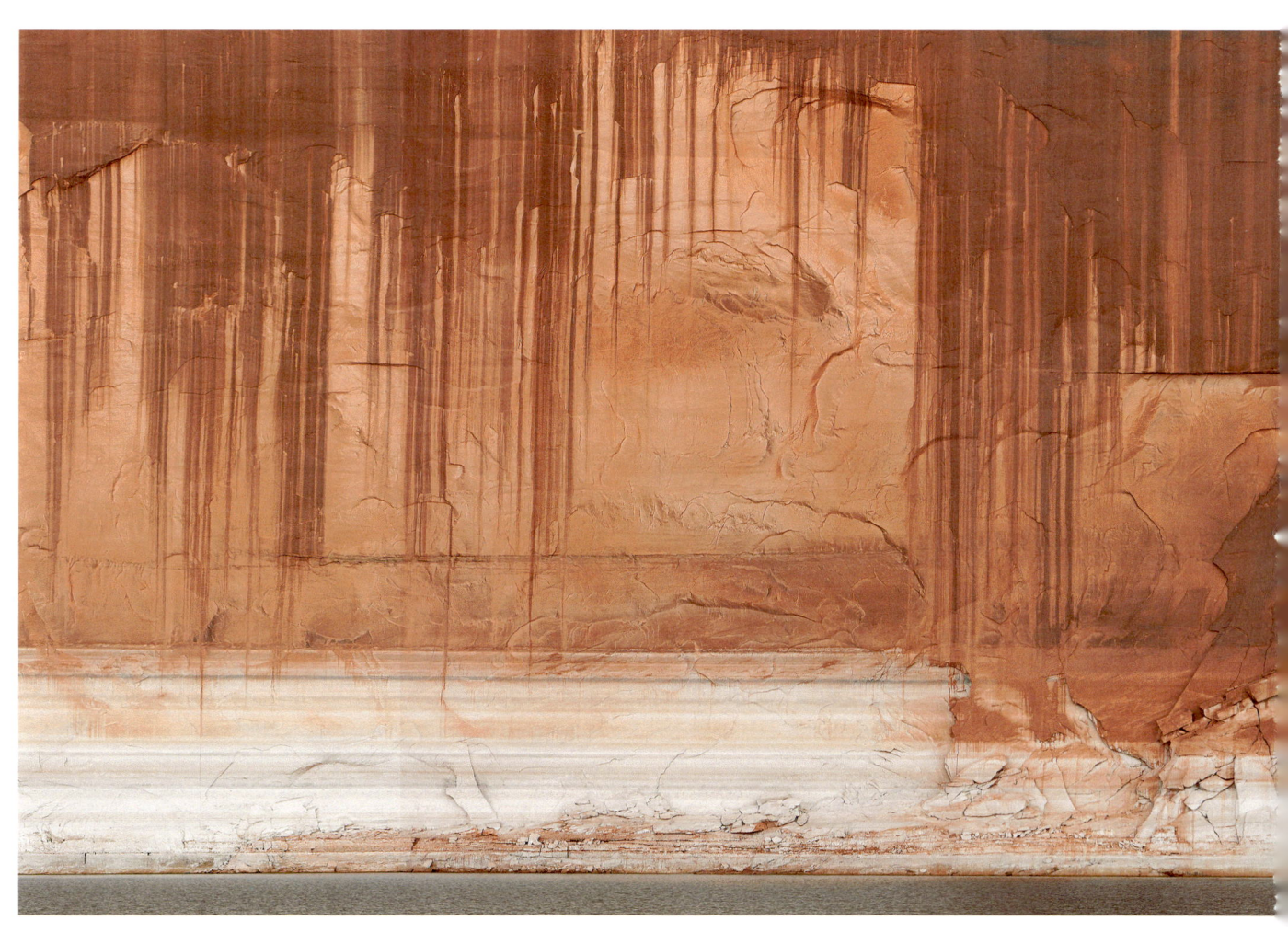

20. Peter Goin   Born Madison, WI, 1951 – lives Reno, NV
Tapestry Wall, Colorado River, Lake Powell, Utah, 2013

Alluvial fan   Alluvium is the sediment deposited by the flow of a river, so an alluvial fan is the mass of sediment, sand and gravel, silt and clay, deposited in a fanlike shape by the flow of a mountain stream or river when it has left a confined channel and opened onto a broad plain. Alluvial fans occur in humid as well as arid and semiarid landscapes, although the most prominent ones are in deserts. A series of fans, formed by parallel streams flowing out of a range of mountains, sometimes forms a continuous and overlapping apron of sediment which is called a bajada or alluvial apron. Norman Hinds notes an instance in his *Evolution of the California Landscape*: "Because of the height of the ranges around Death Valley and their consequently steep slopes, a host of valleys has been eroded into them and the streams have carried quantities of debris into the basin forming alluvial fans and aprons." —Robert Hass

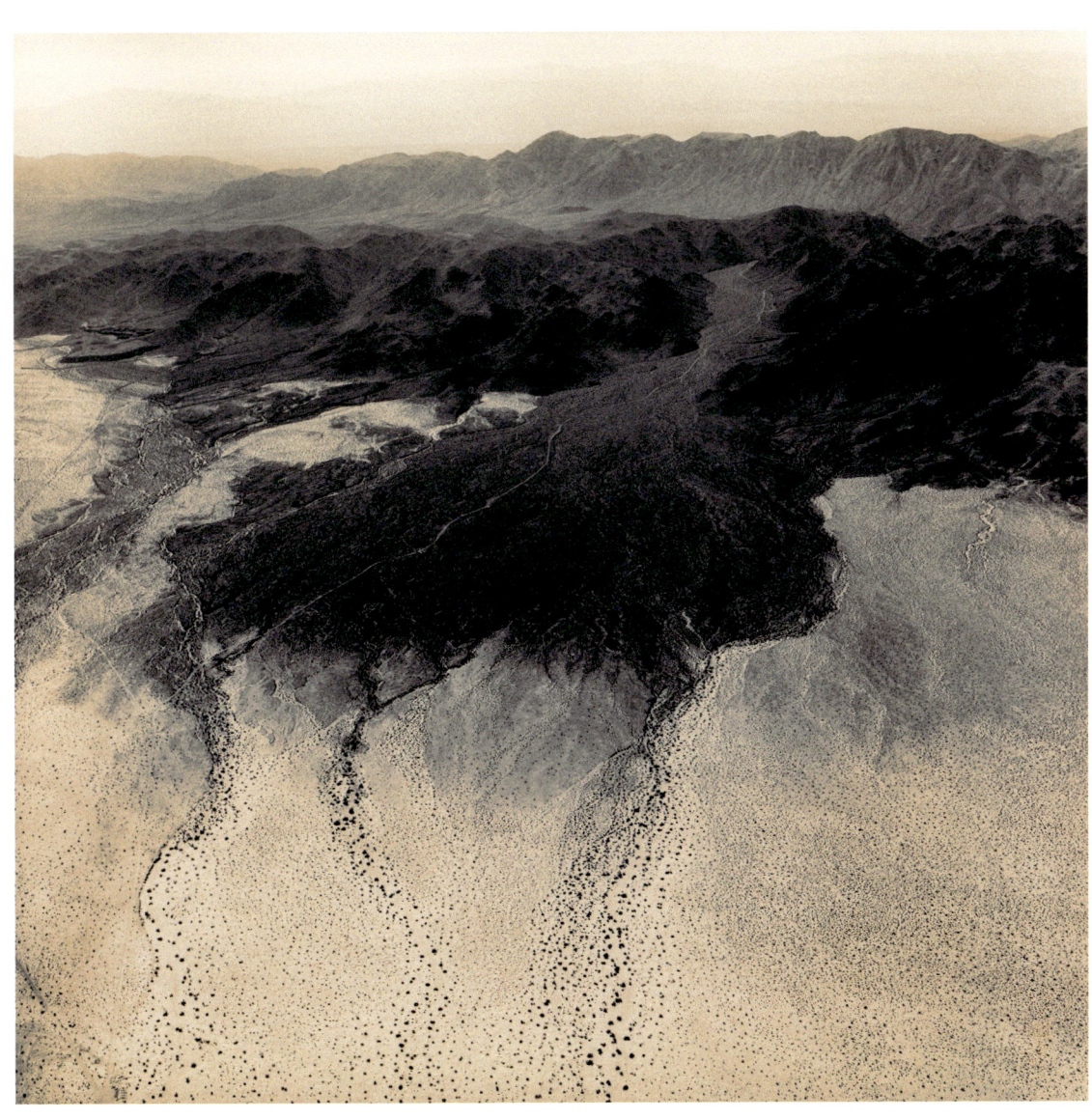

21. Emmet Gowin   Born Danville, VA, 1941 – lives Newtown, PA
*Alluvial Fan, Natural Drainage, near the Yuma Proving
Ground and the Arizona-California Border*, 1988

Floodplain The area of a flat valley floor that a river, swollen by spring melt and spring rains in some parts of the country, and by hurricanes and tropical storms in others, will cover when it overflows its usual course or banks is a floodplain. It is an area in which you will probably not be able to buy flood insurance from a private company. Floodplain incursions are measured according to a river's history—a variety of frequencies depending on the region's hydrology and the upstream control by dams. The hundred-year floodplain is inundated once a century; the one-year floodplain, annually. The means of managing floodplain regions include dikes, floodways, and zoning and building codes—these regulated by community or state laws, unless they do not meet federal government, especially Federal Emergency Management Agency (FEMA), minimum standards; then federal law applies. —Larry Woiwode

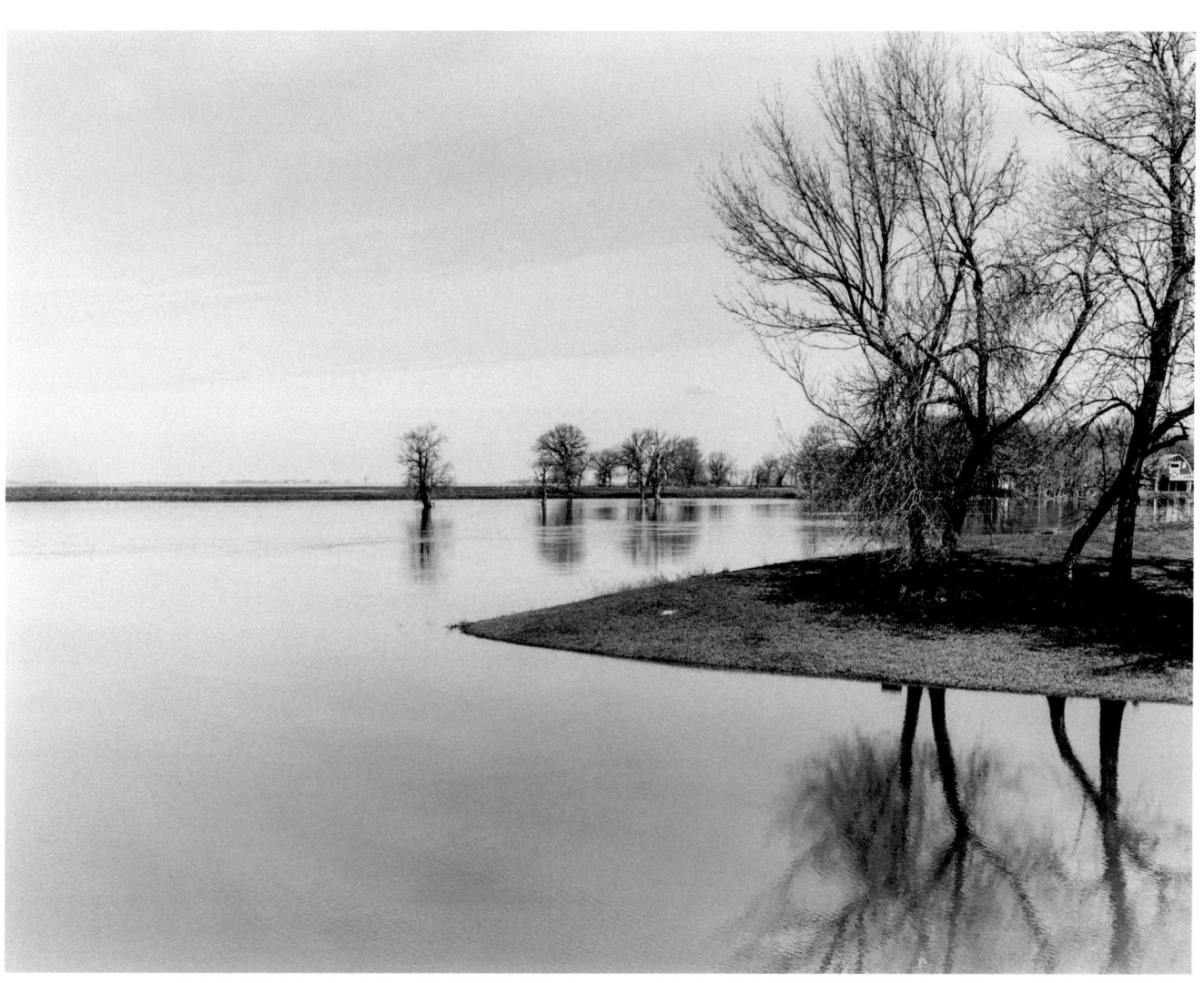

22. Wayne Gudmundson   Born Fargo, ND, 1949 – lives on Bad Medicine Lake, MN
and Tucson, AZ
Red River, North of Georgetown, Minnesota, 2013

Tailings pile   After a mineral ore has been mined, crushed, and stripped of all concentrates valuable enough to be smelted, the remaining pulverized rock debris is called tailings. Being of no economic use, these loose waste materials are dumped near an active mine into tall, barren tailings piles, whose sides slope according to the angle of repose. A large mining operation turns the earth inside out as it buries surrounding landscapes under vast, pyramid-shaped mountains devoid of vegetation. A tailings pile is typically the most prominent physical evidence of a mine. —Barbara Kingsolver

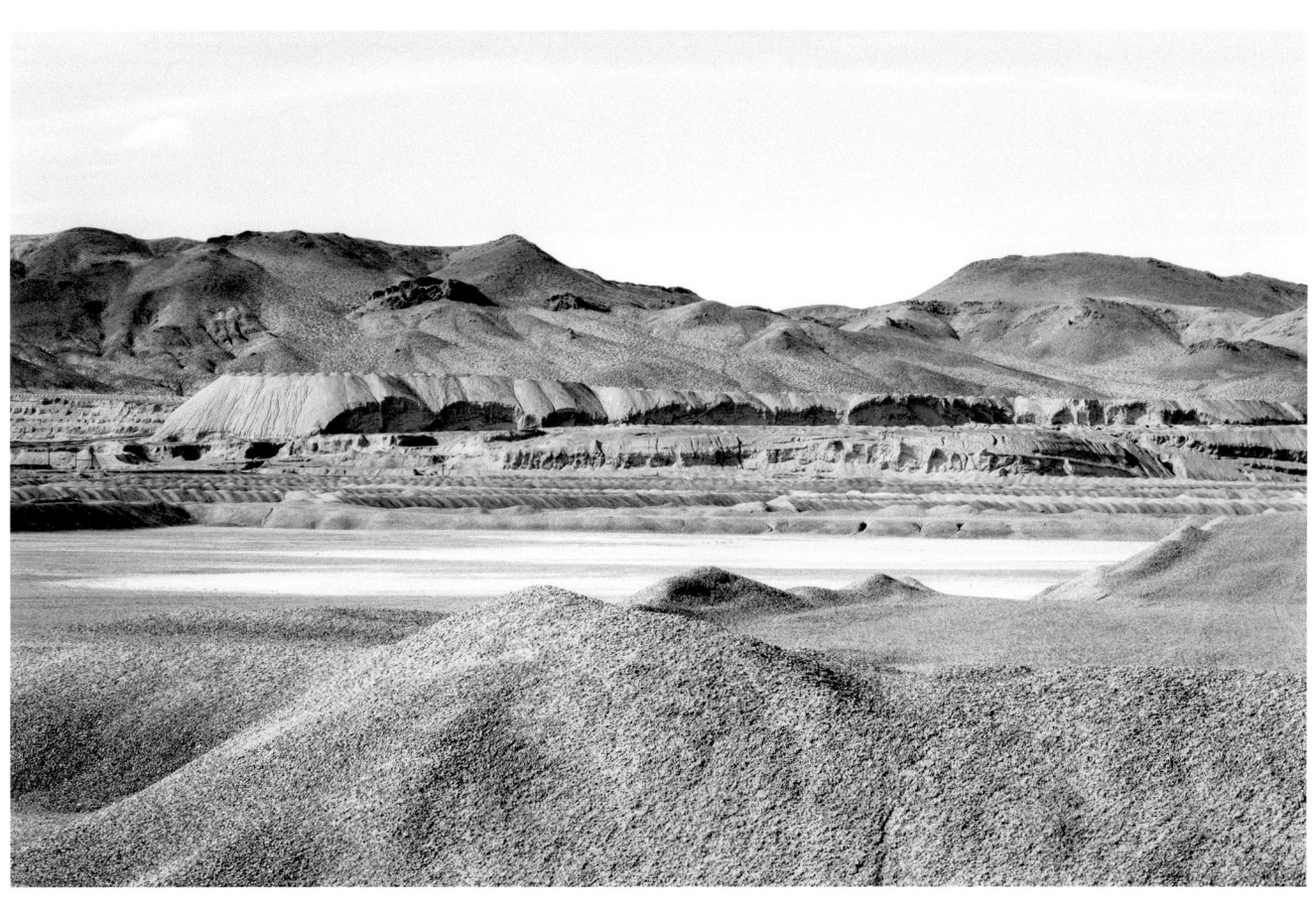

23. Owen Gump Born Kentfield, CA, 1980 – lives Northern CA
Mine Tailings, Lyon County, Nevada, 2018

Tailings pond   Modern mining operations in the United States are required to contain and treat their waste piles because of the toxic cocktails they contain: zinc, copper, mercury, cadmium, lead, and other heavy metals are commonly present, along with the acids of cyanide and sulfur that are used in slurry extraction processes. The resulting dammed depressions are not ponds in any sense dreamed of by Thoreau at Walden, but rather, immense puddles of suspended pollutants. The hazards of holding volumes of poisonous fluids above ground are obvious: foundation seepage, seasonal flooding, or structural collapse will release the concentrated toxins into groundwater or the receiving watershed. —Barbara Kingsolver

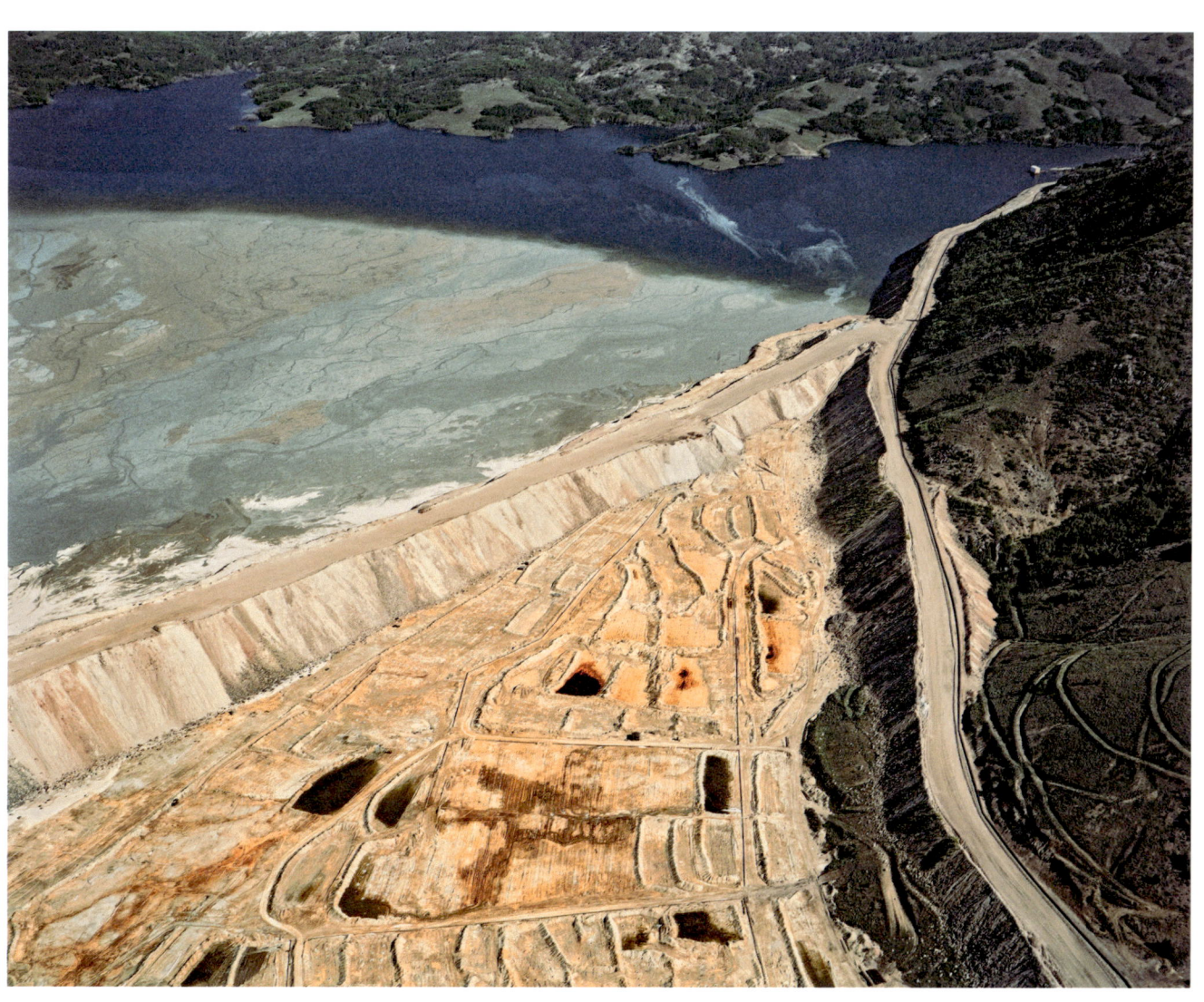

24. David T. Hanson   Born Billings, MT, 1948 – lives Fairfield, IA
*Yankee Doodle Tailings Pond, Tailings Dam, and Leach
Pads, Butte, Montana*, 1991

Mesa　In the North American landscape a mesa, which in Spain is merely a dinner table, occupies a grander scale: a flat-topped mountain or rock mass, usually capped with a weather-resistant rock stratum, it stands above an arid plain as a remnant of eons of erosion. Mesas and their smaller relatives, buttes—a butte is taller than it is wide, a mesa wider than it is tall—figure in place-names throughout the semiarid lands of Utah, New Mexico, Arizona, and Colorado. The world's most famous mesa-and-butte landscape, in the Navajo Nation Monument Valley Tribal Park of northeastern Arizona and southeastern Utah, has so regularly served as the backdrop of cowboy movies and other manufactured visions of the American West that these unusual landforms are mistakenly assumed, throughout the world, to be the dominant feature of the western landscape. Mesas, in art, also commonly co-occur with another cliché of the Southwest, the saguaro cactus with its pair of raised arms, even though that plant has a limited range and does not grow within two hundred miles of Monument Valley. —Barbara Kingsolver

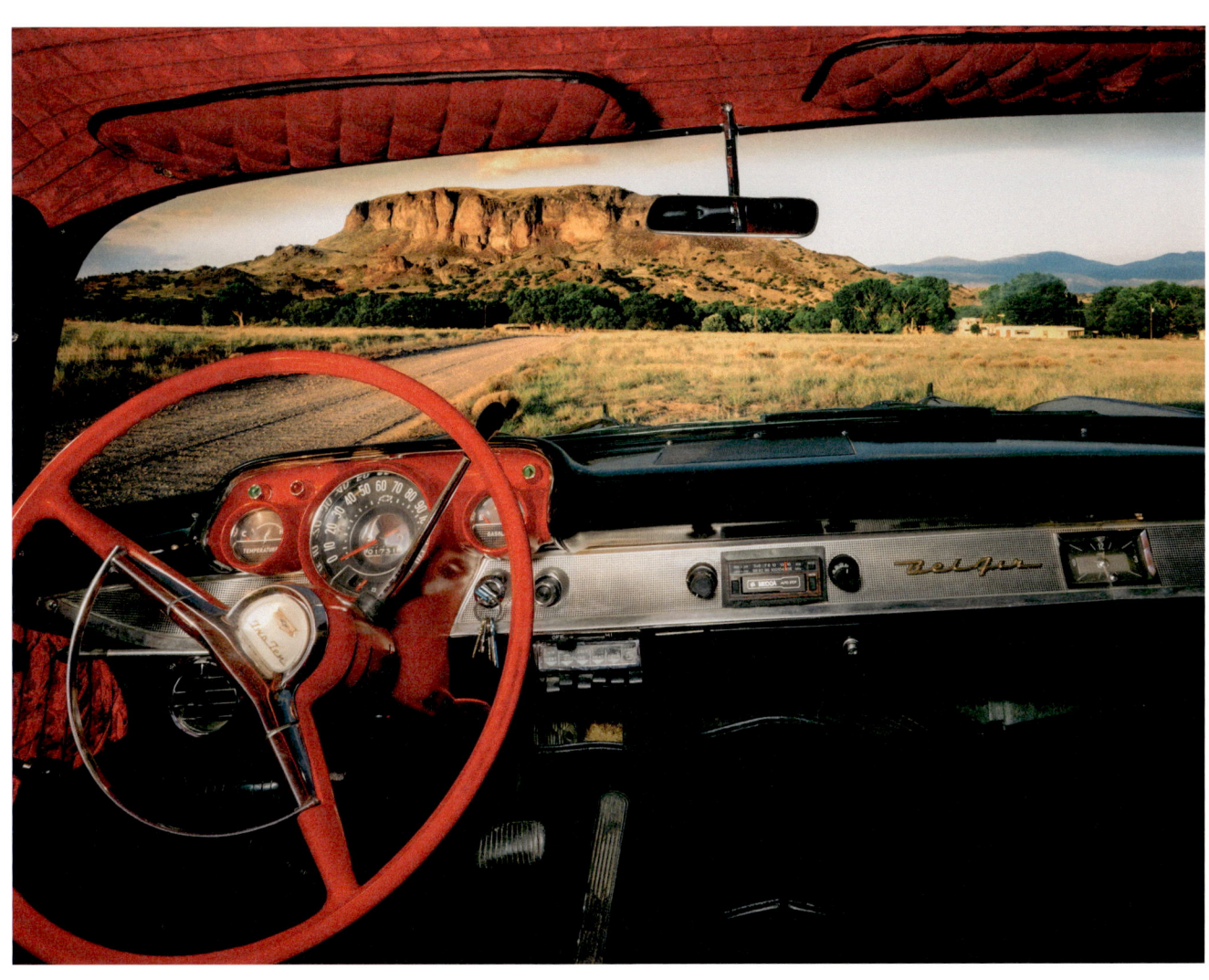

25. Alex Harris   Born Atlanta, GA, 1949 – lives Durham, NC
Black Mesa, New Mexico, Looking East from Fred Cata's
1957 Chevrolet Belair, 1987

Levee   A levee is an embankment along a river that resists the overflow of the stream. Derived in the eighteenth century from the French *levée*, meaning "act of raising," the word refers in modern times especially to the elevated ground along the Mississippi and its tributaries. Natural levees are built up year after year by the deposit of sandy soil on the banks of the flooding river. As the floodwaters rise over the banks, no longer held by the channel, the velocity of the current drops, along with the water's ability to hold sediment. Coarser materials fall out first, and finer silt and clay are carried into the back swamp areas of the floodplain, where they drop out of suspension as the water slows even more. The levees themselves are made of sand and coarser sediments. Man-made levees are constructed to control flooding and protect populated areas along the river. Extensive levees have been built along the Mississippi system. The most famous use of the word is perhaps the Don McLean song celebrating rock and roll and lamenting the death of Buddy Holly: "Drove my Chevy to the levee/but the levee was dry." —Robert Morgan

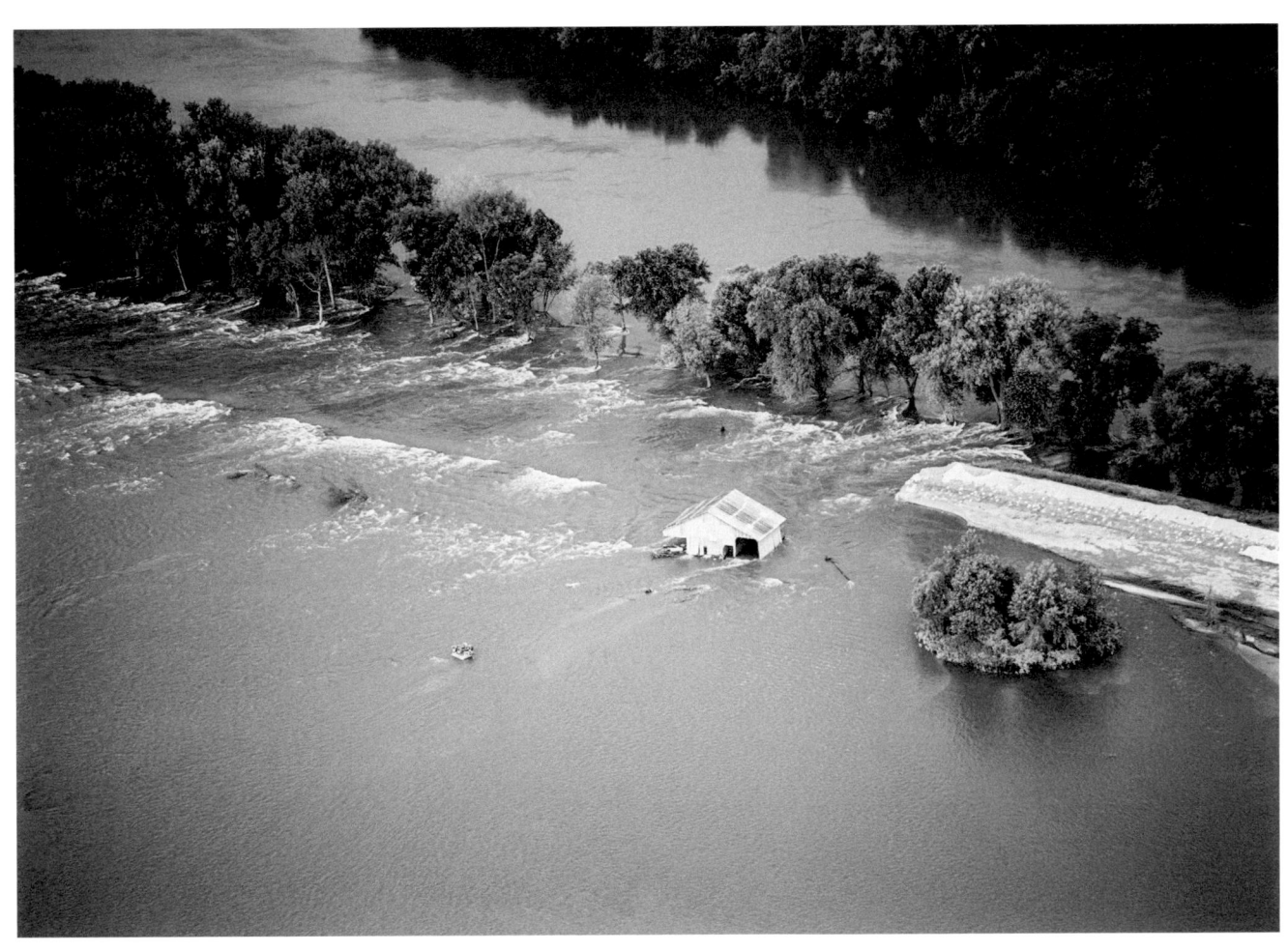

26. Allen Hess   Born Dayton, OH, 1950 – lives Bethlehem, PA
Levee Break, Quincy, Illinois, Mississippi River Flood,
August 27, 1993, 1993

Nunatak   Nunatak is from an Inuktiut (Inuit Eskimo) word, *nunataq*, meaning "something prominent standing alone" or, more prosaically, "lonely peak." (In the Iñupiaq language of the Iñupiat, who live on the Alaska coastal plain far from mountainous terrain, nunataq refers primarily to a cache of meat in the ground.) In its Anglicized form, the word refers to an isolated island of bedrock jutting out from a sea of glacial snow and ice. Nunataks are landforms that existed before glaciation, and within North America they are scattered in Alaska and Canada, and throughout the high-altitude, glacier-bound landscapes of the Rocky Mountains. One might think that these rock outcroppings sequestered in ice would be barren of life, but they have been found to be refuges for a diversity of species. Researchers studying nunataks in Canada's Yukon Territory have found miniature meadows and gardens of sedges, moss campion, mountain heather, tiny poppies, saxifrages, daisies, and other plants that host rare insects and a species of wolf spider and attract occasional butterflies. The collared pika, a tough little mammal, has also found its way to these nunataks and made them home. All too often, nunataks are the final resting place for straying migratory birds seeking an oasis in the vast stretches of snow. —Carolyn Servid

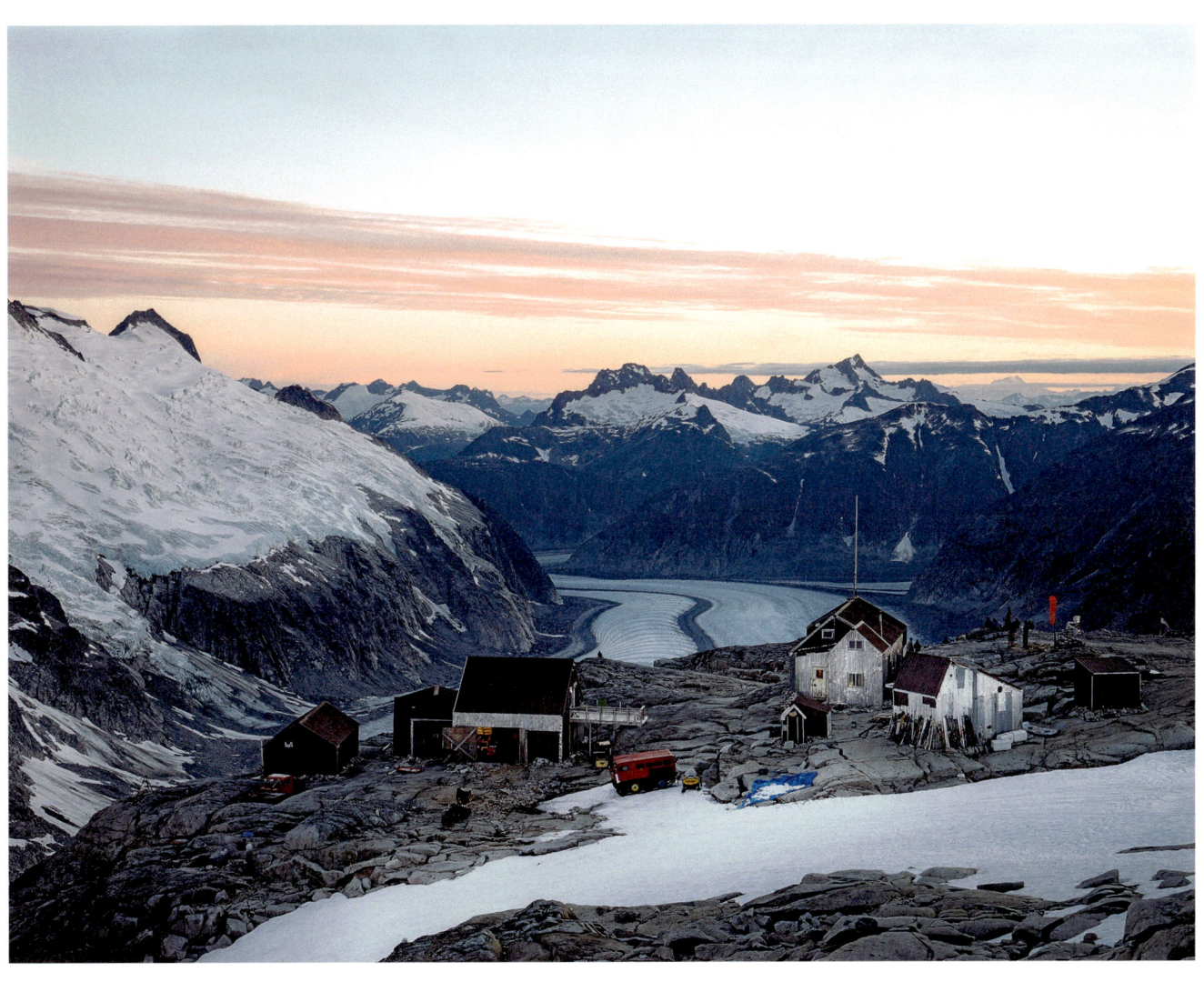

27. Ben Huff   Born LeClaire, IA, 1973 – lives Juneau, AK
*Above the Gilkey Trench, Camp 18, Juneau Icefield,
Alaska*, 2018

Turbulent flow   In contrast to laminar flow, in turbulent flow any particle of a body may move in any direction with respect to any other particle. Hydrologists and river scientists, as well as the curious, beginning with Leonardo da Vinci, have studied turbulence in the Earth's water and atmosphere, and all have found such movements difficult, if not impossible, to predict. Turbulence in a river occurs when rocks, holes, or sudden changes in the river channel obstruct the flow of the water. River rafters characterize turbulent flow by its irregular velocity and movement, reserving the term chaotic flow to describe the most dangerous parts of a whitewater river, where the river's movement cannot be anticipated. —Lan Samantha Chang

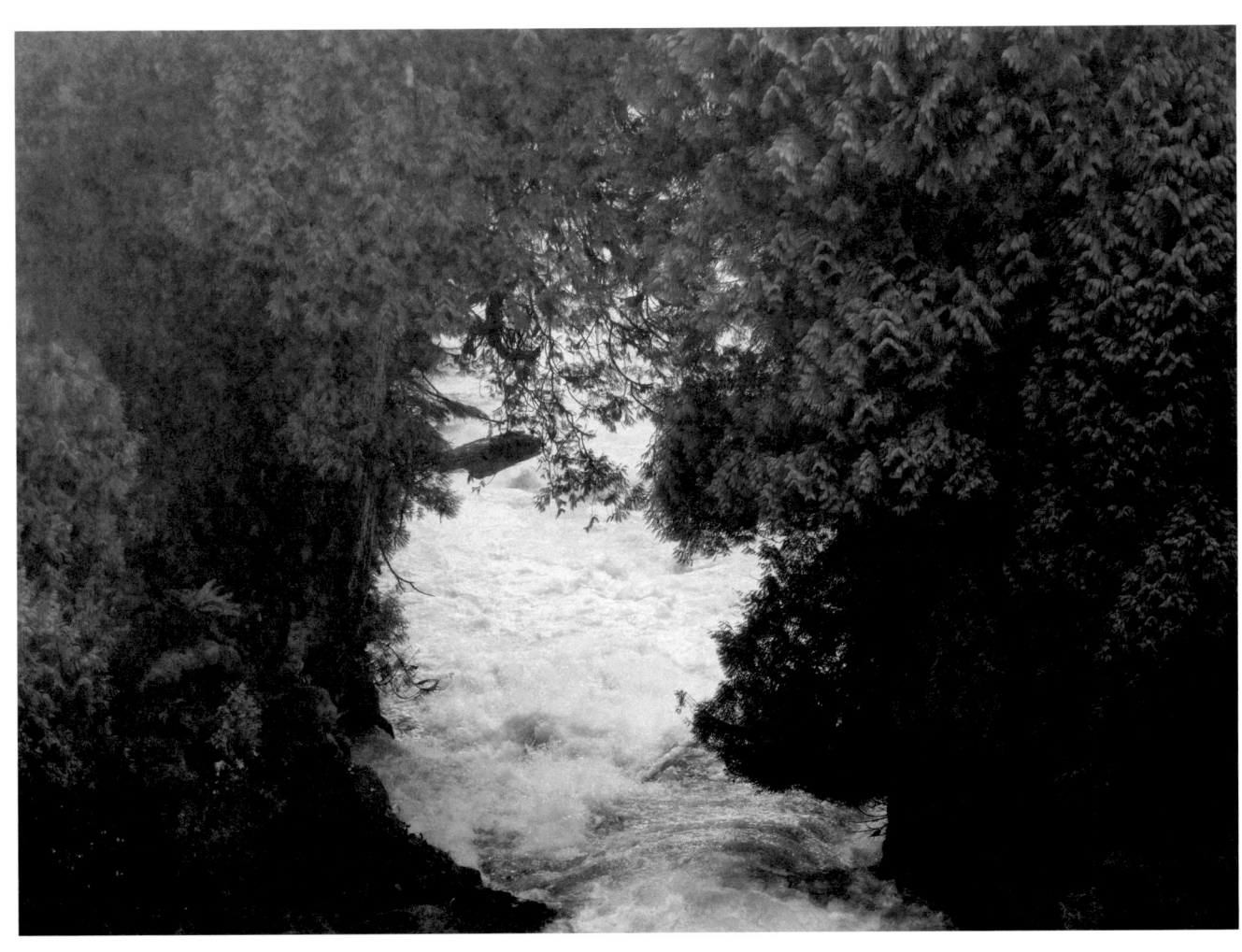

28. Ron Jude   Born Los Angeles, CA, 1965 – lives Eugene, OR
River, 2017

Glacial valley   A glacial valley is distinguished by its distinctive U-shape: a broad flat floor flanked by high walls of rock. Such a valley has been bulldozed wide by a glacier scraping its way down an existing V-shaped valley, created by a preglacial river. Glacial valleys are common in the mountains of the American West and Alaska. In Prince William Sound and southeast Alaska, some of these classic-shaped valleys start deep in coastal mountain ranges and run into the sea later to become water-filled fjords. California's Yosemite Valley is one of the United States' most celebrated glacial valleys, and John Muir was the first to explain its icy origins. In his 1912 book *The Yosemite*, he writes: "These bald, westward-leaning rocks, with their rounded backs and shoulders [facing] the glacier fountains of the summit-mountains, and their split, angular fronts looking in the opposite direction, explain the tremendous grinding force with which the ice-flood passed over them." —Carolyn Servid

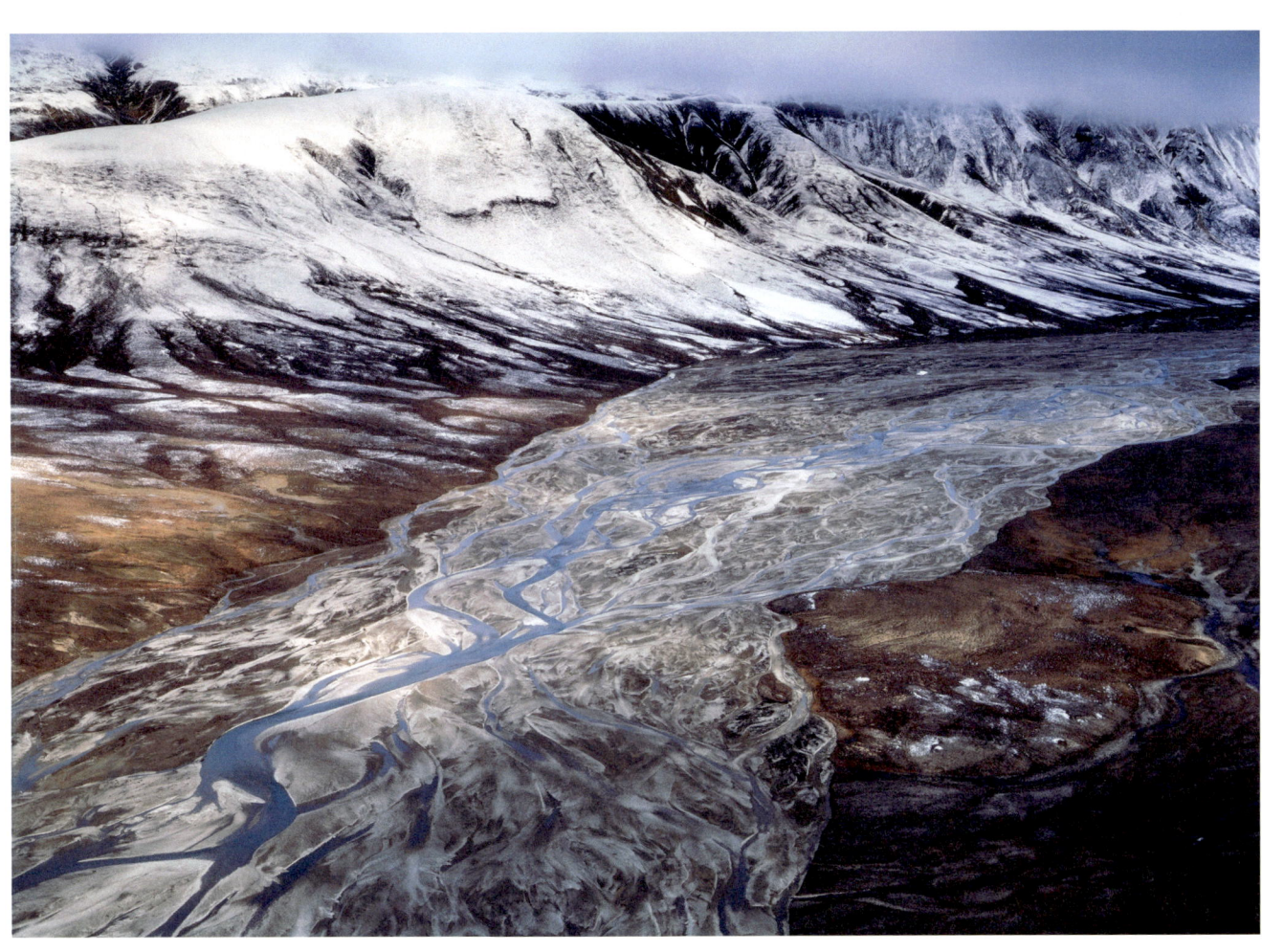

29. Robert Glenn Ketchum   Born Los Angeles, CA, 1947 – lives Los Angeles, CA
Glacial Outflow, Otto Fjord, Ellesmere Island, Canada, 1994

Swell Though many first picture a swell as a feature of the ocean's surface, the term is also used to identify a long, roundly arched, often isolated elevation on the surface of the Earth, created where soil absorbs a great deal of water. Used in this way, the term usually includes an adjective, such as broad, bulging, undulating, protruding, round, or oval. Isolated swells are sometimes called domes or arches, though these terms are technically inaccurate. Swells are correctly called rises when found on extensive plains in combination with the depressions known as swales, the rises being part of an undulating, wet-and-dry, swale-and-rise topography, formed by the differential melting of glacial ice, which once stretched for hundreds of miles across the Midwest. Perhaps the best-known swell in North America is the domal San Rafael Swell in southeastern Utah. From the air, its eastern front resembles a fifty-mile-long wave advancing across the desert, even to its seeming to break in a sea of froth over a spectacular "reef" of white Navajo Sandstone along its eastern perimeter. Formed forty to sixty million years ago, this two-thousand-foot-high swell bowed up so slowly that three rivers in the area—the San Rafael, the Muddy, and the Price—were able to maintain their courses across the uplifted land. They continue to cross the swell today. —Terry Tempest Williams

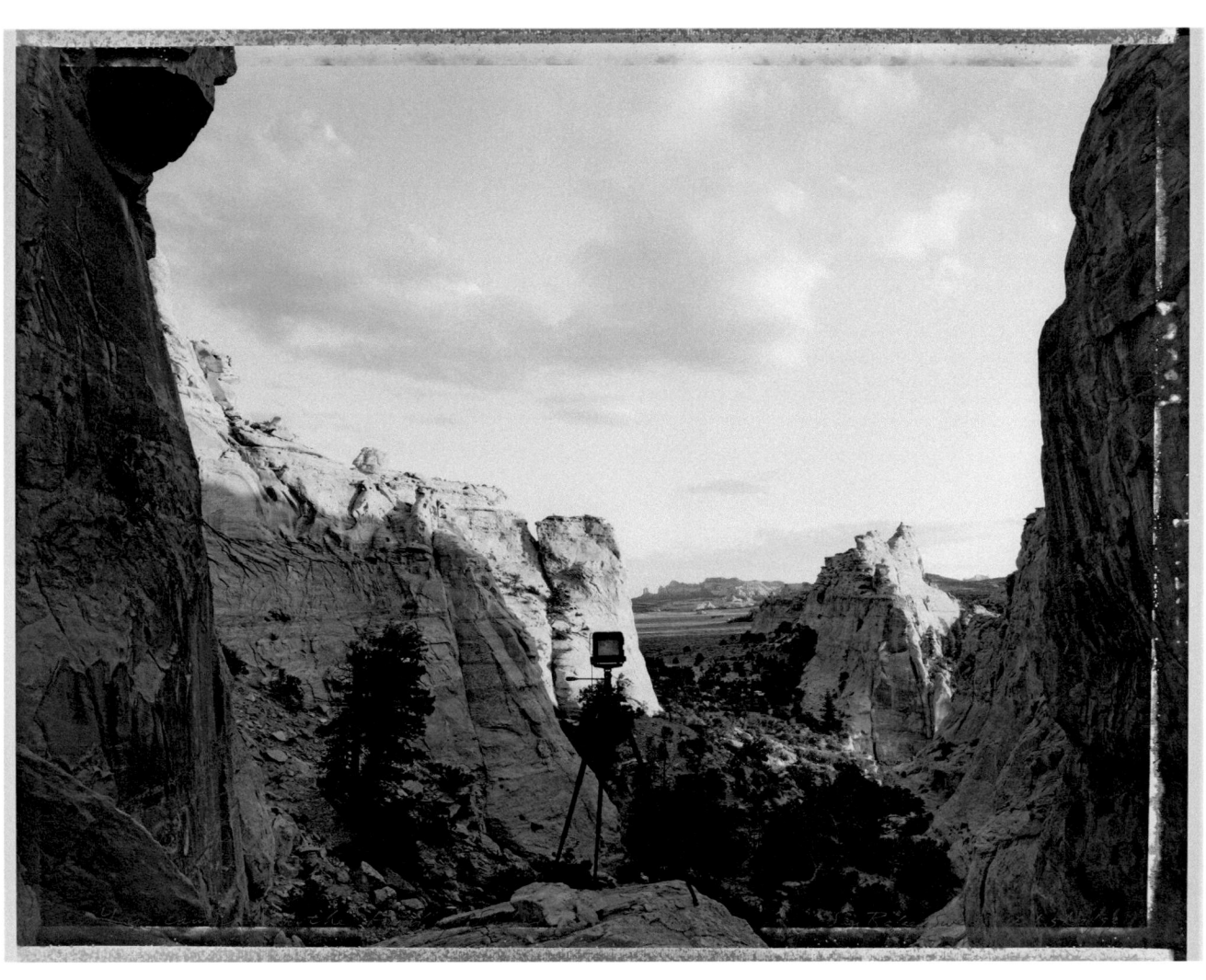

30. Mark Klett   Born Albany, NY, 1952 – lives Tempe, AZ
*My Camera at the Head of Sinbad, San Rafael Swell,
Utah 5/22/93*, 1993

Confluence   The place where streams converge and unite is their confluence. North America's two great rivers, the Missouri and the Mississippi, meet on the northern edge of St. Louis. The confluence of the Allegheny and Monongahela Rivers in Pittsburgh forms the Ohio River. Similarly, the Kansas River, formed by the confluence of the Republican and Smoky Hill Rivers, flows about 169 miles eastward to its confluence with the Missouri River at Kansas City. And a place called The Confluence, in Canyonlands National Park and named by John Wesley Powell, is where the Green and Colorado Rivers meet. Many of the early thriving communities in the American colonies began at a confluence, since rivers were necessary for trade and the transportation of goods. Such trade often required the construction of forts to protect traders from the real or perceived threats of local Native Americans or competing settlers and traders. Hence, Washington Irving notes in his book *Astoria; or, Anecdotes of an Enterprise beyond the Rocky Mountains* (a glorified history of John Jacob Astor's fur trade empire): "At length it was found necessary to establish fortified posts at the confluence of the rivers and the lakes for the protection of the trade, and the restraint of these profligates of the wilderness." Writing about confluence sites in the Great Plains, Ian Frazier notes: "The reason no city grew at the confluence of the Missouri and the Yellowstone is that in 1866 the Army built a post called Fort Buford a few miles east of Fort Union, and in 1868 created a thirty-mile-square military reservation with the post at the center. Since the reservation was closed to all settlement, the city which people eventually built was farther down the Missouri, at the junction of the Little Muddy River. Today this city is called Williston, North Dakota, and it gets much of its income from oil, and its long commercial highway strips wax and wane." —Jeffery Renard Allen

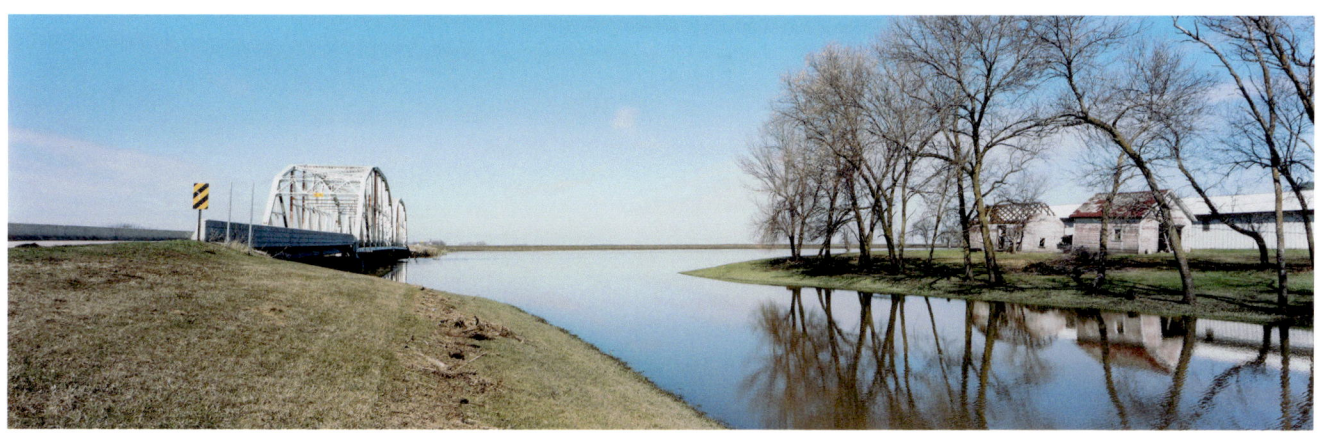

31. Stuart Klipper   Born New York, NY, 1941 – lives Minneapolis, MN
*Confluence of the Buffalo River (Flooded) and the Red
River, Clay County, Minnesota*, 2013

Swale In *The Land of Little Rain*, Mary Austin describes a typical Paiute encampment as being "near the watercourse, but never in the swale." In constructing his "campoodie," Austin goes on to say, "the Paiute seeks rising ground, depending on air and sun for purification of his dwelling, and when it becomes wholly untenable, moves." The swale avoided by the Paiute—and every other knowledgeable camper—is a marshy or moist depression (sometimes mimicking a stream course) in a gently rolling landscape. These elongated hollows were likely created by fingers of glacial ice that melted more slowly than the rest of an ice sheet, depressing the ground beneath them as they did so. (At the same time, the ground between the swales absorbed some of this meltwater and rose). In Florida, poorly drained swales alternate with beach ridges to form dune-and-swale topography. In the midwestern prairies, a series of swales in an area of little vertical relief, and with only slight rises above the general horizontal line of the glacial plain, is called swale-and-rise topography. Hoosier Prairie, on the southeastern shore of Lake Michigan, is a typical example. With less than a ten-foot change in elevation across its 430 acres, the nearly treeless plain is equal parts dry and wet, its swales harboring ecosystems of great biological diversity. Rich plant communities, including bracken and sweet ferns, originally established thousands of years ago on sand dunes above the prairie, survive today in the protection of the damp swales. Another example of extensive swale-and-swell topography, which disappeared almost completely with agriculture in the late 1880s, is the area around Dallas and Guthrie Counties, Iowa, which was carved during the Wisconsin glaciation. Once a mosaic of wetlands and rolling savanna bordering the Mississippi River, the area must have been a hush of relief to migrating waterfowl. —Terry Tempest Williams

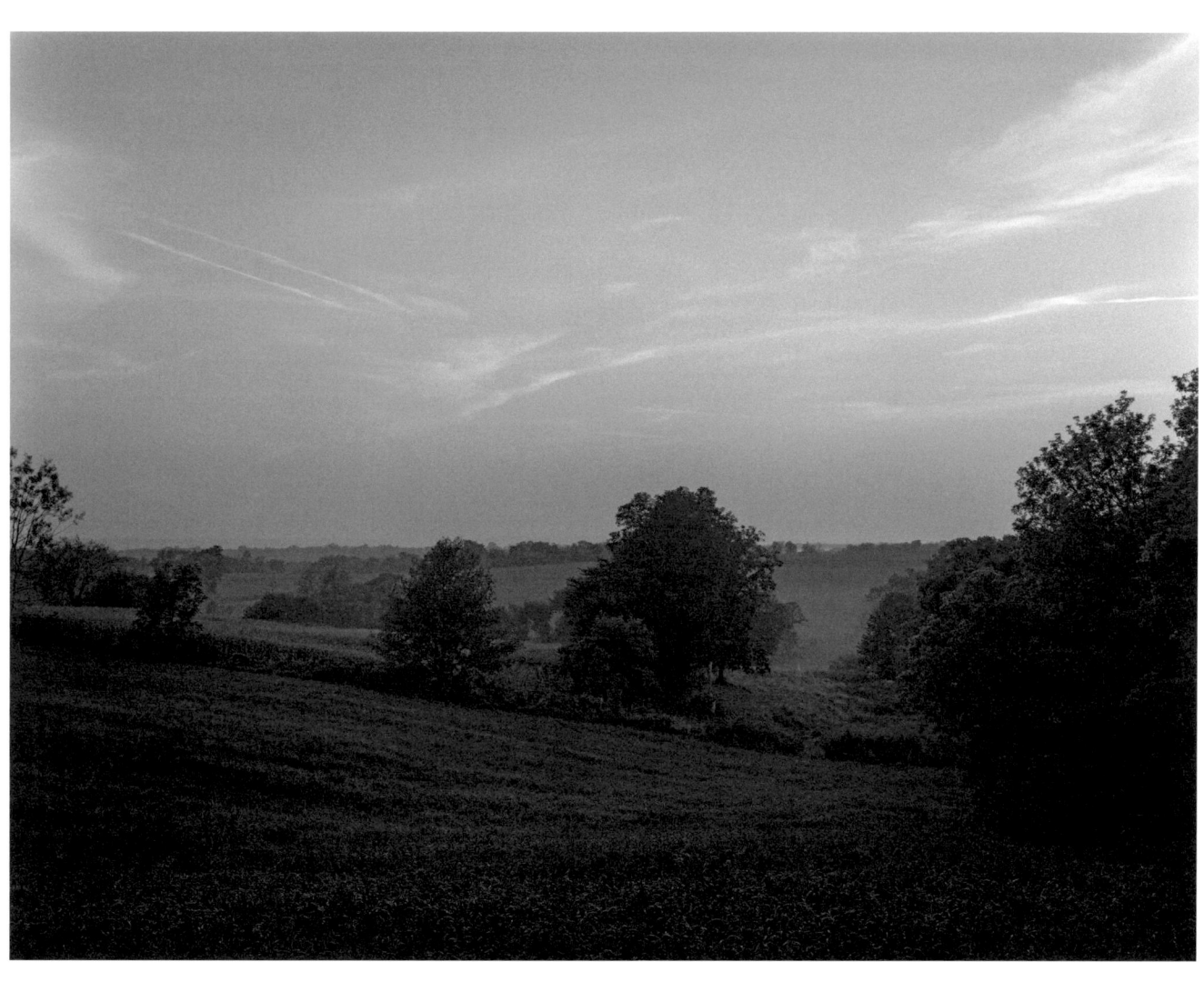

32. Peter Latner   Born New York, NY, 1950 – lives Minneapolis, MN
*Mississippi River Valley at Dusk, La Crosse County,
Wisconsin,* 2000

Salt lake A large body of water with a high salt content, situated in a sere landscape, with no outlet to the sea, is known as a salt lake. Utah's Great Salt Lake, the shrunken remnant of Pleistocene Lake Bonneville, is so salty a swimmer can float on its surface without effort. In her poem "Salt Air," Sharon Bryan writes: "You cannot sink into this 25 percent solution,/it hosts no life but the microscopic/brine shrimp's, which must trace a narrow path/through blazing crystal knives." In his essay "The World's Strangest Sea," Wallace Stegner described Great Salt Lake as a thin horizon line "of quicksilver, of lead, of improbable turquoise, of deep-sea cobalt, or of molten metals, depending on the conditions of the day." Because it's part of a closed system (the Great Basin), Great Salt Lake rises if rainfall exceeds the rate of evaporation and recedes if evaporation exceeds rainfall. This shifting shoreline plays havoc with local roads. The Salton Sea, created in 1905–1907 when the Colorado River burst through poorly constructed and maintained irrigation controls south of Yuma, Arizona, and flooded an ancient lake depression in the Sonoran Desert in California, is another inland salt sea or saline lake. Mono Lake, near Lee Vining, California, on the rain shadow side of the Sierra Nevada, is an alkaline lake. Here, evaporation concentrates naturally occurring alkali salts that form a thin crust on the surface of the water. Nevada's Carson Lake, whose waters contain a high concentration of sodium sulfate and lesser amounts of the carbonates and chlorides found in all briny lakes, is the archetype of a bitter lake. Many mineral lakes, strangely to some, teem with bird life. In *Salt Dreams*, William deBuys's finely observed account of the Salton Sea, he describes the mismanagement of water, the response to cycles of drought, and the population and development pressures that are a part of the social history of the West's mineral lakes. —Terry Tempest Williams

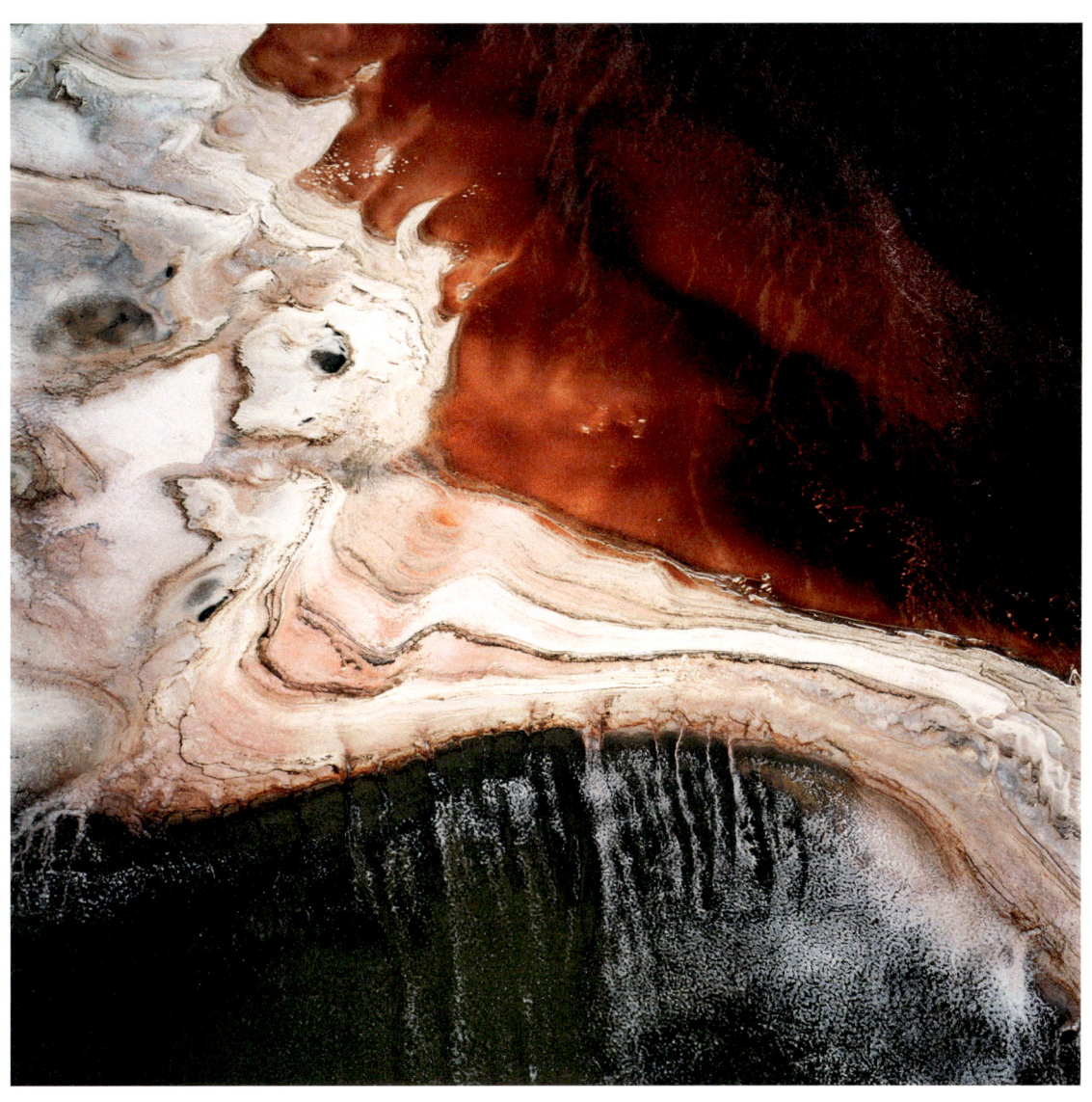

33. David Maisel　　Born New York, NY, 1961 – lives north of San Francisco, CA
Terminal Mirage 14, 2003

Sawtooth   Sawtooth is an adjective used to describe a range of mountains or a single ridge in a series of peaks that resembles the jagged edge of a saw. "The best place I have found to glimpse the western land as it was in the last [the nineteenth] century, without squinting too much, is in the Sawtooth-Stanley country in south central Idaho," writes Harlan Hague in his article "The Sawtooth-Stanley Basin Country." In addition to this classic range of sawtooth mountains, other examples include the ancient Sawtooth Mountain Range that anchors the coast of Lake Superior along the north shore, and Sawtooth Mountain, found in the Indian Peaks Wilderness Area south of Rocky Mountain National Park in Colorado. In his poem "Steel Mountain," from *Sawtooth Country*, David Beisly-Guiotto writes of standing atop this mountain in Idaho: "sheer sky, blue air chipped by white peaks/far as we can see." Those jagged sawtooth peaks. —Pattiann Rogers

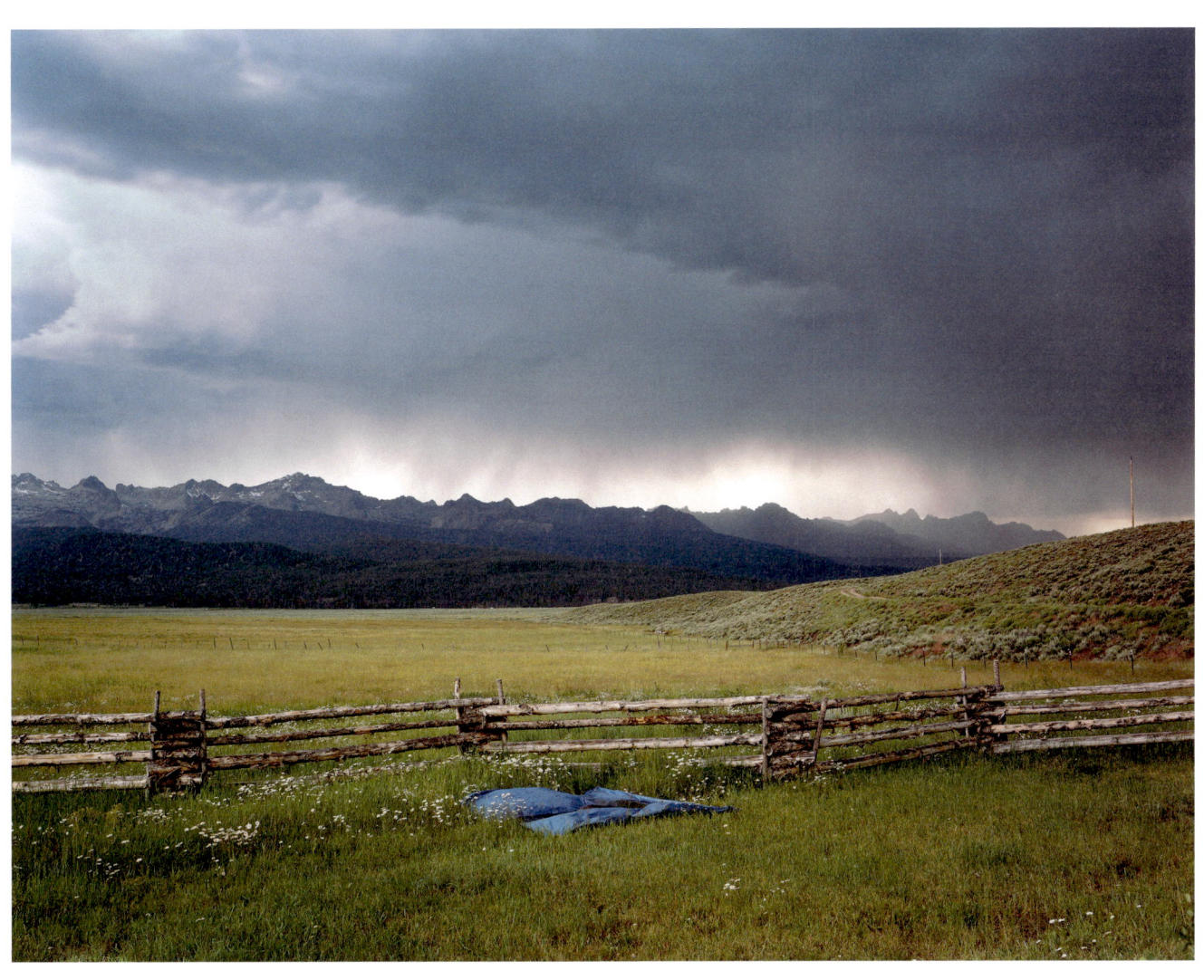

34. Laura McPhee   Born New York, NY, 1958 – lives Wood River Valley, ID and
New York, NY
Irrigator's Tarp Directing Water, Fourth of July Creek Ranch,
Custer County, Idaho, 2004

Aquifer Water, the treasure of the Earth, covers two-thirds of the planet. Some is visible, but much lies beneath the surface, hidden waters traveling through sand, rock, and gravel. These hidden seas are created in part when rain and snow trickle downward. Sometimes rivers dive deep and enter holds of water beneath even parched ground. These stores of water are called aquifers. The Ogallala Aquifer is the largest on the continent, reaching from the plains of South Dakota to Texas. The aquifer is declining by an average of 1.74 feet a year—over one million acre-feet—so excessive is the demand for agricultural and domestic purposes. In places in this region the land is actually collapsing. Native American people of several tribal traditions have long said that prairie dogs "call the rain." Like all Earth's waters, aquifers rise and fall with the moon, and as it turns out, this slow, strong pumping in the aquifers beneath prairie dog towns is what draws rainwater into those aquifers, replenishing them. Where prairie dog holes have ceased to exist, due to land development that has destroyed their habitat and the slaughter of prairie dogs for sport, the soil has become so hard rain can no longer reach the aquifer. The rain in fact has disappeared. —Linda Hogan

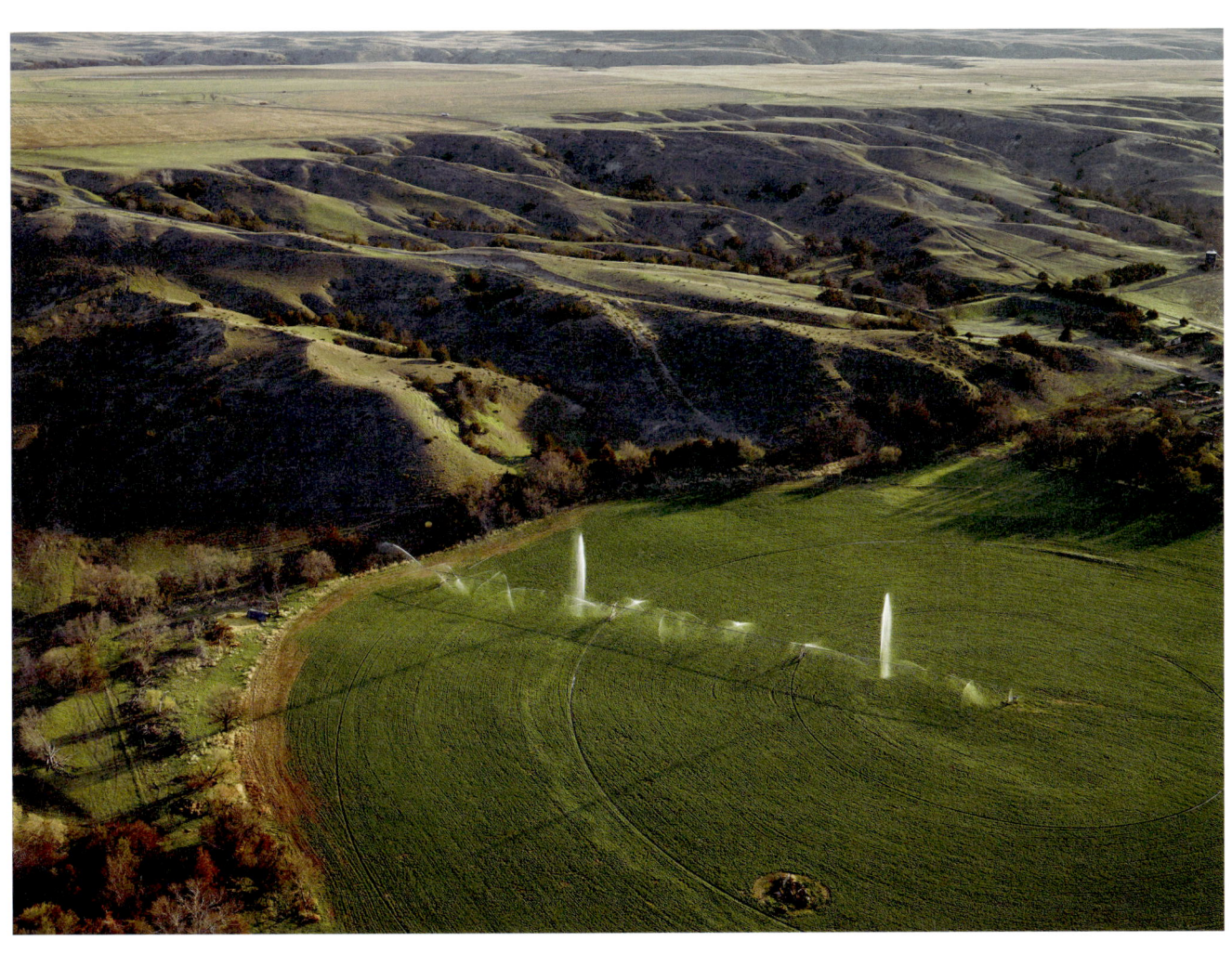

35. Andrew Moore   Born Old Greenwich, CT, 1957 – lives Kingston, NY
Broken Pivot, Cherry County, Nebraska, 2013

Shoulder A bench running along a slope, parallel to a valley below, is called a shoulder, as is a short, rounded spur on a mountainside. The term is also used to designate the crease in a glaciated valley where its steeply eroded lower slopes meet the gentler angle of its upper slopes, land that remained above the ice flow. The margins of a road are also called shoulders, if they're flat enough and wide enough for a vehicle to pull over safely. —William Kittredge

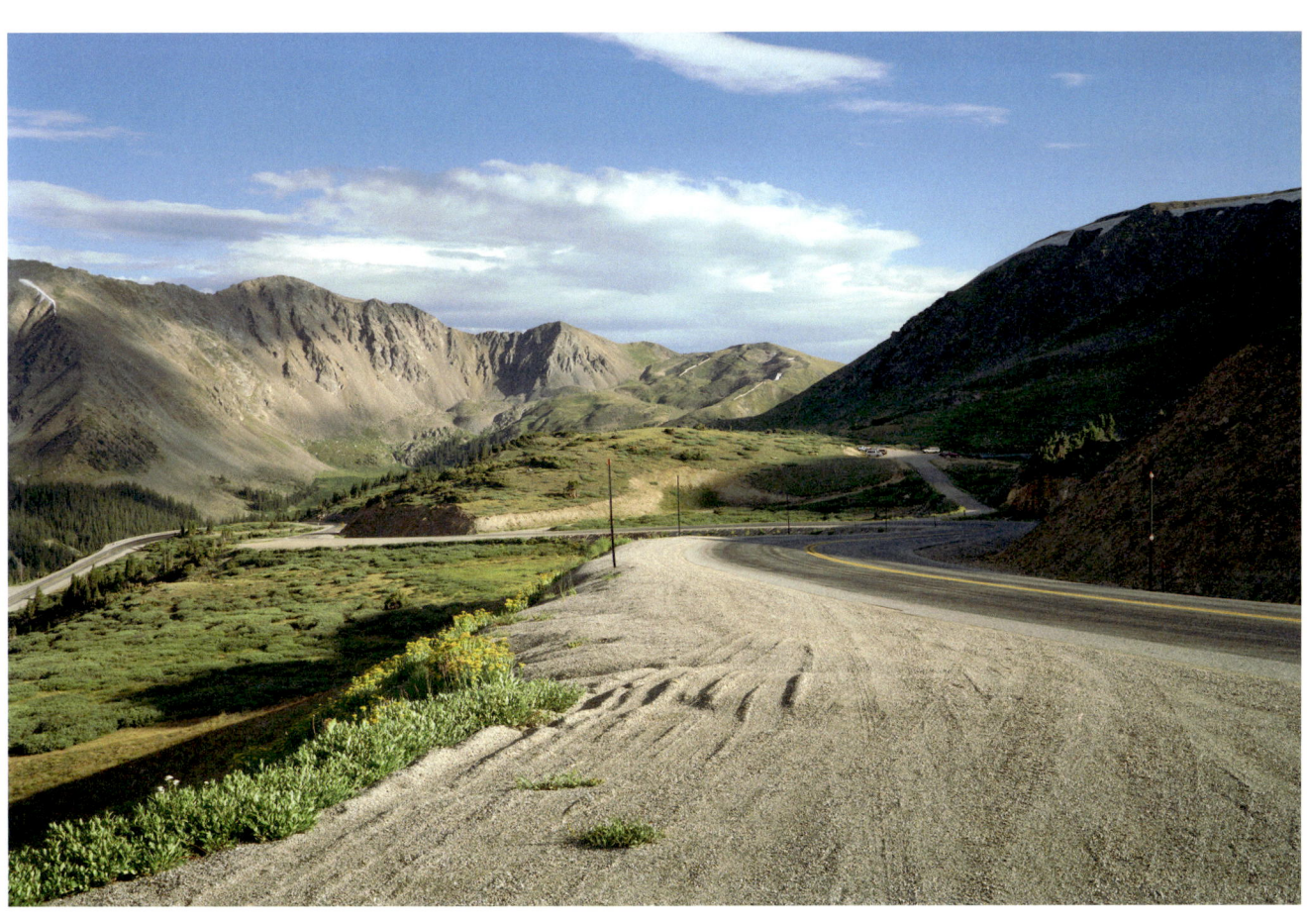

36. Eric Paddock   Born Boulder, CO, 1954 – lives Denver, CO
Loveland Pass, Colorado, 1994

Boreal forest   South of the treeless Arctic tundra, a forest shawl wraps eleven percent of the Earth's northern terrestrial surface. This circumpolar boreal forest is white spruce-dominated, carpeted with lichens, moss, orchids, heaths, quilted with peat bogs, and cut by cold, silty rivers. In *Crossing Open Ground*, Barry Lopez describes one view of this landscape: "a backdrop of hills: open country recovering from an old fire, dark islands of spruce in an ocean of Labrador tea, lowbush cranberry, fireweed . . . each species of leaf the invention of a different green: lime, moss, forest, jade." Boreal forces shape this forest: hot summers of endless daylight; frigid, dark winters; spring floods; permafrost; cycles of insect infestation and fire that decimate vast acreages. Yet fauna thrive: red squirrel, mink, moose, bear, wolf, lynx, marten, red fox, vole, muskrat, beaver, grouse, ptarmigan, porcupine, caribou, snowshoe hare, salmon, sheefish, whitefish, northern pike. And flora: spruce, tamarack, paper birch, quaking aspen, balsam poplar, blueberry, crowberry, Labrador tea, willow, cranberry, saxifrage, prickly rose. Indigenous people, to this day, rely on an intimate knowledge of geography to subsist on these animals and plants. Some non-Natives also pursue this intimate geographic knowledge of the boreal forest. For several years, the poet John Haines homesteaded in the boreal forest south of Fairbanks, Alaska, hunting and trapping for subsistence, receiving the forest's spiritual and artistic sustenance. Of this time Haines wrote, "I am living out a dream in these woods. Old dreams of the Far North."
—Eva Saulitis

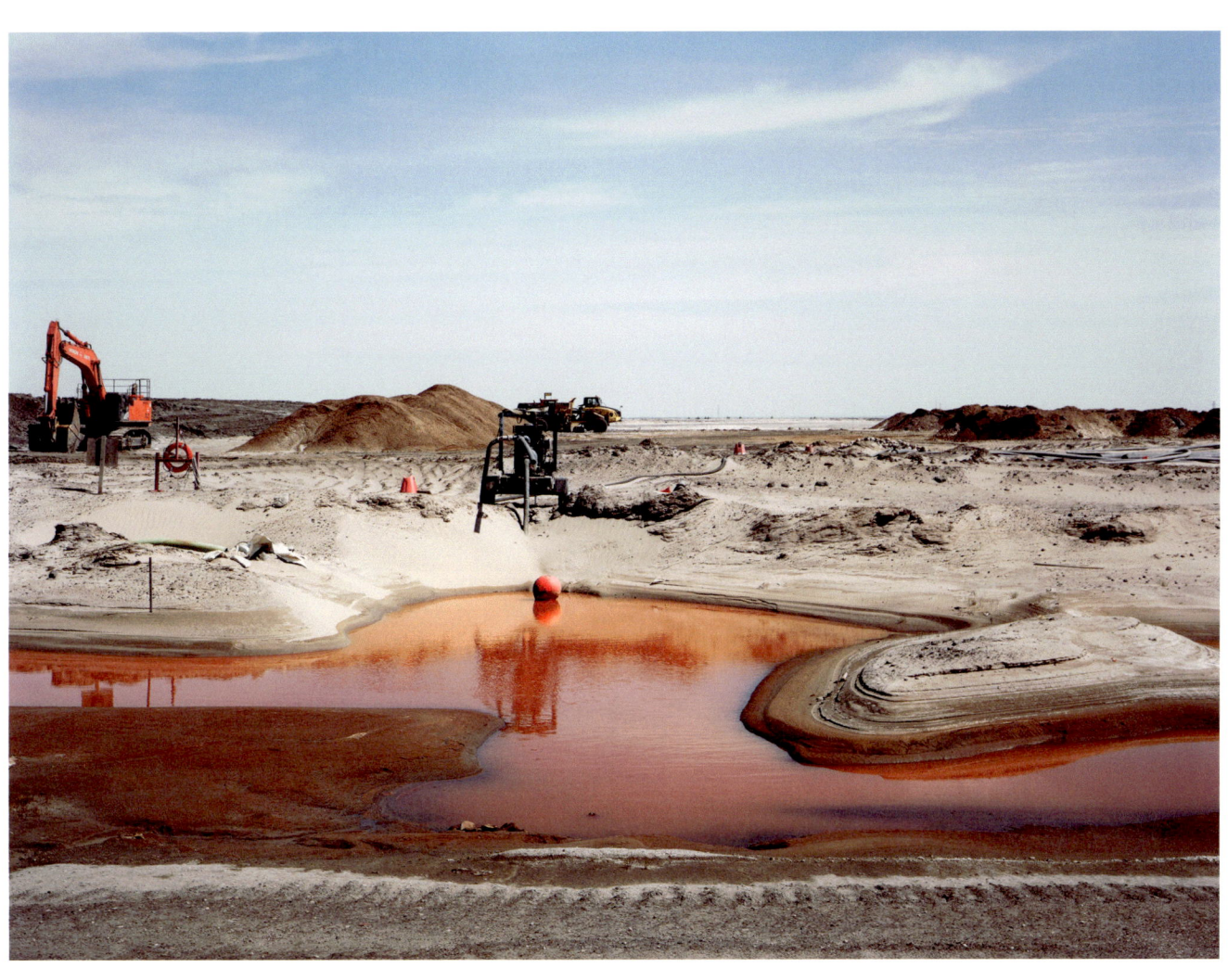

37. Mary Peck Born Minneapolis, MN, 1952 – lives Santa Fe, NM
*Following the Route of the Keystone XL, Syncrude Tailings
Pond, North of Fort McMurray, Alberta*, 2017

Canyon Canyon is a general term with a heady array of specifics. It may be as "simple" as a cleft between steep walls or as complex as the Grand Canyon or Mexico's Barrancas del Cobre—miles across, layered in their depths like ragged, inverted cordilleras. In the Southwest, canyons are assertive landscapes. Aridity sharpens their bones. Rivers may run through them—open arteries in a carapace of rock; others flow only with blow-sand and chokestones. Canyons come blind, box, side, slot, hidden. They stair down and pour off. They gooseneck. They hang. Muley Twist, Desolation, Snap, Lavender, Blue Canyon, Rain Canyon—canyons are where you want to live merely on behalf of their names. The Hopi word *pösövi* means "canyon corners," as if one quirky, prismatic facet at a time were all you could manage in this seemingly irrational geography of space and rock. —Ellen Meloy

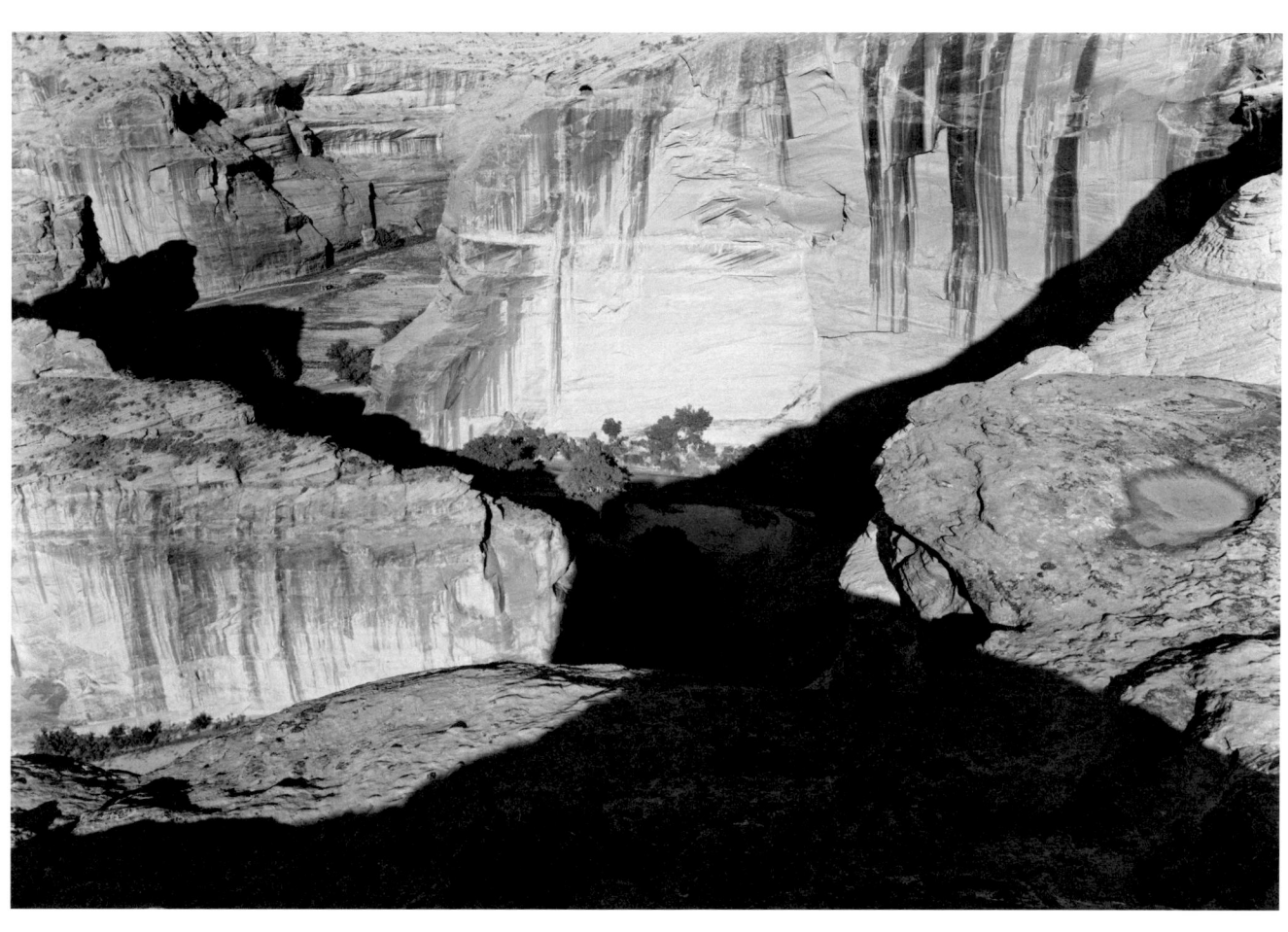

38. Edward Ranney   Born Chicago, IL, 1942 – lives Santa Fe, NM
Canyon del Muerto, Arizona, 1987

Slough   A slough—also slow, slew, sloo, slue—is a narrow stretch of sluggish water in a river channel, inlet, or pond. A slough can also be a marsh, swamp, bayou, or any soft, muddy, or waterlogged ground. The great, flat city of Chicago is built on filled sloughs, or swampy bottomlands. Slough is also a verb, meaning to mire in a slough or swamp, and "to be sloughed" can mean "lost in a swamp." Used as slang, "to slough in," or "slough up," is to arrest or imprison, to be inhibited, or bogged down. Nineteenth-century travelers reported horses sinking up to their necks in sloughs that looked no deeper than a puddle. Prairies, especially those radiating from the Mississippi, are (or were) riddled with sloughs, and sloughs run along the St. Paul, Pacific, and Sioux City Railroad tracks and other elevated rights-of-way, providing ideal homes for muskrats. —Donna Seaman

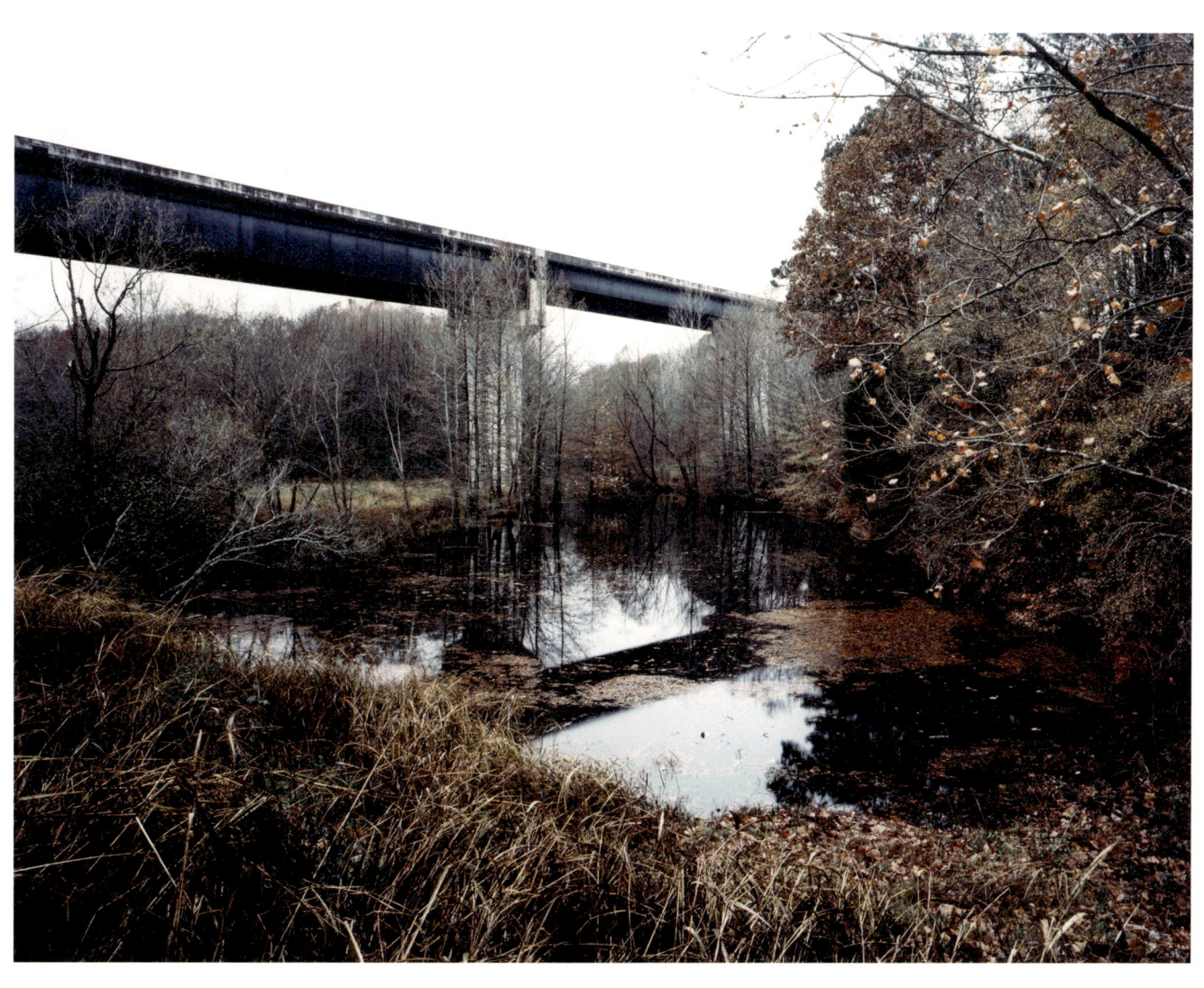

39. Jeff Rich   Born Atlanta, GA, 1977 – lives Atlanta, GA
Slough and MS-25 Bridge, Iuka, Mississippi, 2013

Littoral drift   Littoral means of or pertaining to the shore, and littoral drift is material moved along a beach by a littoral current, a current carried by waves breaking at an angle to the shoreline and moving parallel to and adjacent to the shoreline within the surf zone. Littoral drift is, then, the material waves and wind work to shape coastlines, depositing and rearranging the sand, rock, gravel, bits of shell, and other debris to form shoals, spits, bars, and beaches. One example of a high-littoral-drift zone is California's Santa Cruz Harbor, where up to 327,000 cubic yards of drift is deposited each year, enough to cover a football field to a depth of 184 feet. —Gretchen Legler

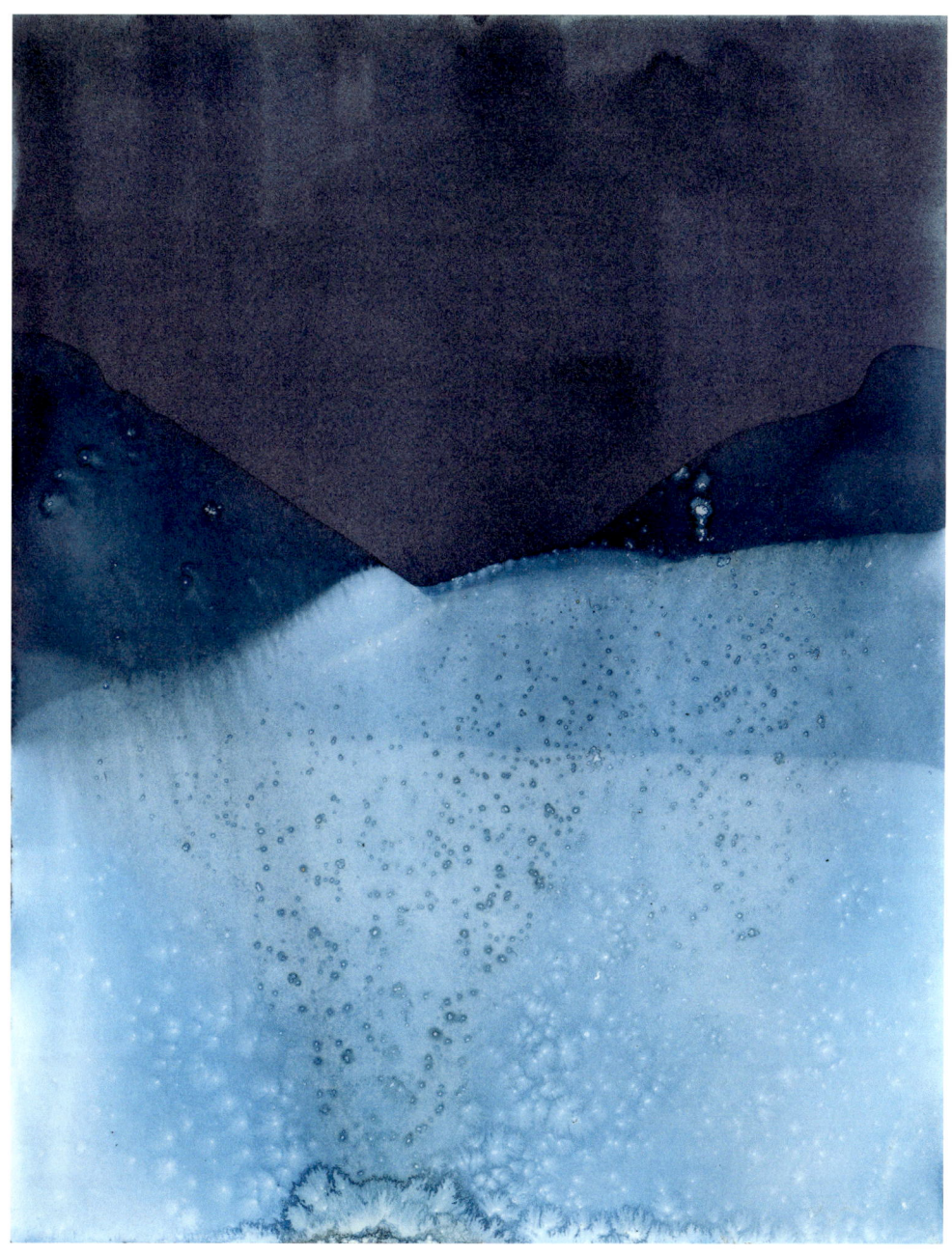

40. Meghann Riepenhoff   Born Atlanta, GA, 1979 – lives Bainbridge Island, WA and San Francisco, CA
Littoral Drift #1223 (Chattahoochee River, Atlanta, Georgia 09.26.18, Draped on Long Island at Confluence of White Water Creek), 2018

Hell In nineteenth-century America, hell was a generic term for a rough or difficult stretch of country, such as the wildly eroded Hell's Half-Acre in Wyoming. Similarly, the thermal features of Yellowstone Park were originally called Coulters Hell, after the explorer and mountain man John Coulter. The word was also used to designate the most lawless sections of frontier towns like Fort Worth and San Antonio, as well as particularly dangerous and rough parts of the urban landscape, such as Hell's Kitchen in New York City. In the southern Appalachians, a hell is a dense, extensive growth of laurel or rhododendron. Horace Kephart, in *Our Southern Highlanders*, defined the term this way: "A 'hell' or 'slick' or 'wooly-head' or 'yaller patch' is a thicket of laurel or rhododendron impassable save where the bears have bored out trails." —Charles Frazier

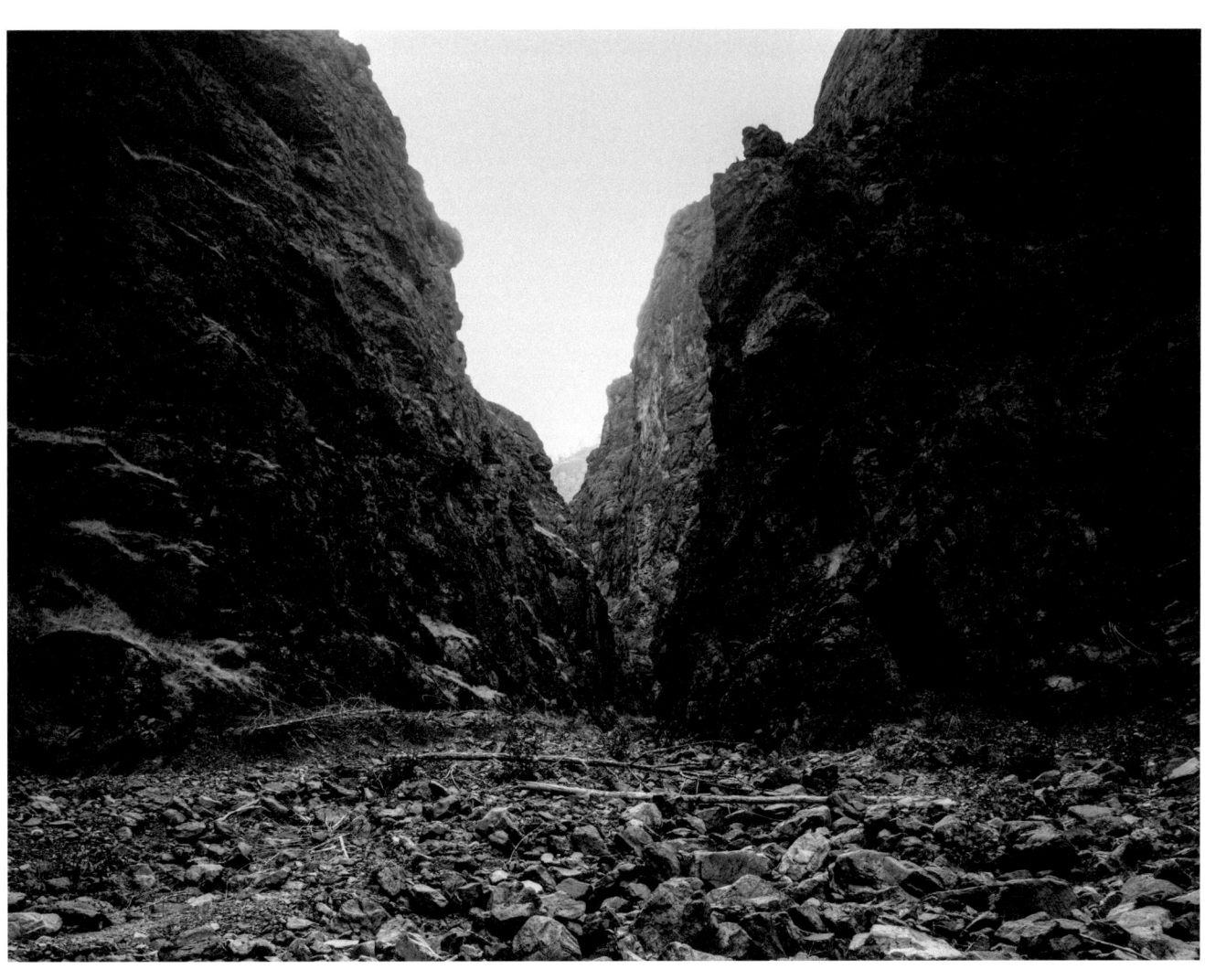

41. Mark Ruwedel   Born Bethlehem, PA, 1954 – lives Long Beach, CA
Hells Canyon Creek, Snake River Drainage, 1999

Blue hole   Blue holes, deep depressions filled with water sometimes so intensely blue they appear bottomless, are one of the spectacular formations of karst topography: limestone bedrock sculpted by the dissolving effects of rainwater or groundwater. Though there are many North American examples, such as the Blue Hole in northwestern Ohio, most famous is the Blue Hole sixty miles off the coast of Belize, a haven for deep-water scuba divers. Located in the aquamarine shallows of Lighthouse Reef, this blue hole is a near-perfect circle more than a thousand feet across, its deep indigo water a result of its four-hundred-foot-depth. Though now submerged, it formed on dry land, either as a cavern whose roof finally collapsed or as a sinkhole. Then melting glaciers at the end of the Ice Age flooded continental margins along the Atlantic coast, turning this land formation into one in the sea. The eerily pure color of a blue hole many not always signal depth: A shallow blue hole in the New Jersey Pine Barrens sometimes called the Jersey Devil's Bathtub owes its saturated hue to the purity of strongly upwelling spring water—undoubtedly also the force that created the formation. —Pamela Frierson

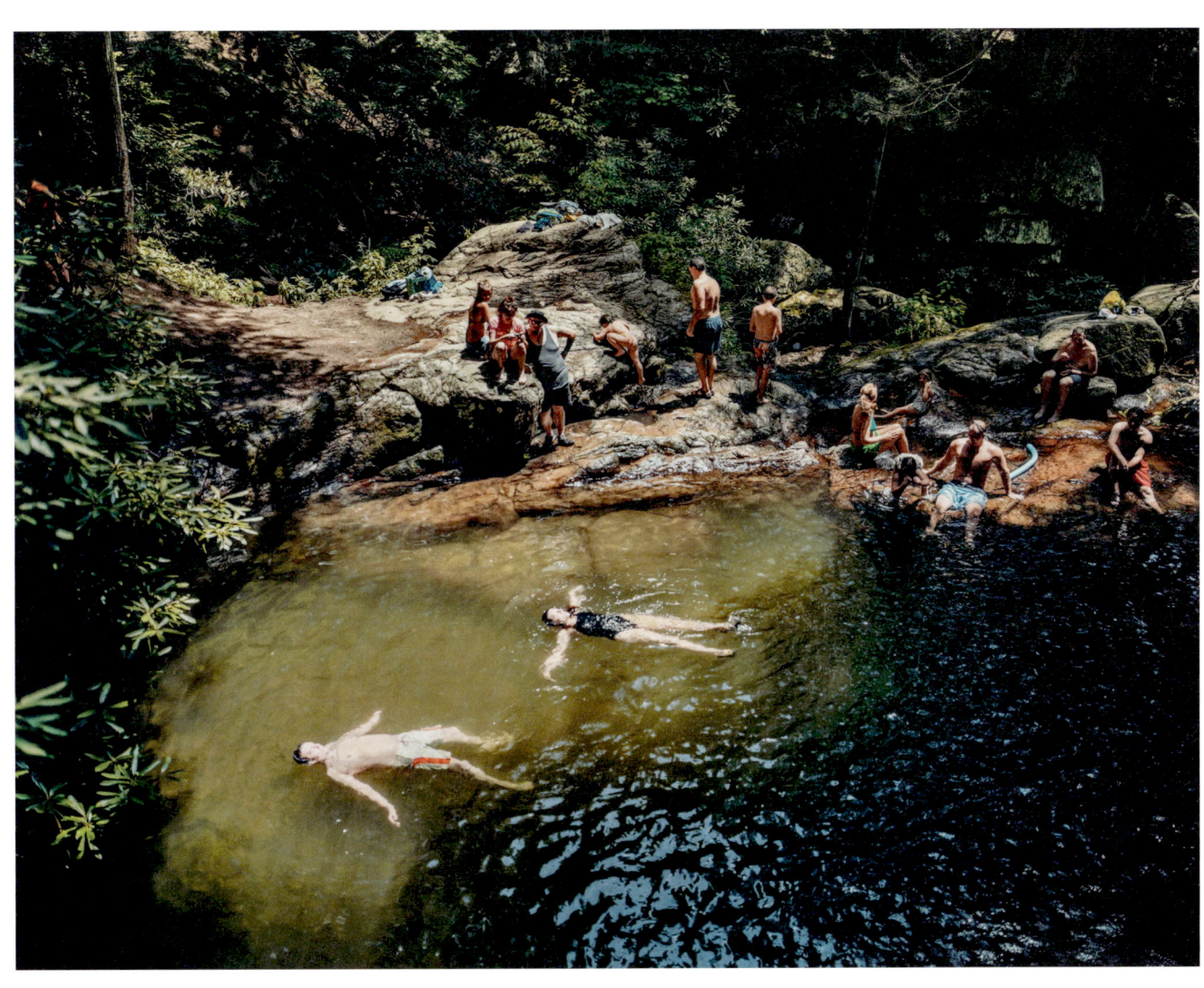

42. Mike Smith   Born Heidelberg, Germany, 1951 – lives Johnson City, TN
Blue Hole, Carter County, Tennessee, 2011

Plateau An extensive area of nearly level land that rises abruptly above a surrounding landscape on at least one side, known also as tableland, is called a plateau. Canyons often encroach on or dissect the plateau's flat surface, and it is distinguished from similar formations by its breadth—the Columbia lava plateau of eastern Washington and Oregon, for instance, is different from the isolated prominence of a mesa, is larger than a butte, is flat, and presents a dramatic vertical fall on all sides. Plateau also designates the American Indians who inhabited the plateau country between the Cascades and Rockies, and the food-gathering culture there. —Larry Woiwode

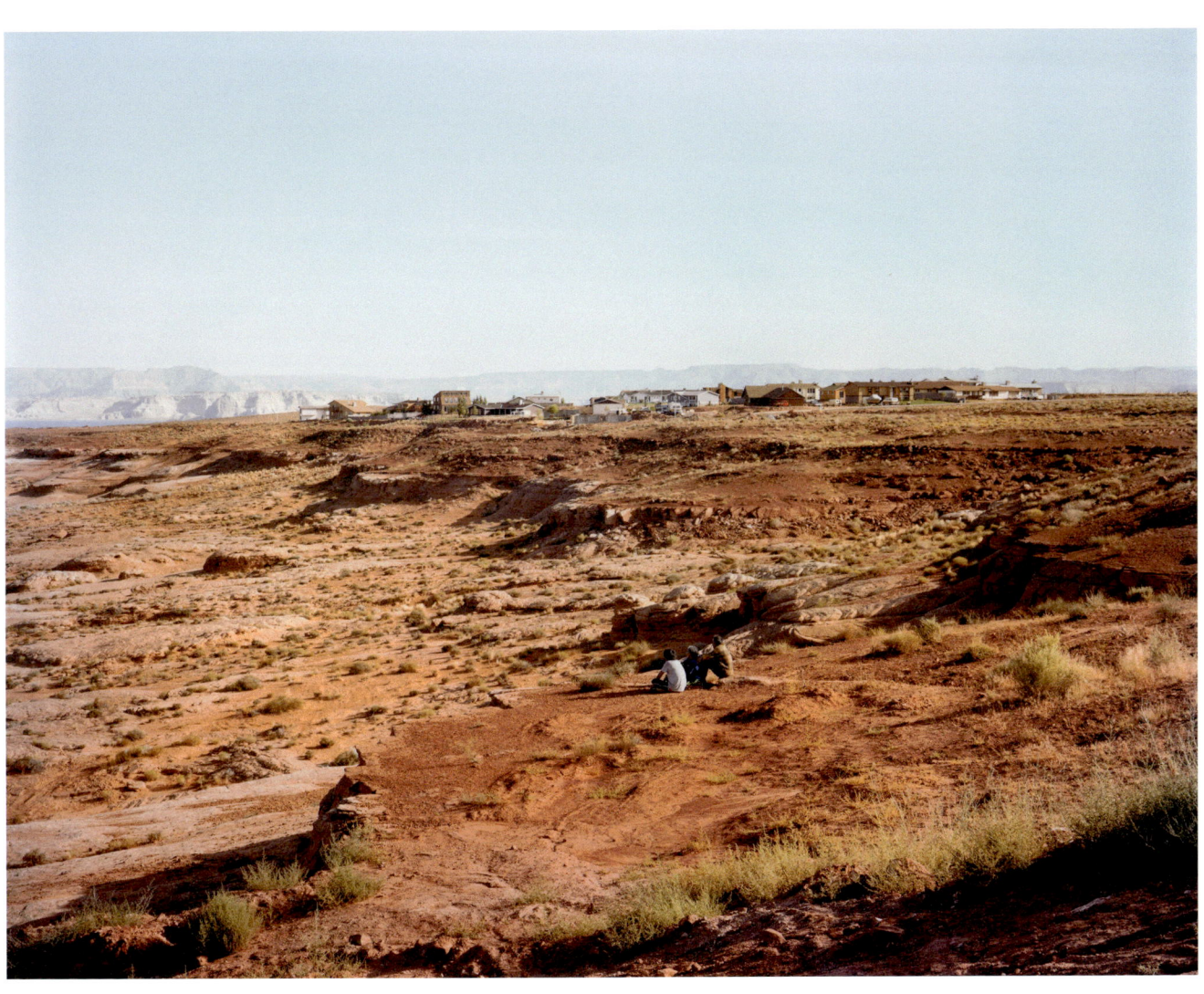

43. Joel Sternfeld   Born New York, NY, 1944 – lives New York, NY
Rim View Trail, Page, Arizona, August 1983, 1983

Dune   Wind and a generous supply of granular material are needed to make a dune, which can arise in arid places or along the shore of a lake or ocean, or even along the banks of a river such as the Arkansas River in western Kansas. Dunes are classified by their shape, which is a function of sand and topography interacting with the wind. Sand particles begin to move when wind velocity reaches about eleven miles per hour. The particles move by skipping over the ground, a motion called saltation. The grains are kicked briefly into the air and then fall with a forward glide, hitting other grains on the ground and putting them into motion as well. Relatively fine sand collects this way to produce dunes with a clearly marked crest that drops off to a steep slip face on the sheltered, leeward side. Coarse sand produces rounded dunes without these features. One of the largest dune fields in the United States is the Algodones Dunes, extending southeasterly more than forty miles from Glamis in Imperial County, California, to the southwestern corner of Arizona and into Mexico. The highest dune on America's East Coast is the 140-foot-high Jockeys Ridge on the Outer Banks of North Carolina; it's an example of a coastal dune. Sometimes, continuing wind causes dunes to move—as at White Sands, New Mexico, where the dunes of loose gypsum sand move twenty-four feet a year. If the winds and sand supply diminish, an advancing or migrating dune might acquire a covering of vegetation and settle down as a fixed or stabilized dune. The dune environment often has unfamiliar acoustic properties and dune-created wind patterns that sculpt the features of the dune field. Wanderers among dunes may feel a thrill in their alien presence, be enchanted, or, like early saints, see visions in mirages and hear voices in the falling sand. —D. J. Waldie

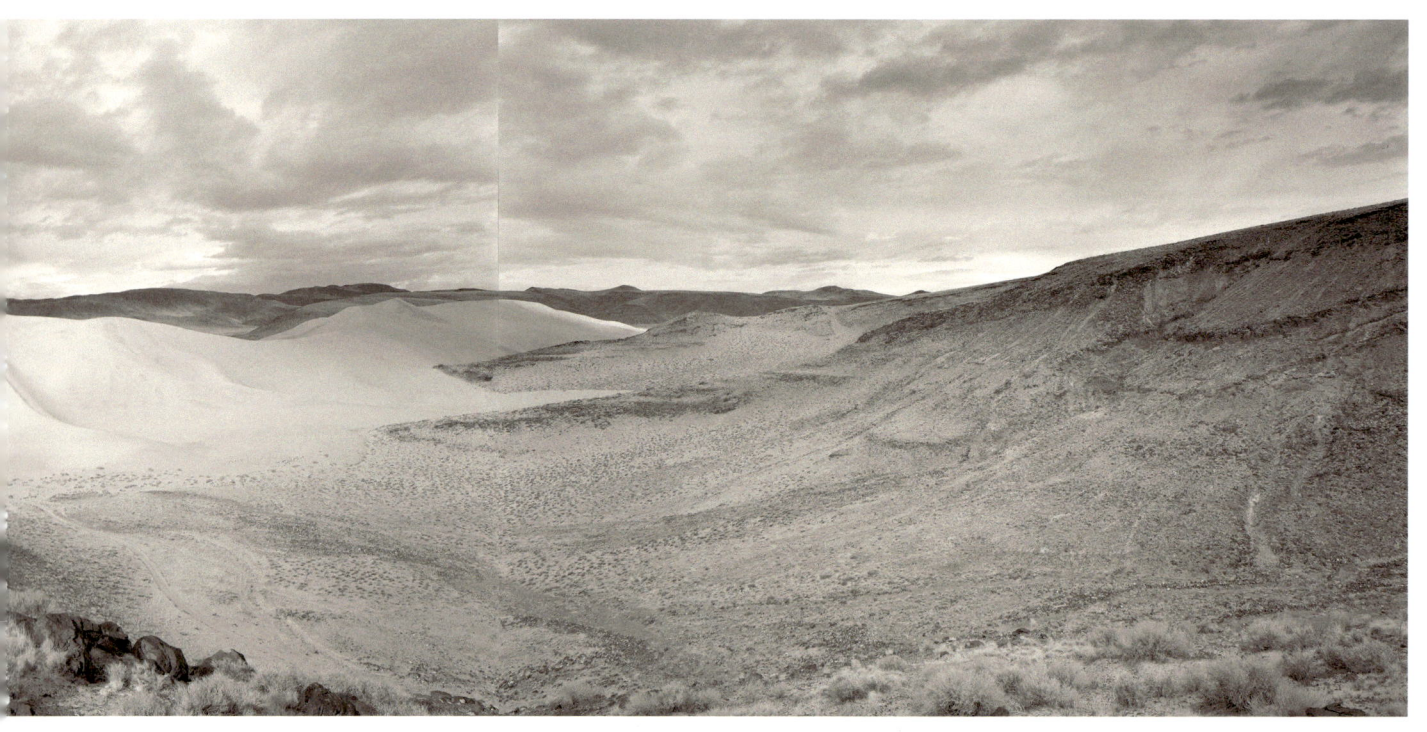

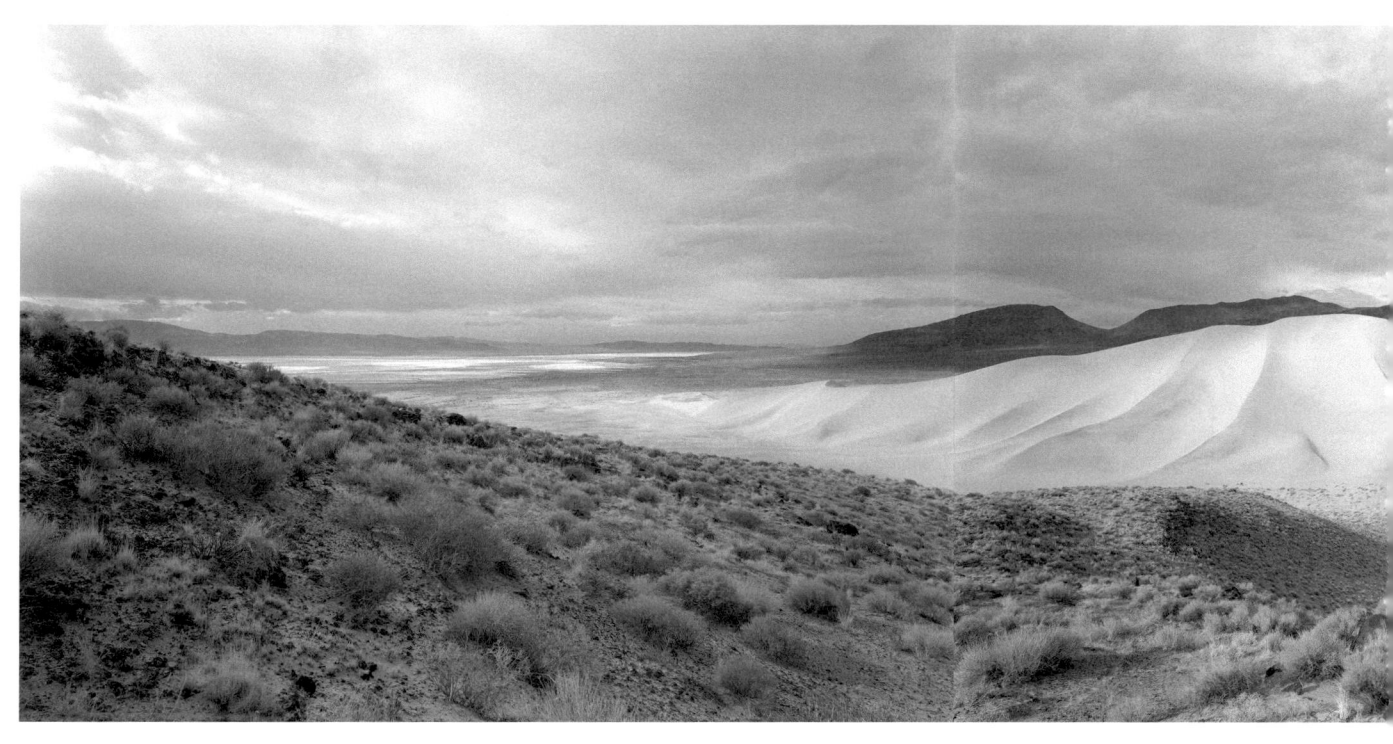

44. Martin Stupich Born Milwaukee, WI, 1949 – lives Albuquerque, NM
Sand Mountain, Nevada, 1980

Comb ridge   A comb ridge is a sharp mountain crest eroded by glaciers or water to look jagged, saw-toothed. Because of the pinnacles and notches along its crest, a comb ridge—the expression is often used interchangeably with arête—resembles a rooster's comb. It is the acute and rugged divide between two aggressive glacial arenas. In the dryland west, a comb ridge is a single fold of upturned rock that has sharp teeth cut by water erosion. An example is Comb Ridge, near Bluff, Utah. Other comb ridges can be seen in Grand Staircase–Escalante National Monument, Utah. —Robert Morgan

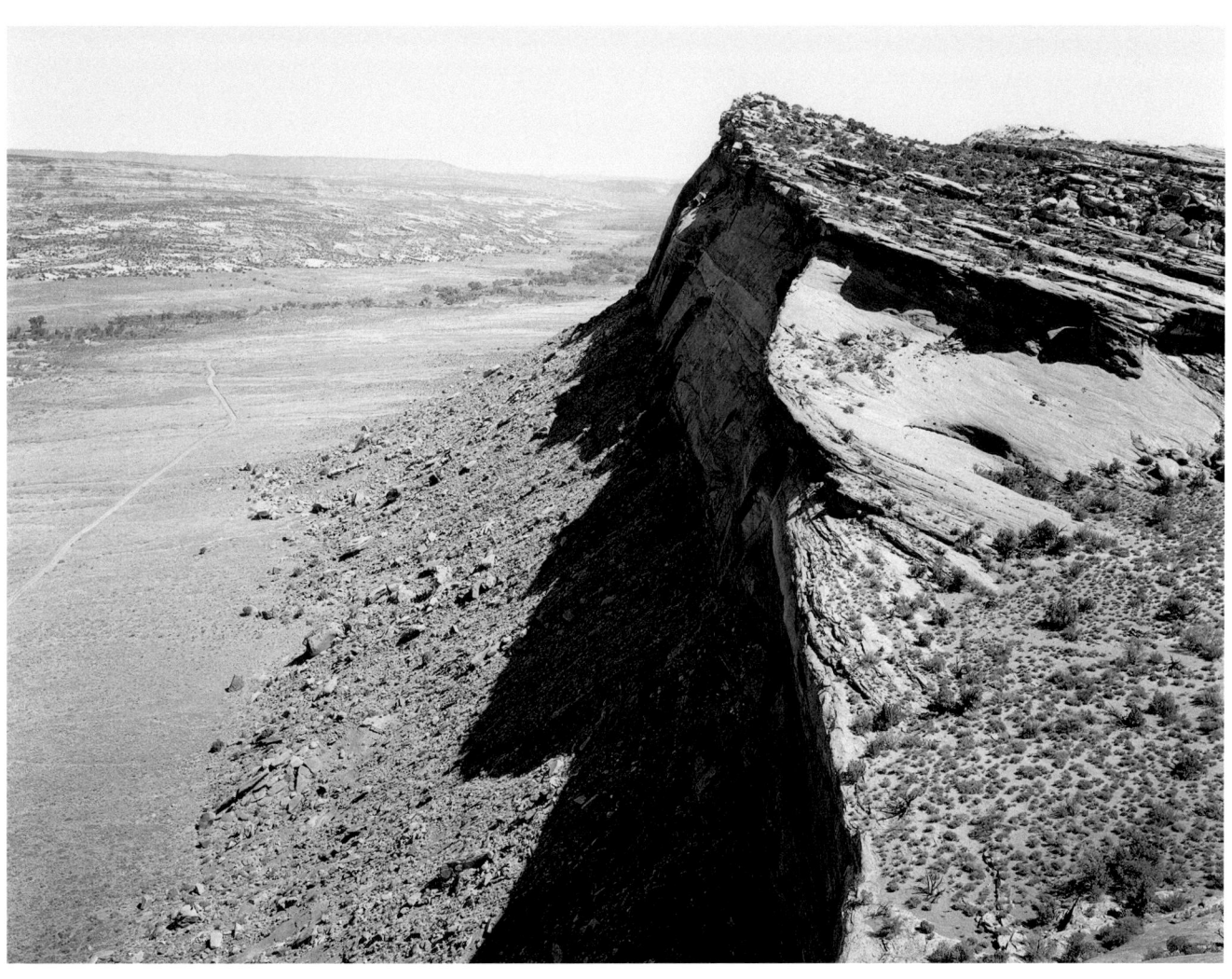

45. William Sutton   Born Toledo, OH, 1956 – lives Boulder, CO
Comb Ridge, Bureau of Land Management, Utah, 1989

Portage A portage is a path or passageway along which canoes or other small boats and goods are carried around obstructions in a stream or between navigable bodies of water. A portage is also a place where such a land route begins or ends, and it refers, too, to the act of carrying or transporting canoes and goods overland, usually to skirt unmanageable rapids or waterfalls. So established a fact of transportation were portages, there existed a portage collar, a strap that passed around the forehead and attached at each end to the burden being carried, which was then supported on the back. A portage was no picnic, but it made traversing the wilderness possible—eventually there were even portage railroads. Most portages were only known locally, but one became famous: the Chicago Portage, which made possible the crucial water route from the Great Lakes to the mighty Mississippi. —Donna Seaman

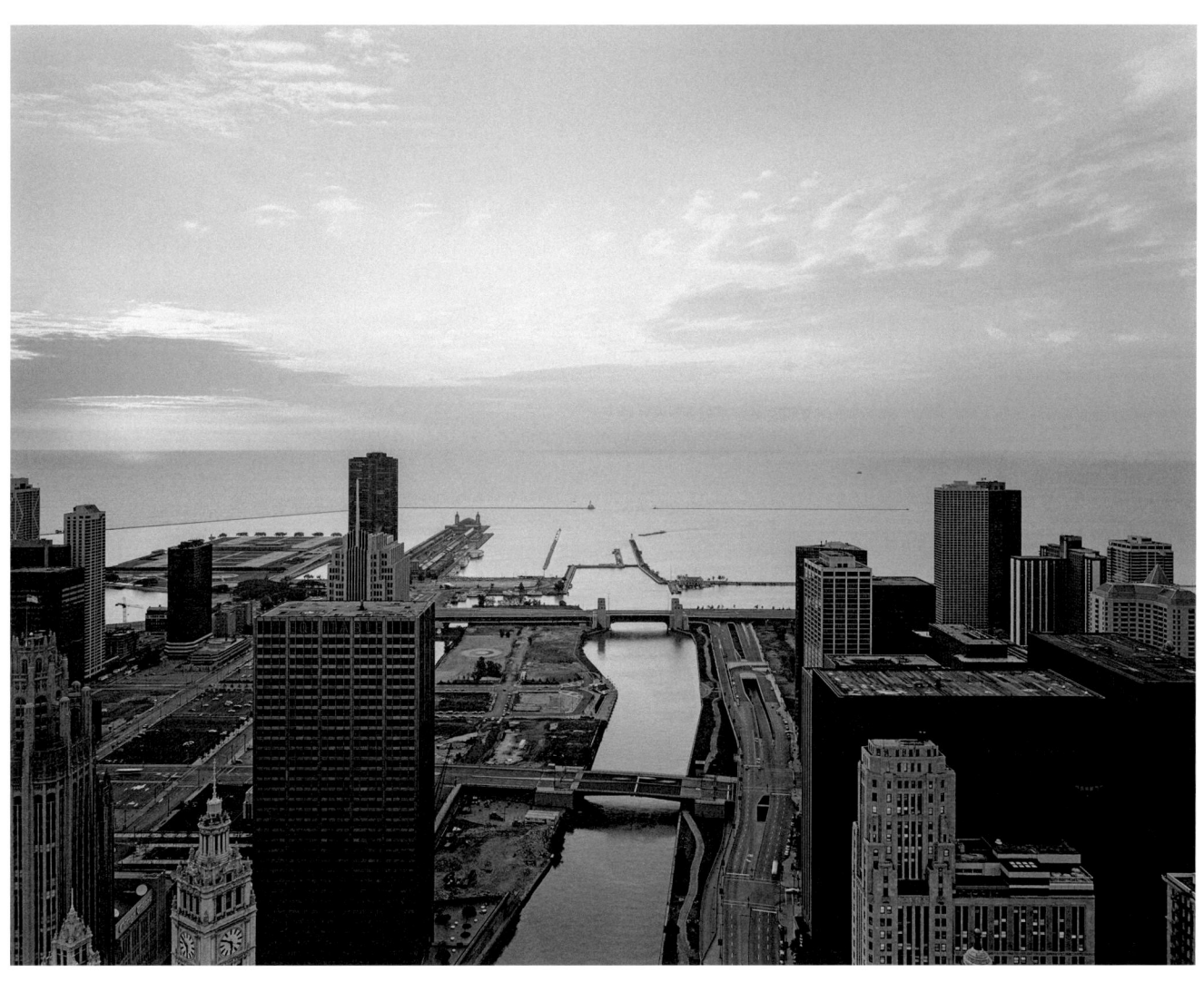

46. Bob Thall   Born Chicago, IL, 1948 – lives Evanston, IL
Chicago (Chicago River. View East from the Roof of the IBM Building), 1989

Basin and range The extension or stretching of the Earth's crust normally results in downfaulted valleys, or grabens, and upfaulted mountains, or horsts. North America's huge geological province of north-south–oriented mountains and valleys created in this way is known as basin and range country (roughly 400,000 square miles) and runs between northern Mexico and southeastern Oregon, and the Sierra Nevada of California and the Wasatch Mountains of Utah. It includes parts of all the major North American deserts—the Great Basin, Mojave, Sonoran, and Chihuahuan. Death Valley, on the Nevada-California border, reaches a maximum of 282 feet below sea level, while the Panamint Mountains just to the west rise to some 11,000 feet in elevation. At the foot of such snowy ranges as the Ruby Mountains in Nevada and Steens Mountain in Oregon, peat-bog marshes form despite the aridity of the basins, providing havens for migrating waterfowl. Runoff from Steens Mountain flows through glacial valleys to the Malheur National Wildlife Refuge and drains into a series of alkaline playas where the waters evaporate. —William Kittredge

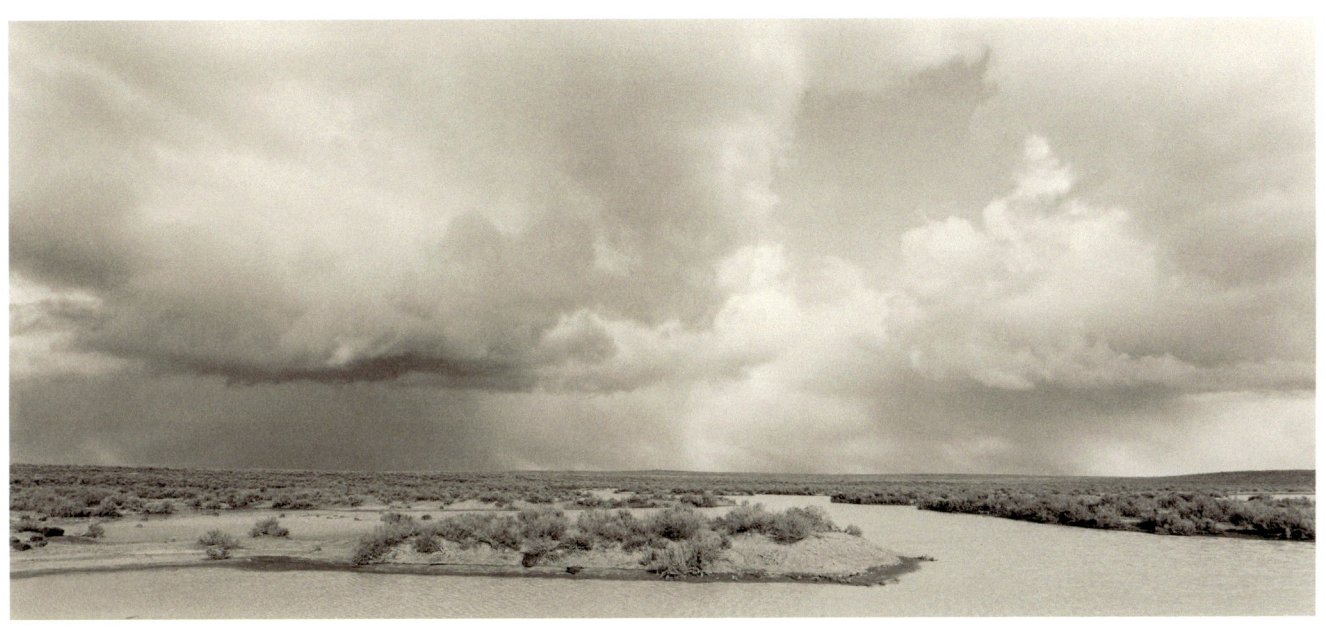

47. Terry Toedtemeier   Born Portland, OR, 1947 – died Hood River, OR, 2008
Palomino Lake, Malheur County, Oregon, 1993

Bayou   Bayou is a word that sounds French but is in fact of Choc-
taw origin, deriving from *bayuk*, meaning "small stream." In
recorded usage since 1818, bayou most commonly refers to
marshy offshoots and overflowings of lakes and rivers in the
delta of Louisiana and the Gulf area. In a region of mostly
swamps and marshy prairies, the bayous are spaces of open
water, sluggish or stagnant, often the abandoned channels
of the river delta cut off into oxbow lakes in the river's vari-
orum history of trial and evolution. Bayou can also refer to a
secondary channel, away from the mainstream, where the
current is slower and the volume smaller. Sometimes a tributary is referred to as a bayou, as is any sluggish stream.
The word can be said to refer to any slow water in a marshy
area, if not dead water perhaps sleeping water, or dreaming
water. —Robert Morgan

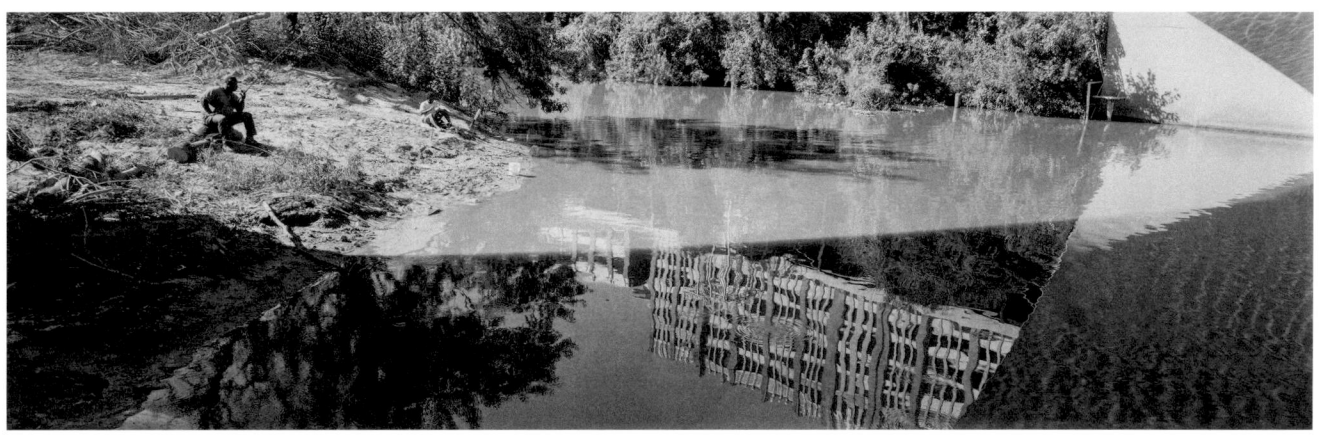

48. Geoff Winningham   Born Jackson, TN, 1943 – lives Houston, TX
Allen's Landing on Buffalo Bayou, Houston, Texas, 2001

Hanging valley A high valley that converges with, and breaks off abruptly into, a deeper valley, often over a cliff, is known as a hanging valley. Hanging valleys occur when glaciations or water flow erode the main valley to a depth well below that of its tributary valleys. A hanging valley might include a hanging glacier, or end in a waterfall such as Bridal Veil Falls in Yosemite or Bird Woman Falls seen from the Going-to-the-Sun Highway over Logan Pass in Glacier National Park. Seacoast streams that fall over sea cliffs, which result from erosions caused by wave action and tectonic uplift, emerge from hanging valleys. Washes in the American Southwest often form hanging valleys, such as the seventy-five-foot cliff where Johns Canyon ends above the gorge of the San Juan River in the Grand Gulch country of southern Utah. —William Kittredge

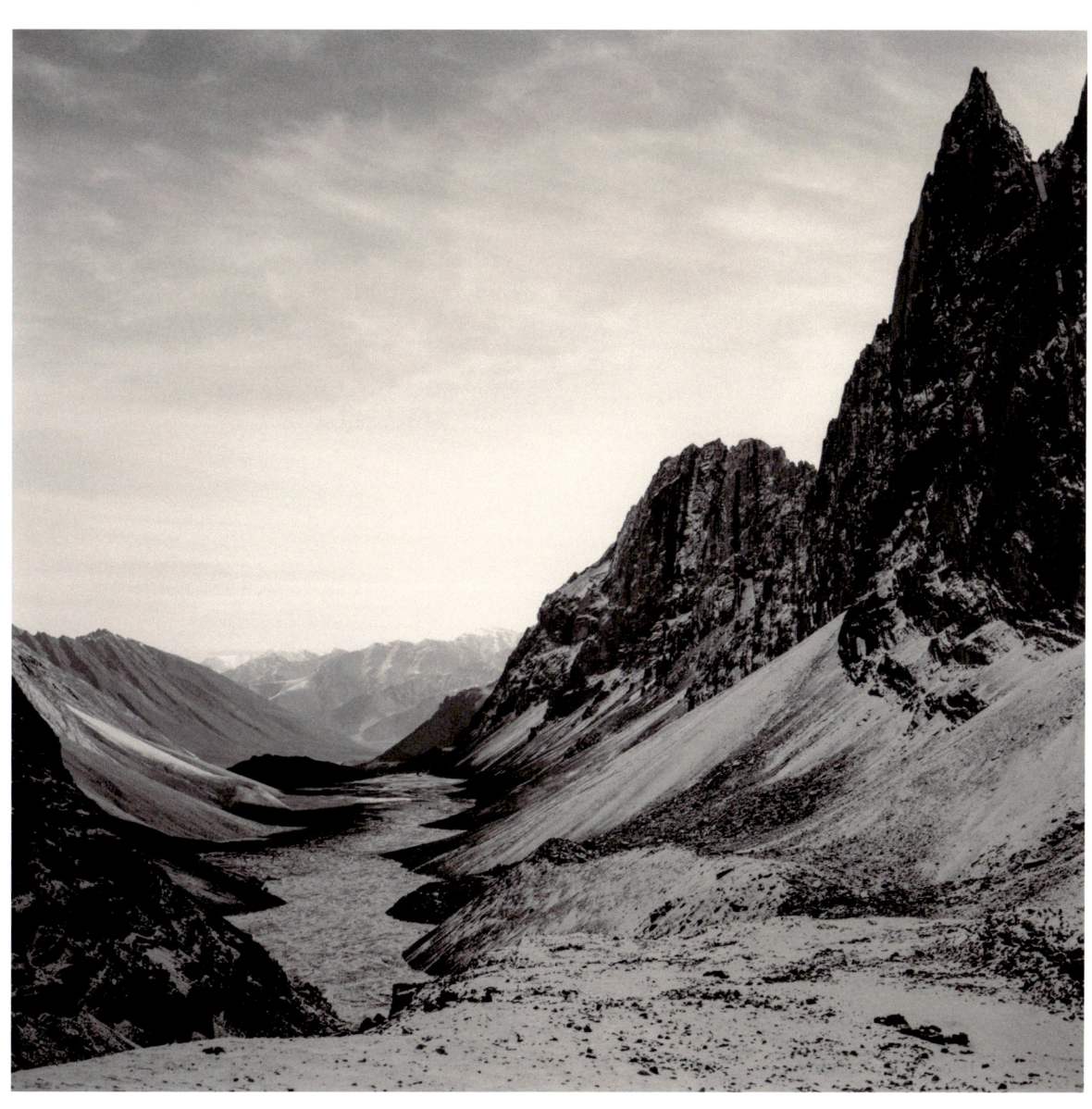

49. Dennis Witmer   Born Lancaster, PA, 1957 – died Spokane, WA, 2022
Hanging Valley, Brooks Range, Alaska, 1996

Stillwater   Stillwater is a term that describes a curious phenomenon of quiet water. In the United States over two hundred places are named Stillwater—including rivers, canyons, streams, ponds, even flats and towns. In the late seventeenth century one such town, bordered by the Hudson River near Saratoga, New York, was chronicled as a place where "the water passes so slowly as not to be discovered, while above and below it is disturbed, and rageth as in a great sea, occasioned by rocks and falls therein." In the late 1800s the best-known city by this name, Stillwater, Oklahoma, formed near a back-eddied place on a creek. Lesser-known Stillwater towns in Nevada, Montana, and elsewhere also grew up around pools of tranquil water. Such cities, because of their names, are often presented as stereotypically tranquil places to live, as depicted in Richard and Florence Atwater's *Mr. Popper's Penguins:* "It was an afternoon in late September. In the pleasant city of Stillwater, Mr. Popper, the house painter, was going home from work." Stillwater is a term also used by meteorologists in predicting storm surges. In deep water they look for the midpoint of the wave crest before it reels down; in shallow water they look for the trough and crest of the wave. The stillwater level is the highest water level measured if wave action were completely smoothed out. —Elizabeth Cox

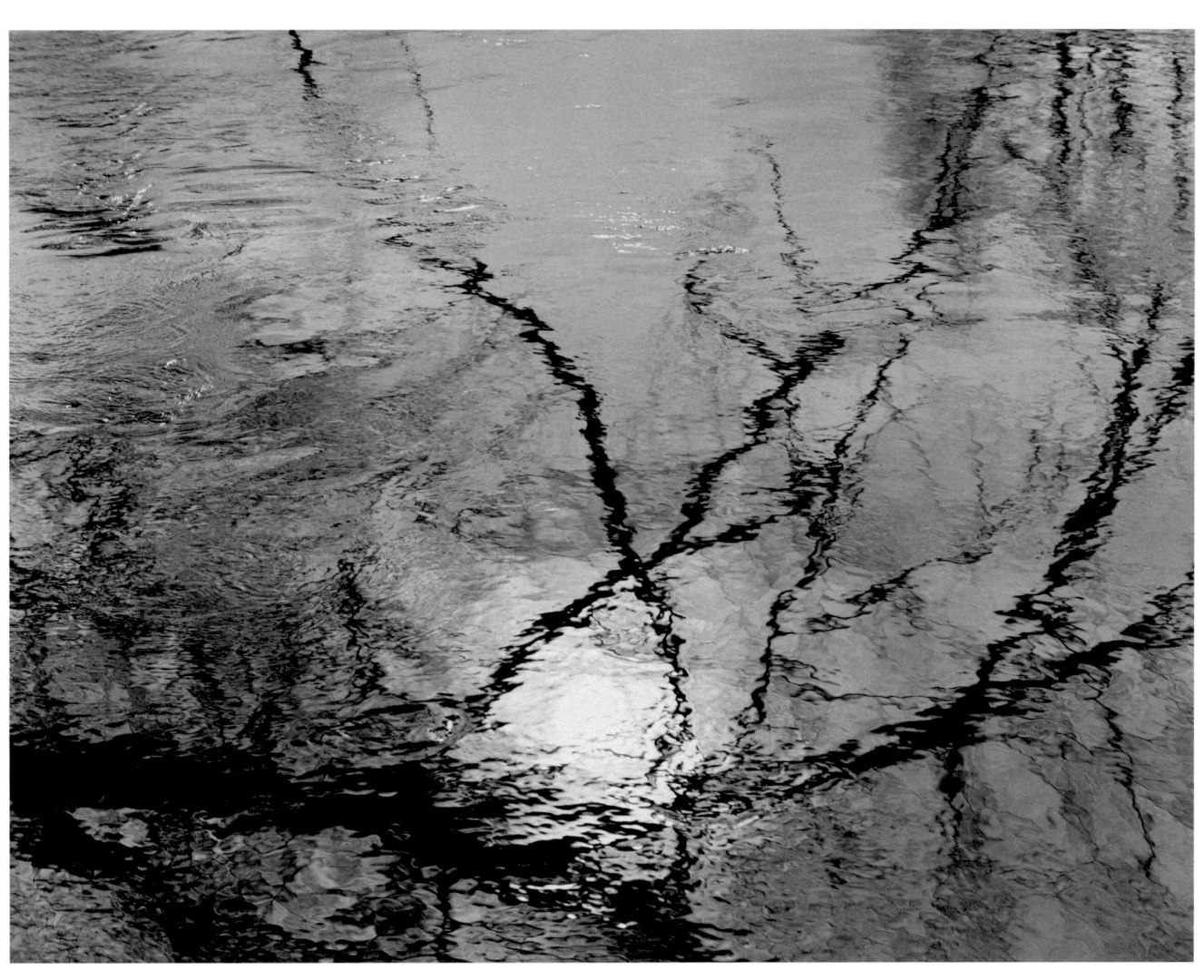

50. William Wylie Born Harvey, IL, 1957 – lives Charlottesville, VA
Cache la Poudre River, Colorado, 2000

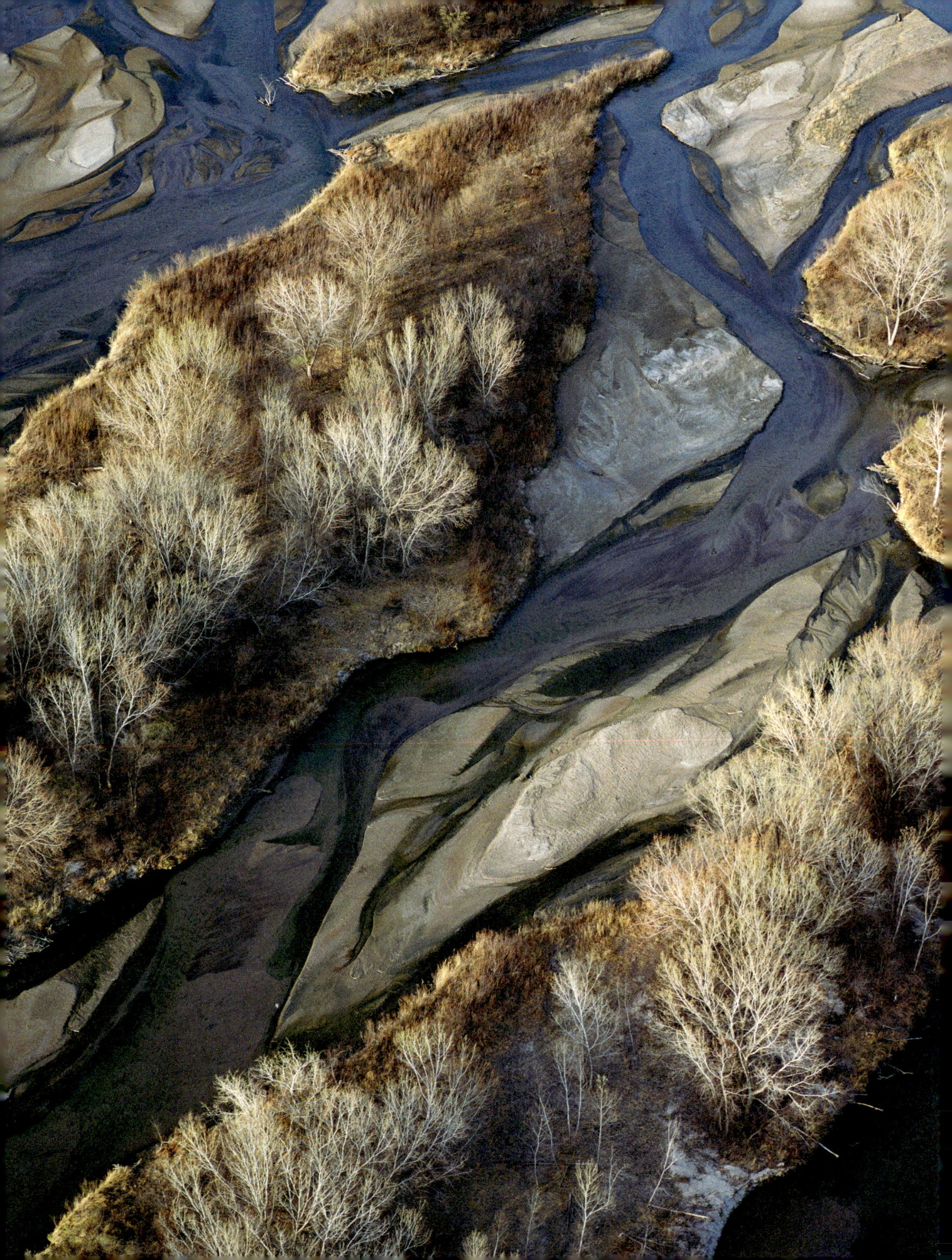

Toby Jurovics   Land, Light, and Film

The Home Ground Collection in honor of Barry Lopez reflects a conversation between the camera and the American landscape that began over one hundred and fifty years ago. The making of these images, during the last decades of the twentieth century and the beginning of the twenty-first, also marks a change in our understanding of the land and all it contains, as photography moved beyond a reflexive association with uninhabited wilderness. While this dialogue was often critical, drawing attention to instances of negligence and abuse, it was also less rigidly constrained, welcoming our presence and, along with it, the possibility of a more intimate relationship with our "home grounds" at a time when we were becoming increasingly distanced from the world around us.

Today, much of our time in the landscape is likely to happen behind the wheel—our lives are mediated by screens, whether the phone or computer or, more prosaically, a windshield—and a long drive remains one of the few times we have the luxury of being able to look without an obligation to do much else. Driving east on I-80 from Colorado toward Lincoln, Nebraska, the Platte River casually weaves alongside the interstate, meandering through sandbars and wooded islands. Its course is given away by the cottonwoods lining its banks, enlivening a landscape that might otherwise be dismissed as flat and featureless, were one also to discount a bright blue sky, sunlight dodging through the clouds, grasses rippling in waves across a windy pasture. About his earliest drives across the country, Barry wrote, "Everywhere I went, state promotional materials touted their home ground as 'the land of contrasts.' Some had more contrast than others, of course, and in a few, like North Dakota, the contrast was subtle. The country as a whole, however, has contrast enough—in its lava fields, alpine tundra, canyons, and barrier islands—to defeat a lifetime of looking"[1] (figure 1).

Selected by the photographers in relation to entries in *Home Ground: A Guide to the American Landscape*, the

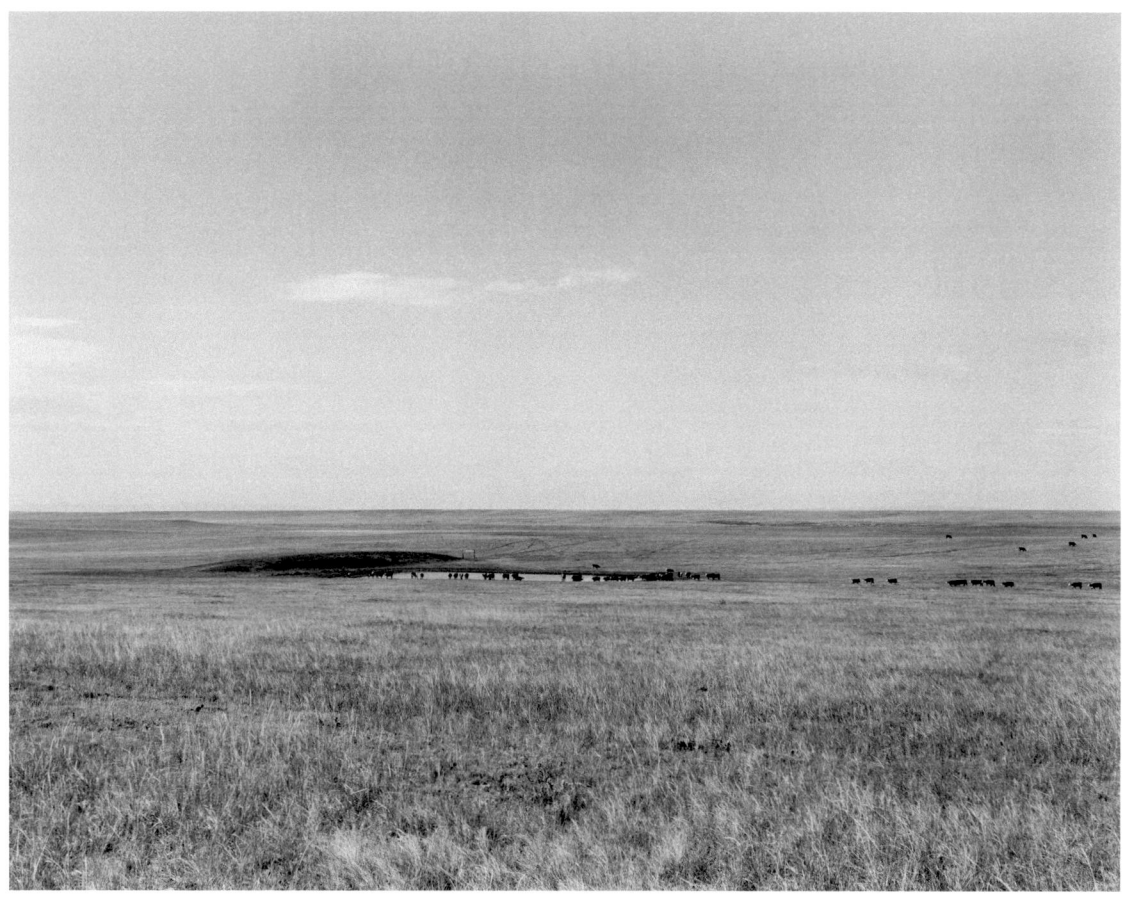

1 Wayne Gudmundson
South of Marmarth, North Dakota, 1983
Sheldon Museum of Art, the Home Ground Collection

Looking-glass prairie

images in this collection are a visual companion to that earlier "reader's dictionary"—a call and response of words and images. In much the same way that Barry observed, "that this seemingly unfettered, nearly immeasurable American landscape I had become acquainted with . . . had distinctively stamped the long line of American literature," photographer Gregory Conniff wrote, "that American space, American light, the things of this country come together to form a voice that shapes how we think and feel, much as our parents' voices shaped us in childhood."[2] And it is in the affection we have for our landscape that American photography discovered its character, speaking with a clarity and precision that reflected the boldness of its geography as well as its elegance and lyricism, even in places that might

134

otherwise be considered ordinary or unremarkable. The rise and fall of our topography, our rivers and canyons, meadows and valleys, the profile of our mountains against the horizon have always been understood to be inspirational and redemptive.

This is the American Earth

Ansel Adams's most important photographs were made before 1960, but few artists remain more firmly fixed in the American imagination. Trading on visual formulas that were already well established in the nineteenth century by painters and photographers including Albert Bierstadt, Thomas Moran, Eadweard Muybridge, and Carleton Watkins, Adams's photographs personified a romanticized wilderness that appeared little changed by the intervening century (figure 2). And with Adams as its leading advocate, the Sierra Club promoted an idealized vision of the American landscape that was largely confined to national parks and public lands defined by their scenery and the recreational opportunities they offered. The mission statement published in *This is the American Earth*, the club's initial "Exhibit Format" book released in 1960, clearly identified its agenda: "The Sierra Club, founded in 1892 by John Muir, has devoted itself to the study and protection of national scenic resources, particularly those of mountain regions. Participation is invited in the program to enjoy and preserve wilderness, wildlife, forests, and streams."[3] David Brower, president of the Sierra Club at that time, went a step further in his foreword to Adams's 1963 biography, *The Eloquent Light*, asserting, "As a photographer of great places, he [Adams] came quickly to discern what did not belong in those places. If something wasn't good on his ground glass, it probably wasn't very good in a national park either, or a forest wilderness."[4] It is as efficient a description of the interdependent relationship between photography and wilderness as one might wish, establishing an ideal of scenic beauty that continues to shape our expectations of the landscape to this day.[5]

The Sierra Club leveraged this vision to build an urgent national awareness of the importance of environmental conservation and encouraged millions of people to visit their national parks. And just as Thomas Moran's watercolors and William Henry Jackson's photographs from their 1871 excursion to the Yellowstone territory were used to lobby Congress for its establishment as the first national park, Adams's photographs were similarly employed to advocate for Kings Canyon

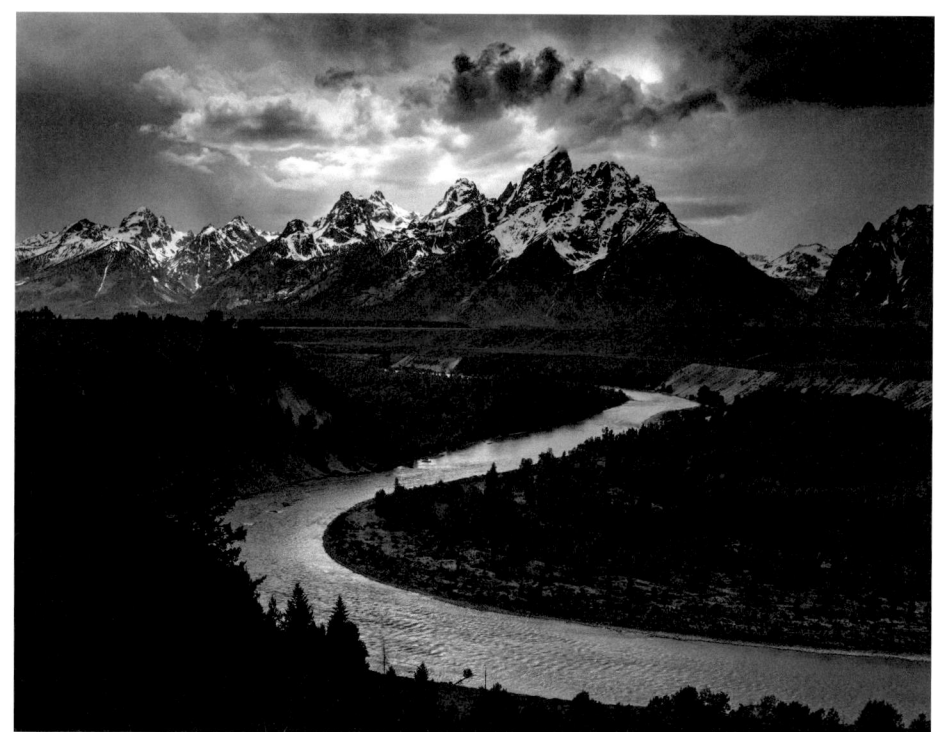

2 Ansel Adams, *The Tetons and the Snake River, Grand Teton National Park, Wyoming*, 1942, printed 1964, gelatin silver print, 15 7/16 × 19 9/16 inches. Sheldon Museum of Art, Nebraska Art Association, Gift of Lawrence Reger in memory of Mrs. Ellery Lothrop Davis, N-227.1970. © The Ansel Adams Publishing Rights Trust

3 Ansel Adams, *Winter Sunrise, the Sierra Nevada from Lone Pine, California*, 1944, gelatin silver print, 14 3/16 × 19 inches. Collection Center for Creative Photography, University of Arizona. © The Ansel Adams Publishing Rights Trust

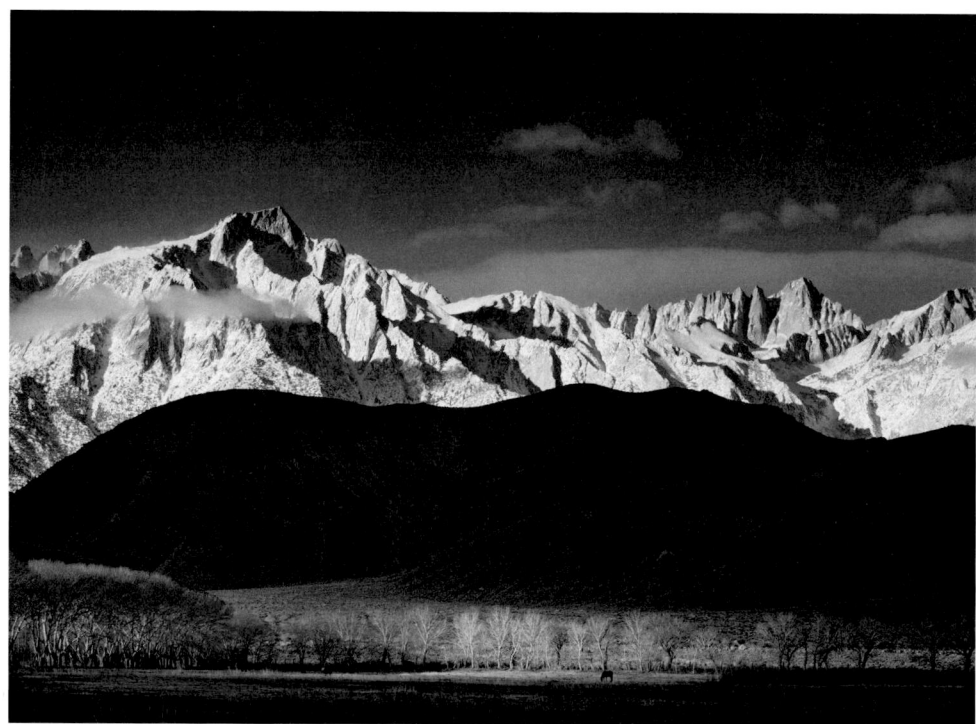

National Park in California and countless preservation efforts led by the Sierra Club and other environmental organizations. But there were also limitations to Adams's style, which by the 1980s had become impossible to ignore. Mark Klett, whose photographs of the Southwest are populated with hikers and tourists, summed up the problem:

> The virtue of Adams's combination of notoriety and longevity was that it helped raise an environmental consciousness about the land. His depopulated scenes suggest that the landscape does best without our presence, and that wilderness is an entity defined by our absence. However, anyone who has visited the site of one of Adams's photographs knows that the romance of his landscapes is often best experienced in the photographs themselves. The reality of the place is quite different.[6]

My Camera at the Head of Sinbad, San Rafael Swell, Utah, 5/22/93, 1993 (plate 30), cleverly undermines the solemnity of wilderness photography, Klett's presumed camera balanced at the edge of an outcropping like a sightseer inching as close to the view as possible. But by this time, Brower's agenda had come full circle, and his insistence on "scenic purity" led to a sense of dissatisfaction with the cities and suburban communities where most people spent their lives. Rather than lay blame at Adams's feet, however, looking at one of his best-known images reveals his understanding that photographs were capable of symbolic possibilities beyond the glorification of mountain scenery. *Winter Sunrise, the Sierra Nevada from Lone Pine, California*, 1944 (figure 3), finds a horse grazing beneath the jagged spires of Mount Whitney, the tallest peak in the continental United States (named for its serrated ridgelines, *Home Ground* tells us that *sierra* translates as *saw* in Spanish).[7] It is majestic and inspiring, but the history of this image has been obscured in the decades since its making. Before appearing as the two-page opening spread of *This is the American Earth*, it was published in *Born Free and Equal: The Story of Loyal Japanese Americans*, Adams's 1944 documentary book about the Manzanar Relocation Center, where the federal government incarcerated over 10,000 Americans of Japanese descent during World War II. The photograph's original caption read, "In the shadow of these mountains, the loyal people of Manzanar await their destiny."[8] Beyond capturing a crisp winter morning under the great flank of the eastern Sierra, Adams's image asserts that the gift of the American landscape comes with the challenge to live up to our highest aspirations, as individuals and as a nation.

Half Wilderness

At the same time Ansel Adams was cementing his legacy in the 1960s and 1970s, a younger generation of photographers was turning its gaze toward the built environment and the familiar surroundings of the everyday landscape. On the surface, their work seemed neither laudatory nor optimistic. Curiously, the slender exhibition catalogue that announced their arrival in 1975, *New Topographics: Photographs of a Man-altered Landscape*, preceded Adams's coffee table-sized *Yosemite and the Range of Light* by four years. A modest, slightly illustrated paperback that was dwarfed by Adams's tome, *New Topographics* was aimed at a more narrowly focused audience of curators, critics, and fellow photographers, and the distinctive style it promoted has yet to achieve the broad public acclaim of its more easily accessible predecessors. Nevertheless, the catalogue's title codified a style and subject matter that guided photography beyond the turn of the twenty-first century. *New Topographics* became a shorthand, suggesting photographs made with a dry and restrained formal style, one that appeared uninflected or detached, without sentiment or emotion. At least superficially, it was a rejection of the visual stamp of Ansel Adams and his peers. Much has been written about the exhibition and its influence, but equally important are the ways in which the era was misunderstood, including the concerns it continued to share with more traditional landscape photography.[9]

Many of the photographs made in the 1970s and early 1980s reflect a familiar reverence for American geography while also embracing evidence of our presence and activity and subjects that weren't considered to be conventionally picturesque. Pointing to these seeming contradictions, Frank Gohlke explained, "I wanted to be anti-heroic, astringent and romantic at the same time."[10] Grounding his images in the spare topography of the Plains rather than the Mountain West, the horizon became the dominant feature in his photographs. An emphatic line evenly dividing the frame, it is also a continually shifting landmark that remains ever in the distance—an especially vivid sensation, Gohlke noted, while driving across the Plains hour after hour. Meanwhile, his photographs located their dramatic energy in the temporal effects of weather—wind, rain, and shimmering heat. Nowhere is this more evident than in *Grain Elevator and Lightning Flash, Lamesa, Texas*, 1975 (figure 4), its familiar, practical architecture as thoroughly American a subject as *Winter Sunrise*: "The dignity of grain elevators, the precision, intelligence and grace of their formal language, their majestic presence within the landscape all seem to confirm the faith that, given the right circumstances, we will make visible the best that is within us."[11]

In welcoming us back into the landscape, *New Topographics* created a sense of balance or reconciliation through images that acknowledged the realities of homes, freeways, shopping malls, and parking lots without discrediting the affection for the land that had always been a hallmark of American photography. This discourse was not free of critique, however. Exploring the sprawling developments of tract homes that had overrun the Front Range north and south of Denver, Robert Adams sharply condemned what he saw as the ugly and uncivil imposition they made on the land. Our view of the summit in *Pikes Peak, Colorado Springs, Colorado*, 1970 (figure 5), is blocked by a gas station and its truncated sign, "Frontie," as if declaring the abrupt end of our Western mythologizing. But the print is also suffused with a soft fluorescent light that cascades over the pumps as the setting sun fills the dusk sky with a radiant glow. Gohlke, Adams, and their colleagues reminded us that signs of human endeavor didn't invalidate a landscape's worthiness of attention and concern, broadening our expectations about where to look and what to look for. In 1978, Adams went so far as to suggest, "Contrary to popular expectations, many of the best nature pictures—often the truest and finally the most reassuring—do contain people and their works. . . . This leaves photography with a new but not less important job: to reconcile us to half wilderness."[12]

New Topographics gave photographers permission to embrace the landscape without hesitation or the need to pause and consider what should be left out of the frame before making an exposure. William Wylie noted, "These landscapes were already familiar to us, and we felt less conflicted—we already knew we loved these places and didn't need to learn how to accept them."[13] Twice walking the length of Colorado's Cache la Poudre River to photograph from its headwaters in Rocky Mountain National Park

139

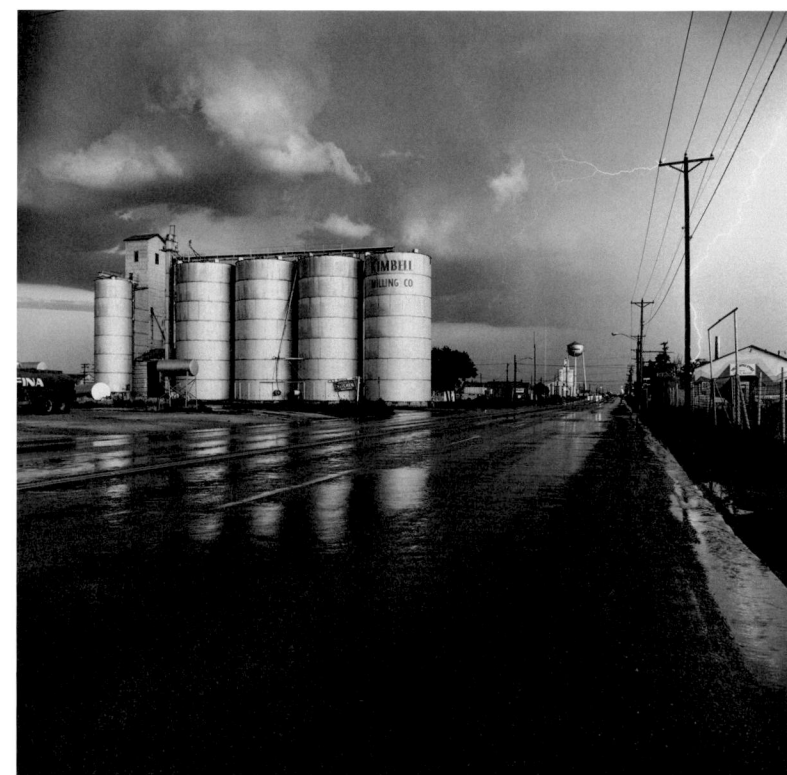

4 Frank Gohlke, *Grain Elevator and Lightning Flash, Lamesa, Texas*, 1975, gelatin silver print, 13¾ × 13¹³⁄₁₆ inches. Sheldon Museum of Art, Nebraska Art Association, Purchased with the aid of funds from the National Endowment for the Arts, N-418.1976. © Frank Gohlke

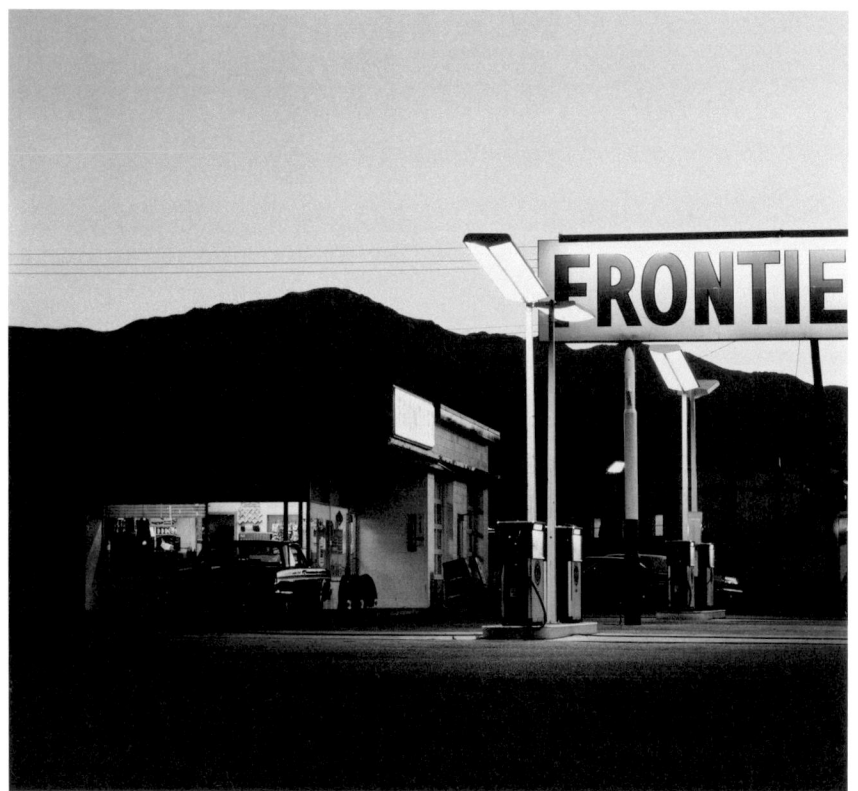

5 Robert Adams, *Pikes Peak, Colorado Springs, Colorado*, 1970, gelatin silver print, 5⅝ × 6 inches. Sheldon Museum of Art, Nebraska Art Association, Purchased with the aid of funds from the National Endowment for the Arts, N-387.1977. © Robert Adams, courtesy Fraenkel Gallery, San Francisco

through Fort Collins and on to its confluence with the South Platte River on the Eastern Plains, he explained:

> The Poudre is in effect a "working" river. Overutilized by agriculture and recreation, threatened by the possibility of a dam, the waterway is the focus of much attention and debate along the Front Range of Colorado. Although many sites retain the marks of human occurrences, the river itself remains wild and full of possibility.[14]

Scaled more modestly than Ansel Adams's view of the Snake River, Wylie's photographs of the Cache la Poudre offer a more trustworthy and reliable account of the river's life as it flows past agricultural fields, barbed wire fences, and railroad tracks. From beneath his dark cloth, Wylie found that irrigation spillways, power lines, and other "human occurrences" were as authentic a part of the river as its sculptured banks and muscular canyon walls (page 10).

Expanding the range of potential subjects allowed for a fuller and more rewarding sense of the landscape to emerge. Eric Paddock witnessed the tail end of Colorado's transition from an extraction to a tourist-based economy, as hiking and skiing supplanted mining and logging. Nevertheless, he hesitated to take sides: "It became too easy for me to be critical of human encroachment and contemporary culture. I wanted to find photographs whose subjects were ambiguous and conclusions tentative. To make photographs that had as little as possible to do with beautiful scenery, recognizing instead the beauty of everyday places."[15] Loveland Pass sits at 11,990 feet, the White River National Forest to its south and the Arapahoe and Roosevelt National Forests to the north. Paddock's view from the top of the pass looks south from its summit into No Name Gulch, toward a series of low peaks along the Front Range (plate 36). Within the frame, the mountains in the distance are no more or less important than the gravel pullout that fills the foreground, its surface mimicking the talus chutes that cascade down the far slopes. Our eyes trace the curve of Highway 6 and the deep afternoon shadows and, were we leaning on the hood of Paddock's car while thumbing through a copy of *Home Ground*, we might just as easily land on the entries for *gulch*, *pass*, *ridge*, or *scree* as on *shoulder* while we surveyed the view. This nondescript roadside is about as far from a scenic overlook at a national park as one might get, but it also offers the possibility of solitude and quiet and, perhaps, when the light is right, an equally satisfying view, reminding us that there is beauty to be found in almost any landscape, even those beyond the imagined boundaries of what we choose to think of as wilderness.

Finding the View

Landscape photography is foremost an art of topography, the objective description of a specific site, depicted in a manner that appears accurate and recognizable. Per Merriam-Webster, *topography* is defined as "2a: the configuration of a surface including its relief and the position of its natural and man-made features; 2b: the physical or natural features of an object or entity and their *structural relationships* [emphasis added]."[16] While contemporary photography has largely dispensed with the heroic and easily romantic, it still takes its formal cues from the beauty of the landscape. Barry often wrote about authority of the land itself—its "factual testimony"—and the intentionality revealed by its form. Recognizing these facts, it is as if the camera and the landscape arrived at a mutual understanding, sharing a confidence that the resulting view would be truthful and reliable. At its most basic, a photograph is a direct report of salient, visible facts, creating a sense of order through the "structural relationships" composed within the frame. The world gives us much to see all at once—the reflection of clouds above a flooded field; shadows bouncing along a picket fence; a braided stream intertwined like a fingerprint—moments that might otherwise have escaped notice had the camera not drawn them to our attention.

Photography has often been said to arrest the "decisive moment," a phrase most famously associated with Henri Cartier-Bresson's gentleman leaping across a puddle in 1930s Paris, the heel of his shoe balanced over its own reflection. We can predict the inevitable splash a frame or two later, but for a fraction of a second, we levitate with him. A landscape photograph, however, often works in the opposite manner, capturing not only the instant the shutter was depressed but a culmination of events—the relationship of topography, light, and weather at the moment of exposure as well as the physical and geologic mechanics that give a place its structure. It is difficult to sit beside a river and not believe it has intention, to trace its course and not imagine some kind of judgment at work. While it is tempting to anthropomorphize the physical world, assigning it a consciousness or narrative, there is also some truth to this idea—a river does think its way through the landscape, guided by gravity and geology as it writes its course. Evidence of this physical intelligence can be seen in Emmet Gowin's *Alluvial Fan, Natural Drainage, near the Yuma Proving Ground and the Arizona-California Border*, 1988 (plate 21). Defining changes in terrain and elevation and the dry shadow of spring run-off that spilled across the desert floor, his split-toned print reads like the contours of a topographic map. Conveying the "factual testimony" of the land as well as a sense of mystery and discovery, Gowin's aerial photographs define relationships otherwise invisible from the ground, revealing what he called "the history of a place"—the physical expression of how it was formed and its geologic structure.[17]

Few photographers understood the intrinsic possibilities a photograph more clearly than Terry Toedtemeier. A geologist by training, his panoramic images of the eastern Oregon desert are at once rigorously descriptive and effortlessly dramatic. Guided by the character of the topography but equally conscious that photographs can carry multiple meanings, he wrote, "The photographs that I create are simultaneously about several layers of beauty: the print, the subject, and the subject context (geology). . . . That the land is beautiful is the strongest clue I have towards a greater sense of unity."[18] Toedtemeier found a consonance between the formal qualities of his prints and their subjects that revealed an intimate physical connection. His use of a panoramic camera was well suited to the low horizon of the Oregon desert, and Toedtemeier believed that an expertly made black-and-white print spoke with every bit the authority of a geologic specimen, its silvery shimmer a double of the land itself (plate 47). His prints can appear so hot, bright, and dry that we can almost feel the dust in our teeth, but they are equally joyful, as if the sky were bursting from the horizon.

Peter de Lory describes a similar interrelationship of photography, biography, and place. A student of Minor White (himself a student of Ansel Adams and Edward Weston), de Lory was inspired by White's use of narrative sequences to create a series of "short stories"—triptych compositions that use the familiar iconography of the West to recount its exploration and settlement, the stubborn grip of its mythology, and the redemptive power of the natural world:

My triptych *Canyonlands Saunter* (plate 13) was compiled in 1997 from hikes made over several years exploring the remote Needles area of Canyonlands National Park, one of the most distilled, isolated landscapes I have found, at once grand and intimate. The Kodak Ektalure G surface paper I used has an unusually warm, milky tone that captured the tactile feel of the rock surfaces. This piece speaks more eloquently than anything I have read as an expression of the land and the experience of moving through it. I think of myself as a "romantic structuralist," a term I coined to describe how I photograph in a very formal straightforward way structurally, freeing the subject up for interpretation and creating an opening for emotion and meaning.[19]

Edward Ranney's *Canyon del Muerto, Arizona*, 1987 (plate 38), creates a similarly tangible relationship between the print and the landscape. Pulling into the canyon overlook early one morning, he recounted how easily the image appeared to him—raking light and graphic shadows defined the shape of the canyon's interior, striking boldly first across the ground glass, upside down and reversed, and later in the print, its surface resonating with the material quality of the sandstone walls. Ranney's understanding of how light reveals the continually shifting appearance of a place draws on his study of Mayan and Incan archaeologic sites in Central and South America, using his camera to define the space, structure, and feeling of these sites as he moved within their surrounding landscapes. *Hungo Pavi to Fajada Butte, Chaco Canyon, New Mexico*, 1983 (figure 6), suggests the simultaneous roles his images play as both archaeological documents and expressive prints reflecting a personal vision. Describing the "Sun Dagger" at the top of Fajada Butte—a shaft of light that penetrates two rock slabs at noon on the summer solstice, striking the center of a spiral petroglyph on the opposite cliff wall—he wrote: "The importance to me of this still living creation, beyond confirming a profound sense of place for the Anasazi, is the actualization of an engaged, resonant symbol, the viewing of which was not unlike experiencing those unique photographic moments when light reveals a distinct sense of visual structure and beauty."[20] Gowin, Toedtemeier, de Lory, and Ranney reveal the range of possibilities in a photographic print: as a mirror of the land and its formal structure; as a kind of mnemonic device,

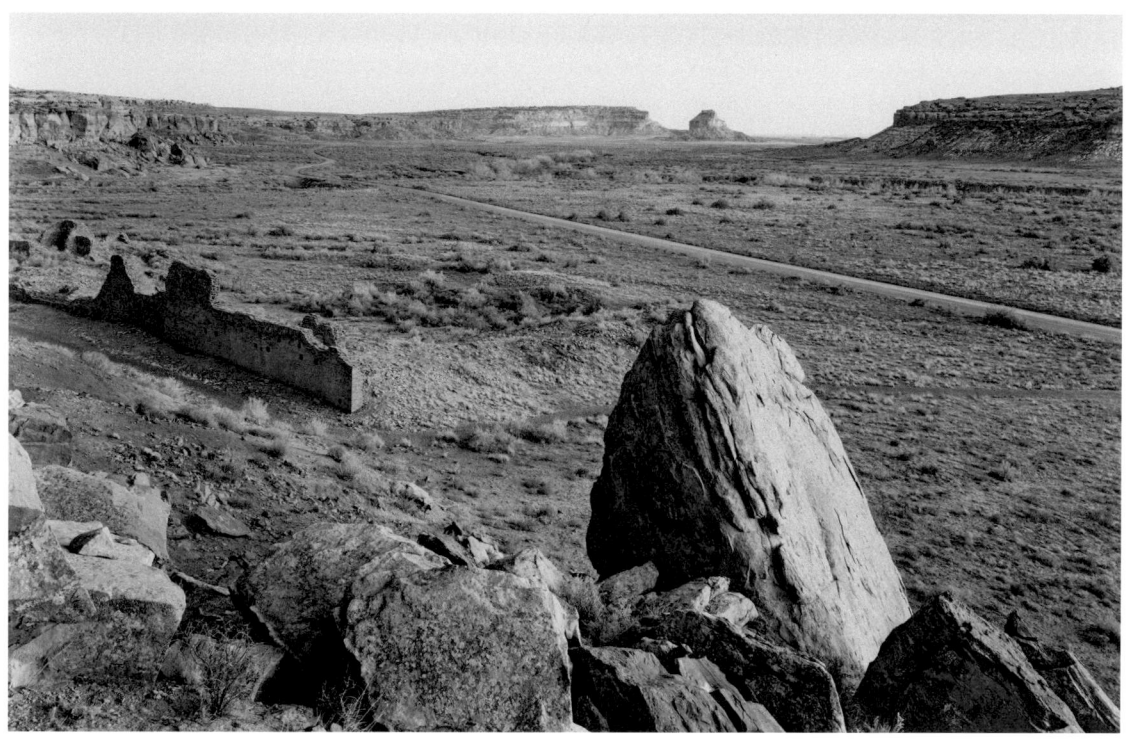

6 Edward Ranney
*Hungo Pavi to Fajada Butte,
Chaco Canyon, New Mexico*,
1982
Sheldon Museum of Art, the
Home Ground Collection

Chaco

reminding us of its tactile and temporal presence; and as a reflection of the emotional resonance of a place and our experience within it.

The Leading Geological Facts
This dual nature of a photograph as an objective visual record and a print reflecting the character of its subject and its maker has been emblematic of American landscape photography since the 1860s and 1870s, when a small corps of artists recognized the camera's ability to document the facts of the landscape as well as the simultaneous geological, historical, and personal narratives it contained. During a time of national trauma, George N. Barnard, Alexander Gardner, Timothy H. O'Sullivan, and Andrew J. Russell left the studio for the battlefields of the Civil War. Working by necessity before or after battle, they saw the human cost of the war mirrored in the landscape: a quiet scene of Antietam Creek whose caption describes hours of fierce combat and the unseen Union soldiers now at rest along its banks; corpses

145

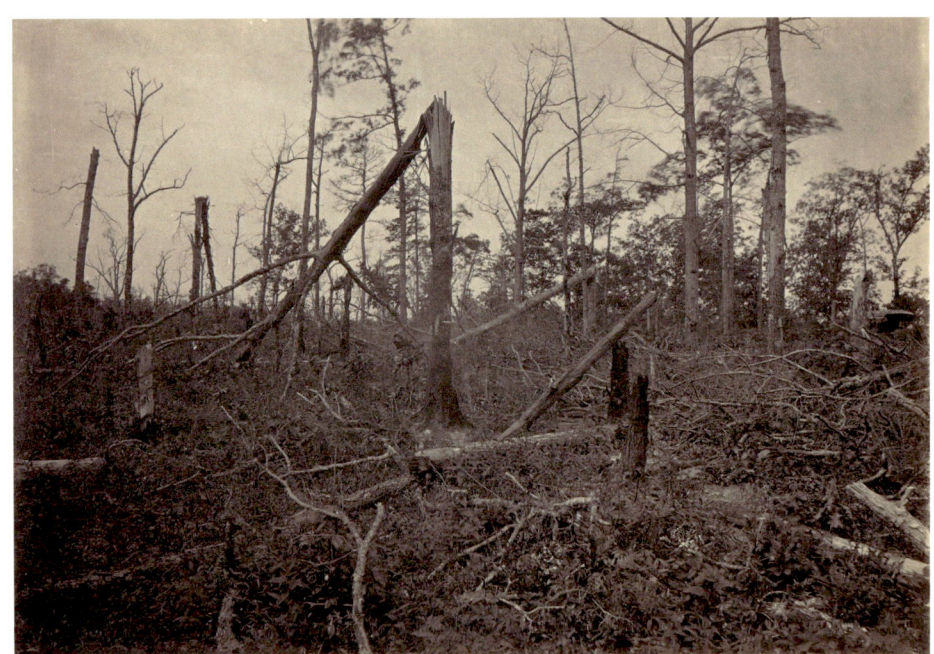

7 George N. Barnard, *The "Hell Hole" New Hope Church, GA.*, 1864 or 1866, albumen silver print, 10¹⁄₁₆ × 14⅛ inches. From the album *Photographic Views of Sherman's Campaign*, 1866. The Metropolitan Museum of Art, Pfeiffer and Rogers Funds, 1970 (1970.525 (27)). Image courtesy the Metropolitan Museum of Art

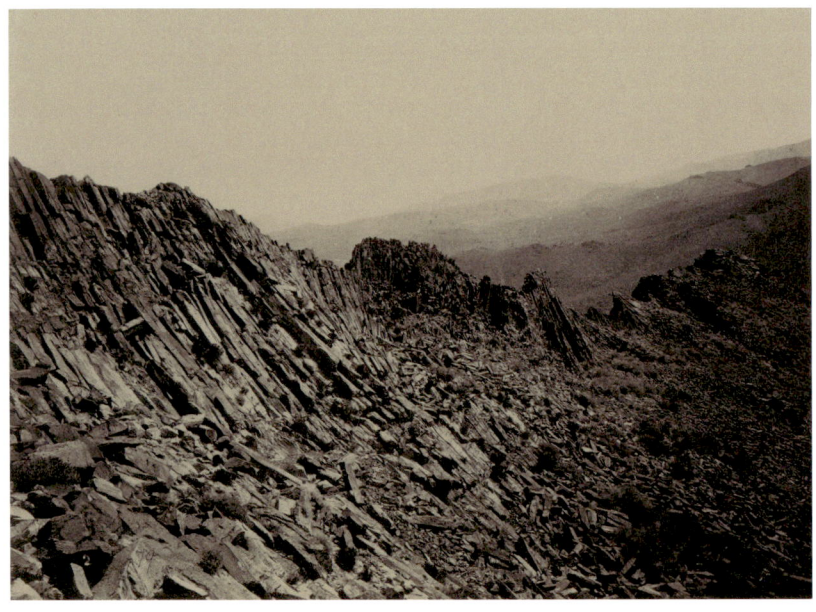

8 Timothy H. O'Sullivan, *Karnak, Montezuma Range, Nevada*, 1867, albumen silver print, 7⅞ × 10⅝ inches. Prints and Photographs Division, Library of Congress, LC-DIG-ppmsca-11862.

photographed where they fell at the Battle of Gettysburg; or a shattered forest offering no safe haven from bullet or cannonball (figure 7). Following the war, many of these photographers headed west on surveys funded by the federal government and the railroads. Their understanding of this still-new medium and the territory beyond the Missouri River matured simultaneously as they explored the interior of the continent, the bold landforms of the Mountain and Desert West inspiring a national style defined by its rigor and clarity. John Szarkowski, the renowned curator of photography at the Museum of Modern Art, spoke of the camera as if in possession of its own intuition: "With no academic authority looking over his shoulder, the photographer was free to give his camera its head, free to discover how it could see most clearly."[21] While it has been assumed that working conditions in the nineteenth century presented a burdensome challenge, many photographers recognized an opportunity when they saw one—upon catching his first view of Donner Lake from the Sierra Crest, O'Sullivan left his companions and climbed the nearest hill to better enjoy the view, a habit he reportedly found hard to break.[22] Many of the earliest images nineteenth-century audiences saw of the American interior were by photographers—Carleton Watkins in Yosemite Valley; William Henry Jackson in the Yellowstone territory; Andrew J. Russell at Promontory Summit; William Bell in the Grand Canyon. Their photographs continue to exert a formidable influence and, in many instances, remain the measure of our landscape.

Although many skilled photographers worked throughout the West in the nineteenth century, no one took advantage of the camera's capacity for description, narrative, and metaphor more intently than Timothy H. O'Sullivan. Working with the geologist Clarence King on the Geological Exploration of the Fortieth Parallel between 1867 and 1872, he made images describing "the leading geological facts" that satisfied the survey's geologists while simultaneously supporting King's belief in Catastrophism—the theory that the earth's history was one of long periods of relative calm, punctuated by unpredictable outbursts of violent geological energy.[23] Investigating a number of sites originally photographed by O'Sullivan in the 1860s, Rick Dingus was the first to decipher his practice of shifting the horizon within the frame to create a heightened sense of instability, supporting King's argument that the landscape was shaped by chaos and upheaval (figure 8). With this background in mind, it is not surprising

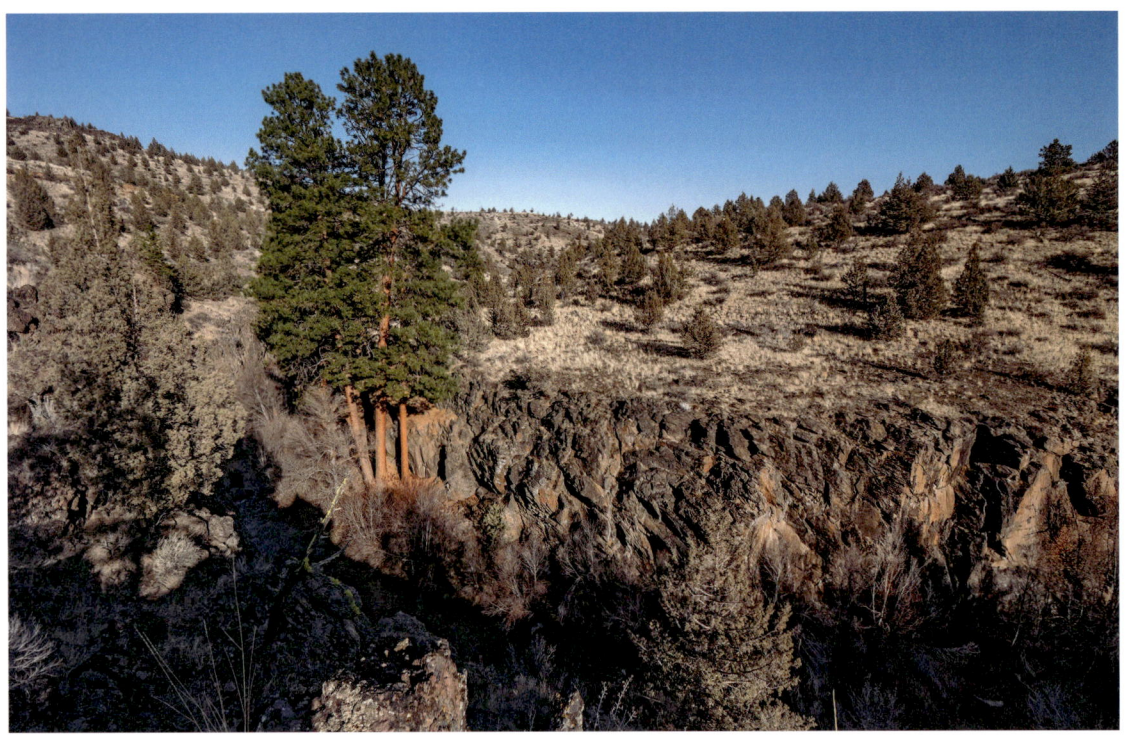

9 Rick Dingus
*Ponderosa Pines in Whychus
Creek Canyon (Upstream from
Where Whychus Creek Merges
with the Deschutes River),
Oregon*, 2020
Sheldon Museum of Art, the
Home Ground Collection

Barranca

that Dingus's most recent photographs were made in col-laboration with scientists from the Deschutes Land Trust, documenting their efforts to restore the Whychus Creek floodplain near his home in Bend, Oregon. Scanning the landscape in *Ponderosa Pines in Whychus Creek Canyon*, 2020 (figure 9), our attention ultimately settles on the cliff face above the creek, contorted by the expansion and cool-ing of the basalt shield that covers eastern Oregon. Dingus offers a topographic description of the land as well as an illustration of how it was formed, above and beneath the surface—a virtual echo of the photographs O'Sullivan made for the King Survey in Nevada.

Coming west under the same circumstances as O'Sulli-van, Martin Stupich arrived in Virginia City, Nevada in 1980 with a contract from the federal government to document the Comstock Mining District, where his predecessor spent the winter of 1867. Since that time, Stupich has photo-graphed nineteenth-, twentieth-, and twenty-first-century industrial infrastructure, drawing little distinction between

148

10   Thomas Joshua Cooper
*Lingering Twilight–The First
View / Shoshone Falls, Centre
Rim Top, The Snake River Basin /
Idaho*, 2003–2004
Sheldon Museum of Art, the
Home Ground Collection

Dry fall

the built environment and the physical landscape. These two are intimately connected in *Dam and Bridge at Glen Canyon near Page, Arizona*, 1992 (page 184), which balances the concave sweep of the dam's face against the arc of the bridge's span, which is mirrored again by the broad curve of the desert basin in *Sand Mountain, Nevada*, 1980 (plate 44). Formed by windblown sand trapped by the Stillwater Mountains to the north, east, and west, the dune is three miles long, a mile wide, and six hundred feet high. It was also the site of one of O'Sullivan's most famous images, his photographic wagon seemingly marooned in an ocean of dunes, yet failing to hint he was only a few hundred yards from a well-traveled road. Pulling back to reveal the dune within a larger context, Stupich undoes O'Sullivan's sleight of hand, relishing a view so expansive it took three frames to contain its wonder, aglow under an overcast sky.

O'Sullivan made his last known photographs of the West at Shoshone Falls, Idaho, in 1874. One hundred and thirty years later, Thomas Joshua Cooper traveled to Idaho to work at one of the sites that had inspired him to become a photographer. He made his first exposures at Cauldron Linn, a narrow basalt channel where the Snake River suggests something of its former authority, before a dozen dams were laid along its course (plate 11). Working above and below Shoshone Falls over the next eight days, Cooper planned his last exposure facing west, as O'Sullivan had, although this time Cooper was able to place his tripod at the brink of the now-dry falls (figure 10). Making a fifteen-minute exposure as the sun dropped below the horizon, his subject was no longer the cascade of the Snake River but the void formed by the fall's enormous basin. Cooper's camera seems to hover above the river, his lens gathering the last light reflecting from its surface, giving material form to empty space as dusk fills the canyon. O'Sullivan's ability to capture what lay between the lens and the horizon has been often noted—something Cooper qualified as the difference between distance and space.[24] More than a century and a half after the first glass plates were exposed in the West, photographers continue to rely on these early views, guided by the apparent straightforwardness of their creation, the self-assurance of their makers, and the distinctive stamp of our geology.

After Landscape

We are entering an era of global trauma, and for many it has become impossible to look at the landscape without feeling an overwhelming sense of loss. We find ourselves no longer able to rely on its steadfast presence or assume that places we have known over a lifetime will continue to reassure and sustain us. Glaciers are swiftly retreating, lakes are rimmed by evaporating shorelines, forests are blackened, and habitats are vanishing at an unprecedented pace. In the fall of 2020, migrating songbirds fell from the sky between Texas and Nebraska—malnourished from a presumed combination of wildfire, drought, and extreme weather.[25] Arctic summers are expected to be ice-free within two decades, and as this essay was written, temperatures ninety degrees above normal were recorded on the Antarctic ice shelf.[26] We cannot help but recognize the transience of this moment and how much has already changed in the years since many of these images were made.

Photographers have sounded the alarm for decades. *Redlands, California*, 1983 (figure 11), from Robert Adams's series *Los Angeles Spring*, does little to suggest the promise

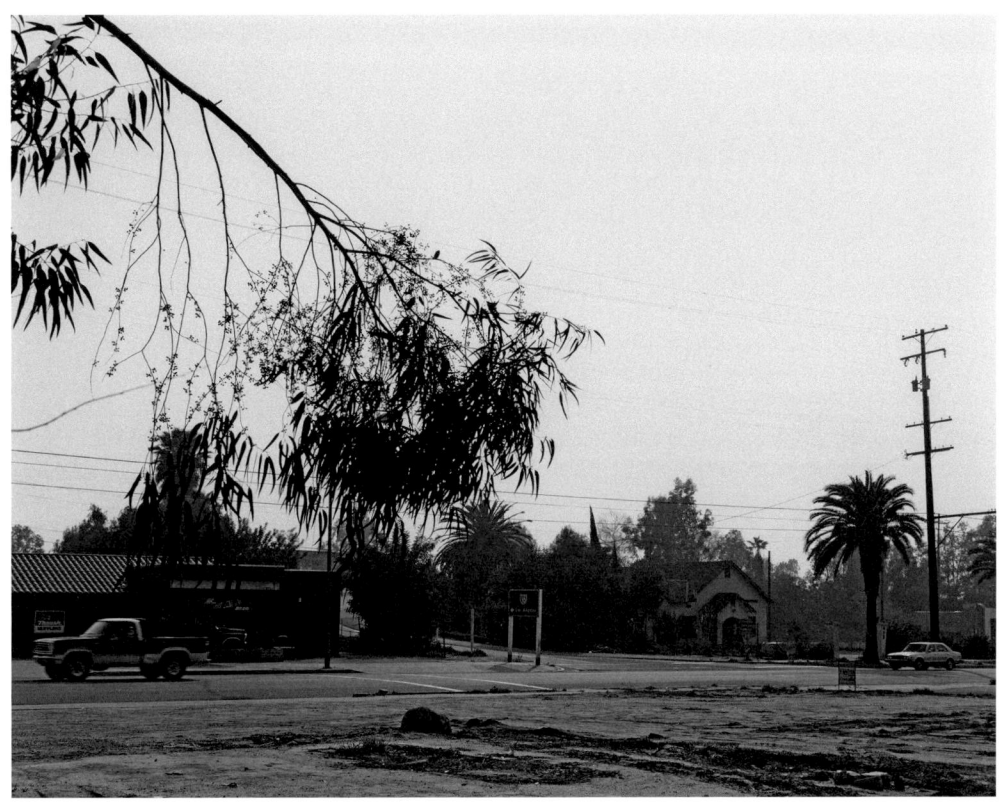

11 Robert Adams, *Redlands, California*, 1983, gelatin silver print, 15 × 18%₆ inches. Sheldon Museum of Art, University of Nebraska–Lincoln, Olga N. Sheldon Acquisition Trust, U-6956.2021. © Robert Adams, courtesy Fraenkel Gallery, San Francisco

of the season or the sea air and citrus blossoms that lent the Golden State its name. Instead, he wrote, "All that is clear is the perfection of what we were given, the unworthiness of our response, and the certainty, in view of our current deprivation, that we are judged."²⁷ Bent under the weight of a dull sky, we are led to ask if it is possible for a tree to mourn? And yet, at the time this photograph was made, it didn't seem unrealistic to maintain hope, and it remains a remarkably beautiful print, sunlight filtering softly through the heavy air. Although one can imagine the rumble of the freeway in the background, the rustle of leaves in the Santa Ana winds and the familiar scent of eucalyptus are enough to offer some solace. Likewise, David T. Hanson's *Yankee Doodle Tailings Pond, Tailings Dam, and Leach Pads, Butte, Montana*, 1991 (plate 24), was made at a time when it was thought that grievances against the land, no matter how brutal, were nevertheless discrete and resolvable. Like so much of the West, Hanson's home state of Montana markets its scenic vistas as a resource while shielding the extractive industries that drive its economy from view. But an abundance of open space, a sparse population, and a disregard for regulation led to the belief that the land would absorb whatever harm was done to it. In 1982, Hanson began making aerial views of industrial and military sites in order to gain access to high-security areas and picture damaged landscapes too vast to be encompassed from the ground. This perspective can abstract the brutality of his subjects, but Butte—"The Richest Hill on Earth"—is also home to the largest Superfund hazardous waste site in the United States. In November 2016, thousands of migrating snow geese died after landing in the toxic waters laden with arsenic, cadmium, zinc, and sulfuric acid that fill the Yankee Doodle pond and the adjacent Berkeley Pit, an abandoned open-pit copper mine.[28] Hanson's photographs capture a legacy we are unlikely to recover from—it is doubtful that this site can be successfully reclaimed—and we now understand that larger global systems have been compromised to a degree that is beyond our ability to redress.

Working at a similarly damaged site, one can imagine how painful it was as Mary Peck set up her camera at the tar sands processing facility seen in *Following the Route of the Keystone XL, Syncrude Tailings Pond, North of Fort McMurray, Alberta*, 2017 (plate 37). By the time she traveled north to photograph the route of the proposed Keystone XL Pipeline (which was ultimately canceled in 2021), no sign remained of the boreal forest that once blanketed the province:

> I wanted to see what was visible aboveground for myself—how the land where the oil comes from is treated would speak to how these companies treat the land. North of the Hardisty refinery in Fort McMurray, Alberta—the center of the tar sands mining industry—I visited a "restoration forest" and "reclamation ponds." It reminded me of looking at a clearcut in the Pacific Northwest with a timber company representative and being asked to believe the horror I saw in front of me was going to result in something remotely resembling the forest that had been removed. I spent six weeks exploring two provinces and three states, driving several thousand miles to see the landscape the 1,100-mile pipeline would go through. My trip involved looking at

water along the way, staying within range—and always downstream—of the proposed pipeline.[29]

Peck followed the Missouri River corridor, also navigated by Lewis and Clark in 1803–1804, camping beside Nebraska's Niobrara River, 1,400 miles south of Fort McMurray yet not beyond its reach (page 6). Like the Platte, it finds its way through a subtle topography—a respite from the barren landscape to the north—but how much more violence the land can absorb remains to be seen.

It is equally heartbreaking to read Benn Huff's account of his initial foray into Alaska, the backbone of Barry's life as a writer: "Several years ago, shortly after moving to Juneau from the Interior, I worked on a set of pictures at the Mendenhall Glacier. I struggled with the landscape, as I tried to illustrate the gulf I felt between the joy of seeing that glacier for the first time, and the sense of mourning I felt with each subsequent trip."[30] Few other places live as vividly in our imagination as Alaska—perhaps because most of us know we are unlikely to see it in person—so we also rely more heavily on what photographs like Huff's or Dennis Witmer's glorious *Hanging Valley, Brooks Range, Alaska*, 1996 (plate 49), can tell us. In 2005, Witmer noted, "That a place such as this should continue to exist seems unlikely. But it does exist, nearly untouched, protected by distance, climate, and luck. It lends a faint glimmer of hope: if this place has survived this long, perhaps, also, we might."[31] Twenty years later, its survival is increasingly in question, and were we to travel there today, our experience would likely be much as Huff described, the joy of recognition tempered by the knowledge that we are also witnessing its end.

Owen Gump's *Mine Tailings, Lyon County, Nevada*, 2018 (plate 23), gives a glimpse of a future where centuries of extractive industry have become so interwoven with the topography that it becomes challenging to distinguish where one ends and the other begins. Once the site of one of the largest open-pit gold mining operations in the state, heaps of ore were sprayed with a cyanide solution to dissolve any residual gold. Visible across northern Nevada, these ore piles mimic the rise and fall of basin and range, creating a "topography in reverse" that blends almost seamlessly into the desert landscape. Gump's *Martin Canyon*, 2017 (figure 12), documents construction of the Alphabet, Inc. (Google) research park outside of Reno, Nevada, a serpentine road graded to drill soil samples. Although building has since

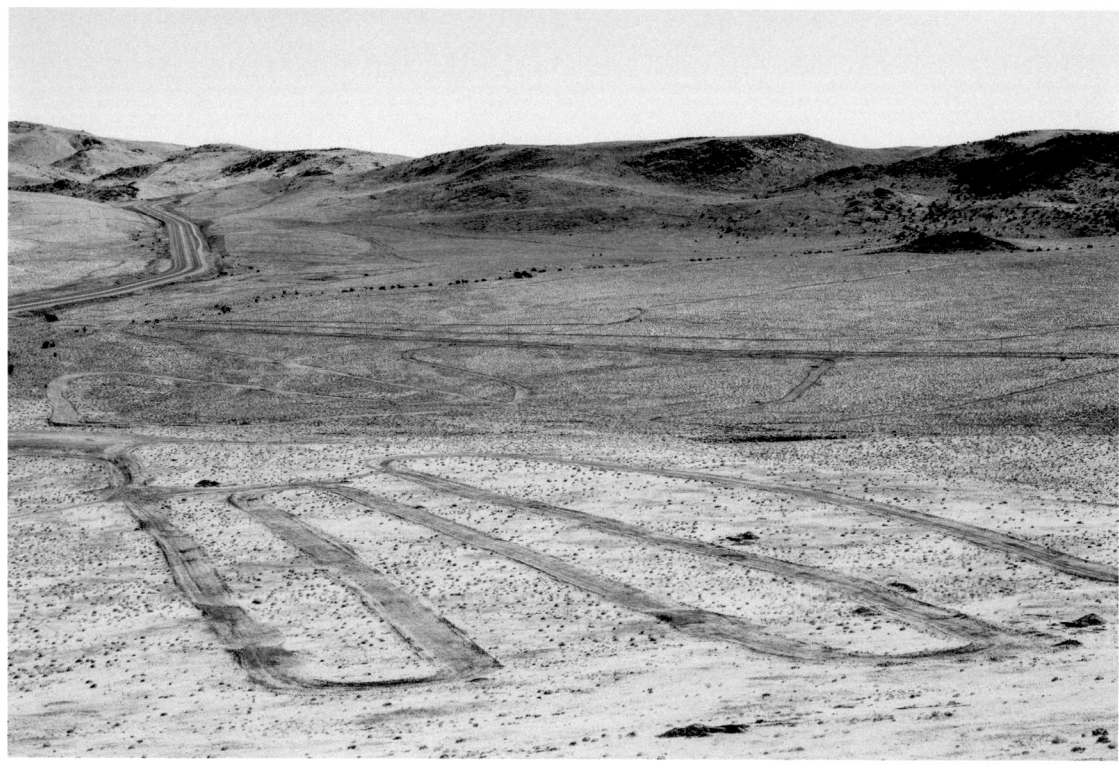

12 Owen Gump
*Martin Canyon, Future Site of
Alphabet, Inc. Research Complex, Storey County, Nevada,*
2018
Sheldon Museum of Art, the
Home Ground Collection

Tool mark

been completed, Gump has been unable to re-photograph the site, which is now protected by locked gates, barbed wire, and aggressive security, speaking to the transfer of public lands to corporate ownership in the name of perpetual economic growth and development.

We have modified and engineered the landscape to our purposes for centuries, although orchards and fields, road cuts, tunnels, rail grades, and riprapped streams fit comfortably within our daily viewshed. Many of these interventions are so familiar that they have disappeared into the background, although were it possible to lay a filter over the landscape, we would likely be shocked at how much has been transformed in ways that we fail to recognize. More disturbing are the open-pit mines, clearcut forests, weapons facilities, chemical refineries, and fracking rigs that lie just beyond the sightline. Taken to an extreme, we are entering an age of what might be considered "synthetic landscapes," places that reveal little of their original character and photographs that trade on the appearance of topographic authority but

154

are entirely fabricated. Using paper, cardboard, and Fome-Cor, which he lights and photographs in his studio, James Casebere recreated Caspar David Friedrich's painting *The Sea of Ice*, 1823–1824 (figure 13). Friedrich's original depicts the hull of a ship crushed in the pack ice of an Arctic sea. In the nineteenth century, this would have been understood as a depiction of the sublime—the experience of awe, terror, or danger in the face of nature. Casebere's twenty-first-century echo suggests the far more alarming prospect of a future where nature has been overpowered, and a frozen Arctic exists only in our memory.

Similarly, Dan Holdsworth's *Argentiere Glacier no. 05*, 2016 (figure 14), sits comfortably alongside the geologic surveys of Timothy H. O'Sullivan and Emmet Gowin, an elegant facsimile of the topography it maps. Working with a geologist, Holdsworth made hundreds of digital captures over several weeks in the field. A computer then generated a "point cloud" correlating the images with their GPS coordinates to create a three-dimensional model of the landscape. Holdsworth refers to his images as "future archaeology," asking us to imagine varying scales of time from the eons it takes to form a glacial valley to the instantaneity of the digital age to a future era with or without humanity's presence.

How will it change us when the landscapes that have shaped our imagination are gone, and the only ice we know is in a photograph of an invented landscape or one produced in a computer? What will be lost when we are required to temper our memories and expectations of the places we most love? In *Horizon*, published the year before he passed, Barry asked, "However it might be viewed, the throttled Earth—the scalped, the mined, the industrially farmed, the drilled, polluted and suctioned land, endlessly manipulated for further development and profit—is now our home. We know the wounds. We have come to accept them. And we ask, many of us, What will the next step be?"[32]

A Society to Match Our Scenery

We live at a time when a cascading series of catastrophes makes it impossible to ignore that the landscape as we wish to imagine it no longer remains—what Barry named an "Era of Emergencies."[33] As remarkable as the scale of the crisis we face is the swiftness with which it has come upon us. In *Arctic Dreams: Imagination and Desire in a Northern Landscape*, published in 1986, Barry warned of the rapid advance of mining and petroleum exploration poised to

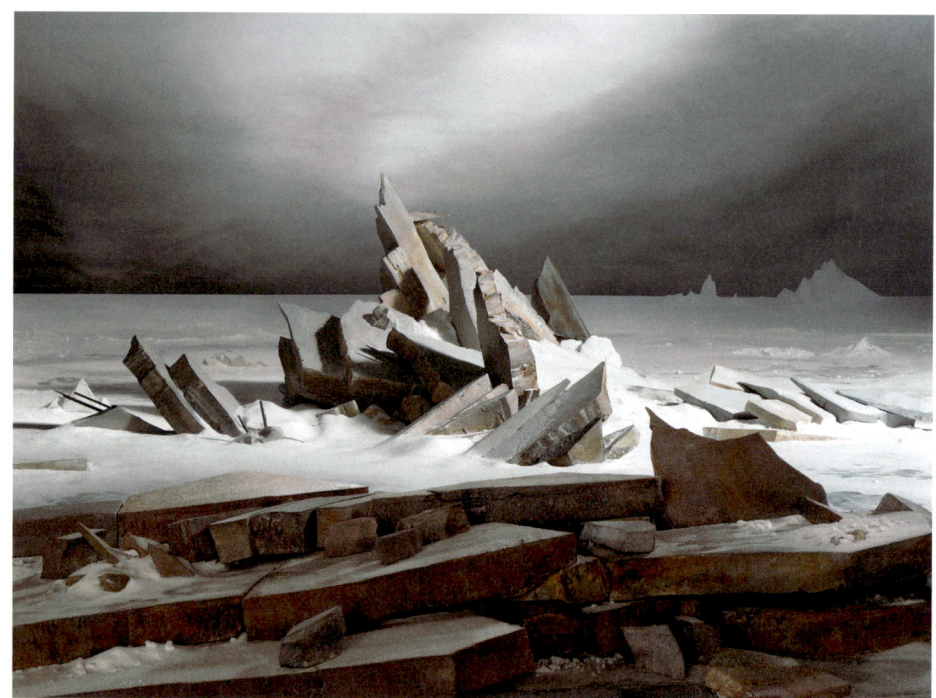

13 James Casebere, *Sea of Ice*, 2014, archival pigment print mounted to dibond, 37¾ × 49¾ inches. © James Casebere, courtesy the artist and Sean Kelly, New York

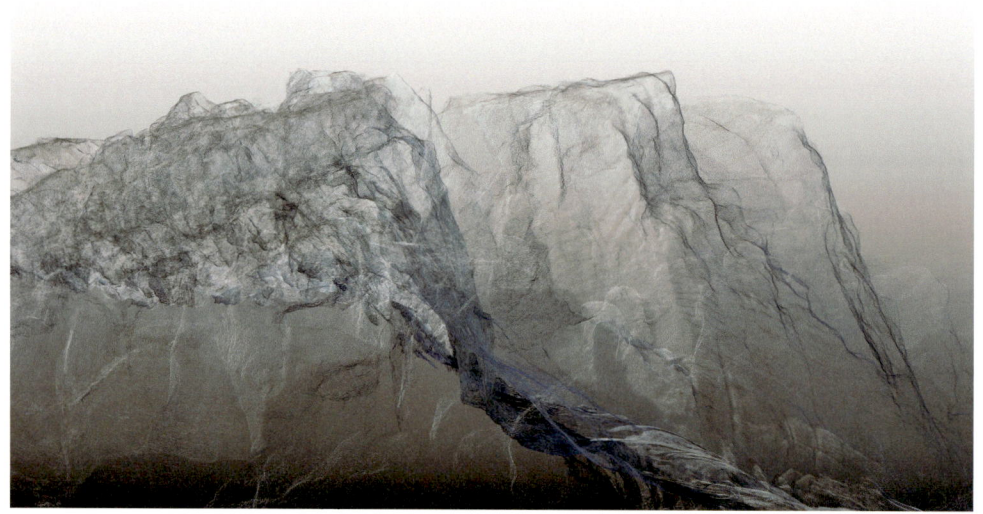

14 Dan Holdsworth, *Argentiere Glacier No. 5*, 2016, from the series "Continuous Topography," chromogenic development print, 48⅜ × 81¹³⁄₁₆ inches. Courtesy Denver Art Museum, Partial gift of the artist and funds from Frederic H. Douglas by exchange, 2018.134. © Dan Holdsworth

devour the Arctic, yet he never made a single reference to human-caused climate change. A little more than thirty years later, the situation had changed so dramatically that Barry uncharacteristically admitted he saw no sign of salvation ahead. Of what we are able to predict with reasonable certainty there seems to be little in the future to offer hope, but we owe the landscape more than to define it solely in response to tragedy.

Barry and I grew up two miles and twenty years apart along Ventura Boulevard in Los Angeles's San Fernando Valley, looking toward the same horizon, although he knew the Valley before the grid of freeways and boulevards and tract houses had replaced its fields and orchards. When I think of my home ground, I remember it looking much like *Redlands, California*, 1983. Nevertheless, I'm comforted by the smog that seems to seep from the edges of Robert Adams's print because it feels familiar, reminding me of glancing towards the San Gabriel Mountains on hot summer afternoons to check on their summits through the amber sky.[34] I also remember the first photography book I purchased, Ansel Adams's *Yosemite and the Range of Light*. Paging through to find *Winter Sunrise*, I recall his friend Wallace Stegner's invocation:

> Angry as one may be at what careless people have done and still do to a noble habitat, it is hard to be pessimistic about the West. This is the native home of hope. When it fully learns that cooperation, not rugged individualism, is the pattern that most characterizes and preserves it, then it will have achieved itself and outlived its origins. Then it has a chance to create a society to match its scenery.[35]

Stegner had a print of *Winter Sunrise* on his wall, of which he reported, "I have looked at it, studied it, scores of times, and every time I do so it lifts me."[36] His quote above touches on two of the things that Barry held most closely: community and the land. It also reminds us that the American landscape carries with it a set of responsibilities, to it and to each other. Of his own correspondence with Stegner, Barry recalled that "[Wally] . . . could pay you a compliment in such a way that you felt you had to continue, and maybe do better just to live up to the implied expectation."[37] I believe Ansel Adams intended *Winter Sunrise* to encourage us in much the same way.

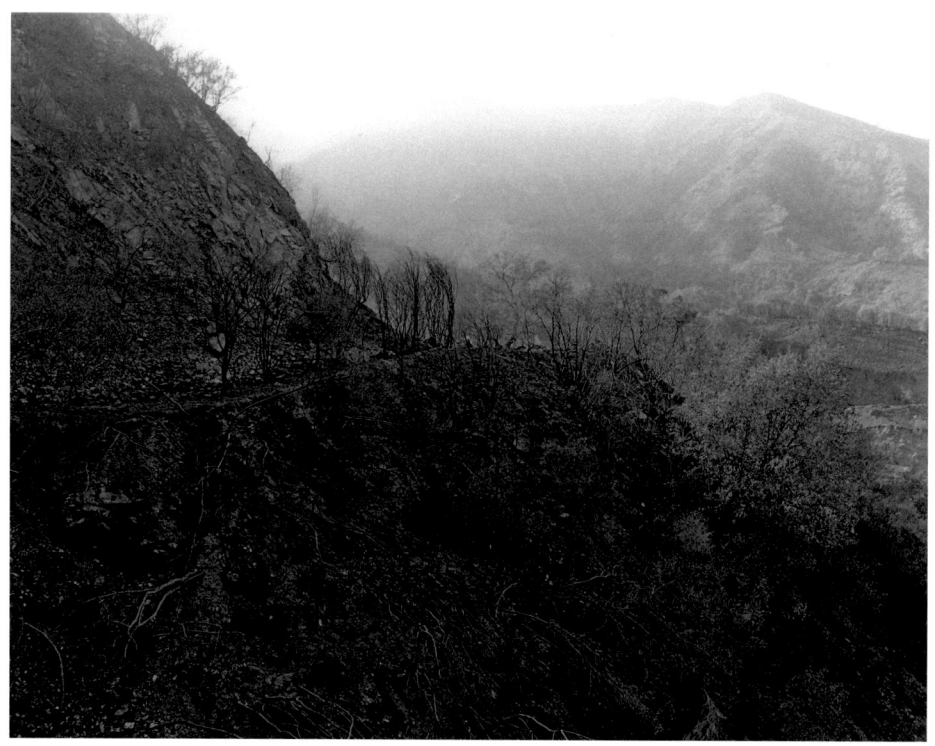

15 Mark Ruwedel, *San Gabriel Fire #11*, 2020, gelatin silver print, 14¹⁵⁄₁₆ × 19⁵⁄₁₆ inches. Sheldon Museum of Art, University of Nebraska–Lincoln, Robert E. Schweser and Fern Beardsley Schweser Acquisition Fund, through the University of Nebraska Foundation, U-6983.2022. © Mark Ruwedel

It is, of course, possible we will wind up with a society that matches our scenery, although not in the way Stegner had hoped for—one that is coarse, combative, stripped of dignity and comity, like the landscapes we have left barren and scarred in our wake. Mark Ruwedel's 2020 photograph *San Gabriel Fire #11* (figure 15) hints at a future where we have little choice but to stand back as the land is consumed before our eyes. A sobering echo of *Los Angeles Spring*, it is the City of Angels reduced to soot and ash as fire becomes the new signature of California's endless summer. Still, as challenging as it may seem, we can do better than resignation, and within these pages, we are offered guidance and reassurance.

"We have a shapely language, American English," Barry reminded us.[38] The same is true of our landscape, full of places that inspire palpable, physical pleasure, bordering on desire. Scanning the view while hiking or driving or gazing out the window during a flight, the land unfolds before us as we trace mountain ranges and watersheds and coastlines.

The sharp strike of a ridge, a tumble of boulders piled at the base of a cliff or the weight of a reservoir bearing against a dam reveal the tension and anticipation within the land, as if Clarence King were right and at any moment something spectacular might happen. Or it may be as simple as watching as evening descends over the Plains to a background of birdsong and the occasional truck shifting gears (figure 16). At the northernmost boundary of the sea ice, miles off the coast of Baffin Island, Barry recalled, "The edges of any landscape—horizons, the lip of a valley, the bend of a river around a canyon wall—quicken an observer's expectations. The attraction to borders, to the earth's twilit places, is part of the shape of human curiosity."[39] Reading this account in *Arctic Dreams*, it is invigorating to imagine what it would have been like to scan that limitless horizon, but Barry also believed it was no more or less thrilling than what we might witness on any given day close to home.

There are photographs in the Home Ground Collection I have returned to repeatedly. Lois Conner's *Badlands, South Dakota*, 1996, seems to be two images slyly combined, the portrait of a hoodoo, its head cocked, posed within a sweeping panorama. The eponymous Sawtooth Mountains in Laura McPhee's *Irrigator's Tarp Directing Water, Fourth of July Creek Ranch, Custer County, Idaho*, 2004—a thoroughly American name that calls to mind the holiday sky filled with fireworks. The New England meadow in Barbara Bosworth's *Moon Rising, the Night the Bird was Singing, Carlisle, Massachusetts*, 2006, washed by the blue night sky. And the damp evening air, sinking low to the ground in Peter Latner's *Mississippi River Valley at Dusk, La Crosse County, Wisconsin*, 2000. Three of these places I know firsthand; the last, Latner's print makes easy to imagine. We are fortunate that everywhere in our country has the possibility of being remarkably beautiful.

Perhaps as an anodyne to other more dispiriting days behind the camera, Robert Adams also wrote the following about the joy of encountering the world through photography:

> One does not for long wrestle a view camera in the wind and heat and cold just to illustrate a philosophy. The thing that keeps you scrambling over the rocks, risking snakes, and swatting at the flies is the *view*. It is only your enjoyment of and commitment to what you see, not to what you rationally understand, that balances the otherwise absurd investment of labor.[40]

I cannot claim that every photograph in this collection was exposed with an explicit agenda in mind, and many of the artists would back away from overt declarations of morality or patriotism. But behind all of these images there is delight in the way that light defines the land, pleasure found in its shape and contour, and the reassurance of photographs that offer us a faithful and perhaps revelatory account of what was discovered before the lens. And I am certain that each was made with attention and care and the good fortune of knowing that there is no better way to understand where we live and who we are—our past and what is waiting over the horizon—than to be able to walk the landscape, camera in hand, and discover the view.

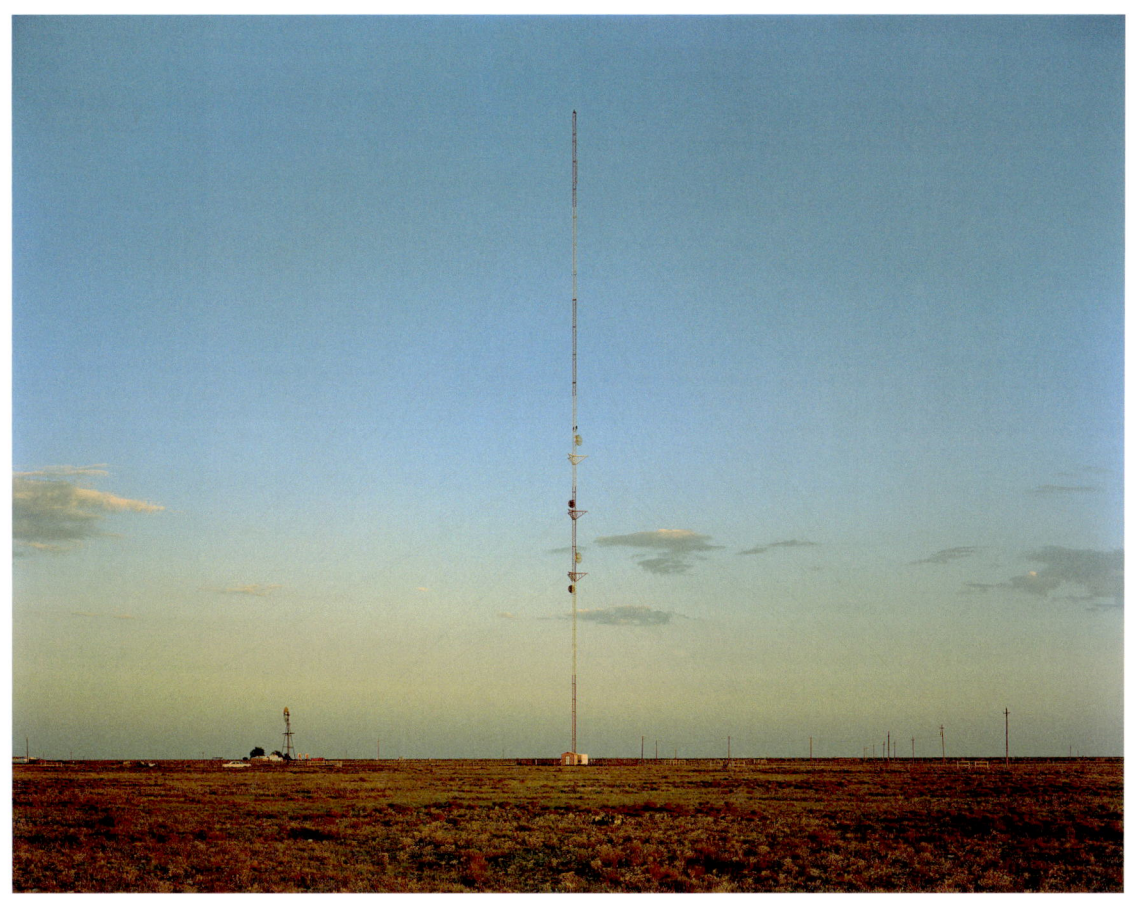

16   Steve Fitch
*Radio Tower on the Llano
Estacado between Caprock and
Maljamar, New Mexico, June 29,
2005*, 2005
Sheldon Museum of Art, the
Home Ground Collection

Staked plain

Notes

1. Barry Lopez, "Introduction," in Barry Lopez and Debra Gwartney, eds., *Home Ground: A Guide to the American Landscape* (San Antonio, TX: Trinity University Press, 2006, 2013), xix. *Home Ground* citations refer to the paperback edition.

2. Lopez, "Introduction," xix. Gregory Conniff, "Introduction," in *Common Ground* (New Haven, CT: Yale University Press, 1985), xi.

3. Ansel Adams and Nancy Newhall, *This is the American Earth* (San Francisco, CA: Sierra Club, 1960), xii.

4. David Brower, "Foreword," in Nancy Newhall, *Ansel Adams: The Eloquent Light* (San Francisco, CA: Sierra Club, 1963), 7.

5. "Wilderness is a cultural, not an ecological, concept," begins William deBuys's entry "Wilderness," a concise summary of the historic, legal, and poetic aspects of this formative American ideal. Lopez and Gwartney, 488–89; this volume, 40.

6. Mark Klett, "The Legacy of Ansel Adams: Debts and Burdens," *Aperture* 120 (fall 1990): 72. This same observation was made earlier by Wallace Stegner, although in a manner that singled Adams out for praise, "a sheet of paper printed in values of gray can actually strike the viewer with more force and suggestiveness than would the natural objects from which it was made. It is Ansel Adams's gift to be able to intensify the emotional effect of visual experience. More than one visitor to the western scenes which Adams has made his own by an act of artistic pre-emption has complained that nothing looks so magnificent as an Adams photograph of it." Wallace Stegner, "Foreword," in Ansel Adams, *Images 1923–1974* (Boston, MA: New York Graphic Society, 1974), 9.

7. Stephen Graham Jones, "Sierra," in Lopez and Gwartney, 410.

8. Ansel Adams, *Born Free and Equal: The Story of Loyal Japanese Americans* (New York: U.S. Camera, 1944), 106–7.

9. See Toby Jurovics, "Same as It Ever Was: Re-reading *New Topographics*" in Greg Foster-Rice and John Rohrbach, eds., *Reframing the New Topographics* (Chicago, IL: The Center for American Places at Columbia College Chicago, 2010), 1–12, for a critical analysis of the reception of the 1975 exhibition *New Topographics: Photographs of a Man-altered Landscape*.

10. Panel discussion, "New Topographics: Landscape Photography Then and Now," The Photography Show Presented by AIPAD, New York, NY, March 20, 2010.

11. Frank Gohlke, "Silos of Life . . . ," *New York Times*, January 18, 1979, sec. A, p. 21.

12. Robert Adams, "Inhabited Nature," *Aperture*, no. 81 (1978): 29–31.

13. Conversation with the author, November 2011.

14. William Wylie, *Riverwalk: Explorations along the Cache la Poudre River* (Boulder: University Press of Colorado, 2000), xiii.

15. Conversation with the author, January 2022.

16. https://www.merriam-webster.com/dictionary/topography.

17. Toby Jurovics, "Introduction," in *Emmet Gowin: Aerial Photographs* (Princeton, NJ: The Art Museum, Princeton University, 1998), 8.

18. Letter to the author, September 8, 1998.

19. Email to the author, January 2022.

20. Edward Ranney, "Excavating the Present," in *Aperture*, no. 98 (1985): 42.

21. John Szarkowski, "Introduction," in *The Photographer and the American Landscape* (New York: The Museum of Modern Art, 1963), 3.

22. Toby Jurovics et al., *Framing the West: The Survey Photographs of Timothy H. O'Sullivan* (Washington, DC: Library of Congress and Smithsonian American Art Museum, 2010), 41–42.

23. Jurovics, *Framing the West*, 17–18.

24. Jurovics, *Framing the West*, 25–26.

25. Phoebe Weston, "Mass die-off of birds in south-western US 'caused by starvation,'" *The Guardian*, December 26, 2020: https://www .theguardian.com/environment/2020 /dec/26/mass-die-off-of-birds-in -south-western-us-caused-by -starvation-aoe.

26. Jason Samenow and Kasha Patel, "It's 70 Degrees Warmer than Normal in Eastern Antarctica. Scientists are Flabbergasted," *The Washington Post*, March 18, 2022: https://www .washingtonpost.com/weather/2022 /03/18/antarctica-heat-wave-climate -change.

27. Robert Adams, "Introduction," in *Los Angeles Spring* (New York: Aperture, 1986), n.p.

28. Ben Guarino, "Thousands of Montana Snow Geese Die after Landing in Toxic, Acidic Mine Pit," *The Washington Post*, December 7, 2016: https:// www.washingtonpost.com/news /morning-mix/wp/2016/12/07 /montana-snow-geese-searching -for-pond-land-in-toxic-mine-pit -thousands-die/.

29. Email to the author, February 2022.

30. Ben Huff, *The Light That Got Lost*, Volume 1 (Juneau, AK: Ice Fog Press, 2020), n.p.

31. Dennis Witmer, *Far to the North: Photographs from the Brooks Range* (Fairbanks, AK: Far to the North Press, 2005), n.p.

32. Barry Lopez, *Horizon* (New York: Alfred A. Knopf, 2019), 65.

33. On December 24, 2020—the day before his passing—Literary Hub published the online essay, "Barry Lopez: An Era of Emergencies is Upon Us and We Cannot Look Away." https://lithub.com/barry-lopez-an -era-of-emergencies-is-upon-us-and -we-cannot-look-away/. This essay later appeared as the introduction to Sandra S. Phillips and Sally Martin Katz, eds., *American Geography: Photographs of Land Use from 1840 to the Present* (Santa Fe, NM: Radius Books and the San Francisco Museum of Modern Art, 2021) and has been reprinted in Lopez, *Embrace Fearlessly the Burning World* (New York: Random House, 2022), 21–26.

34. In his 2002 essay, "A Scary Abundance of Water," Barry made a similar observation, "Robert Adams's *Los Angeles Spring* . . . made palpable a landscape I have never wanted to be too long absent from." In Lopez, *Embrace Fearlessly the Burning World*, 254–55.

35. Wallace Stegner, *The Sound of Mountain Water* (Garden City, NY: Doubleday & Company, Inc., 1969), 38.

36. Stegner, "Foreword," 19.

37. "In Memoriam: Wallace Stegner," in Lopez, *Embrace Fearlessly the Burning World*, 28.

38. Lopez, "Introduction," xxvii.

39. Barry Lopez, *Arctic Dreams: Imagination and Desire in a Northern Landscape* (New York: Charles Scribner's Sons, 1986), 123.

40. Robert Adams, "In the Nineteenth-Century West," in *Why People Photograph* (New York: Aperture Foundation, 1994), 153.

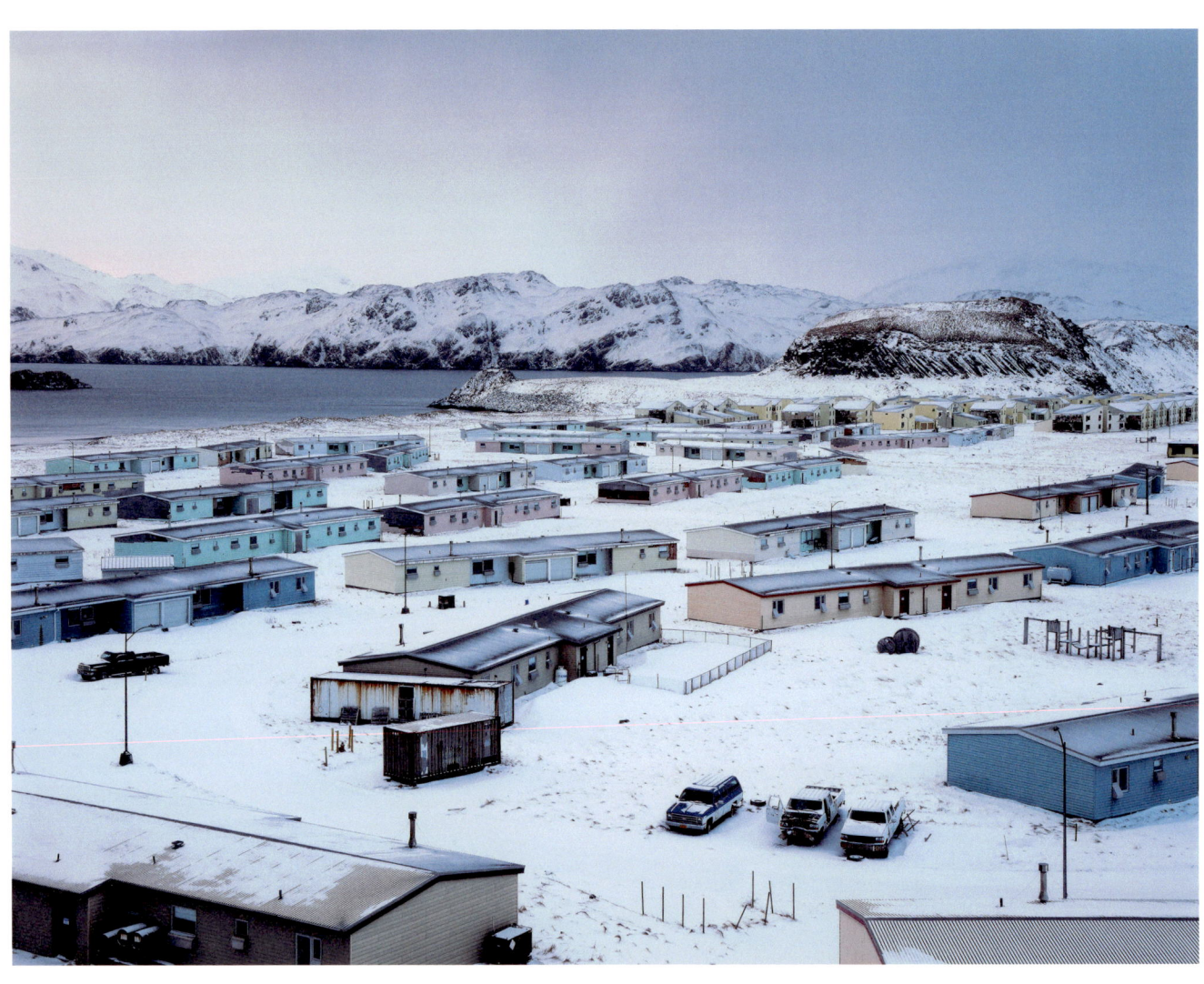

Ben Huff
Kulluk Bay Neighborhood, Adak, Alaska, 2017
Sheldon Museum of Art, the Home Ground Collection

Volcanic plug

Checklist of the Home Ground Collection

All photographs collection of Sheldon Museum of Art, Sheldon Art Association, the Home Ground Collection: Gift of the artist in honor of Barry Lopez.

All dimensions are image size, height followed by width. Complete entries for the landscape terms accompanying each print can be found in *Home Ground: A Guide to the American Landscape* (Trinity University Press, 2006, 2013).

Photographs copyright the artist unless otherwise indicated.

Robert Adams
Born Orange, NJ, 1937 – lives Astoria, OR

Clearcut. Second-growth Stump on Top of Old-growth Stump. Coos County, Oregon, 2013
Gelatin silver print, 11¾₆ × 9 inches. S-1197.2022
© Robert Adams, courtesy Fraenkel Gallery, San Francisco
Old-growth forest

Virginia Beahan
Born Philadelphia, PA, 1946 – lives Lyme Center, NH

17 Palms Oasis, Anza-Borrego Desert State Park, California, 2013
Pigment print, 31⁵⁄₁₆ × 40 inches. S-1276.2022
Oasis

Geothermal Hot Springs Now Visible Due to Reduced Colorado River Streamflow into the Salton Sea, on the San Andreas Fault near Mullet Island, California, 2014
Pigment print, 31⅝ × 40 inches. S-1277.2022
Solfatara

Marion Belanger
Born Willimantic, CT, 1957 – lives Guilford, CT

Mangroves, Everglades City, Florida, 2002
From the series "Everglades"
Pigment print, 17½ × 21⅞ inches. S-1209.2022
Mangrove swamp

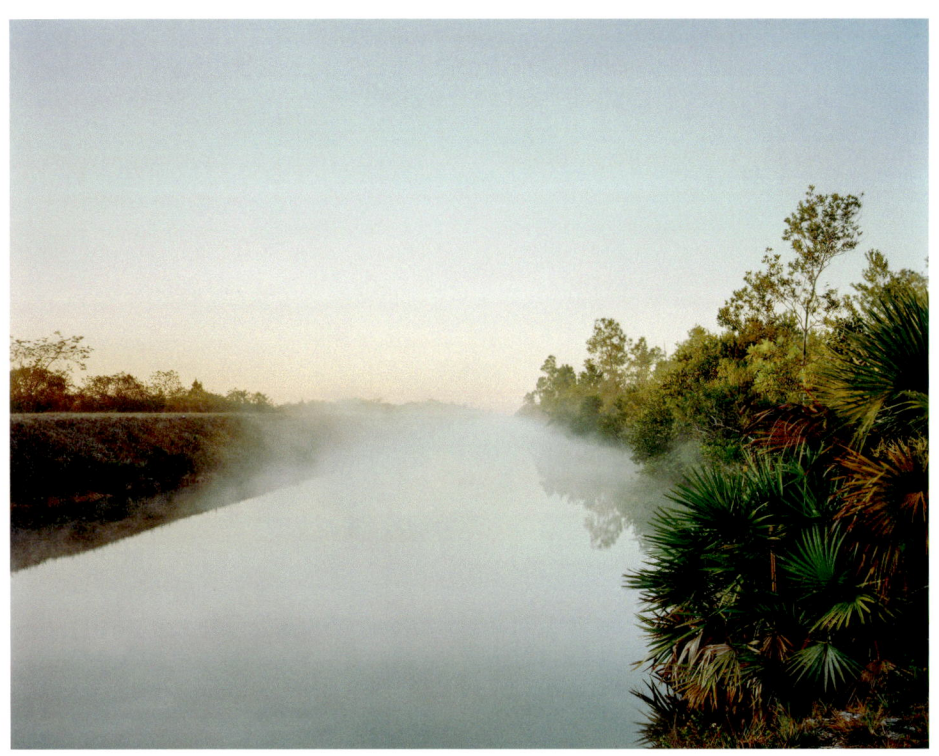

Marion Belanger *Boundary, Everglades National Park, Florida, 2004*

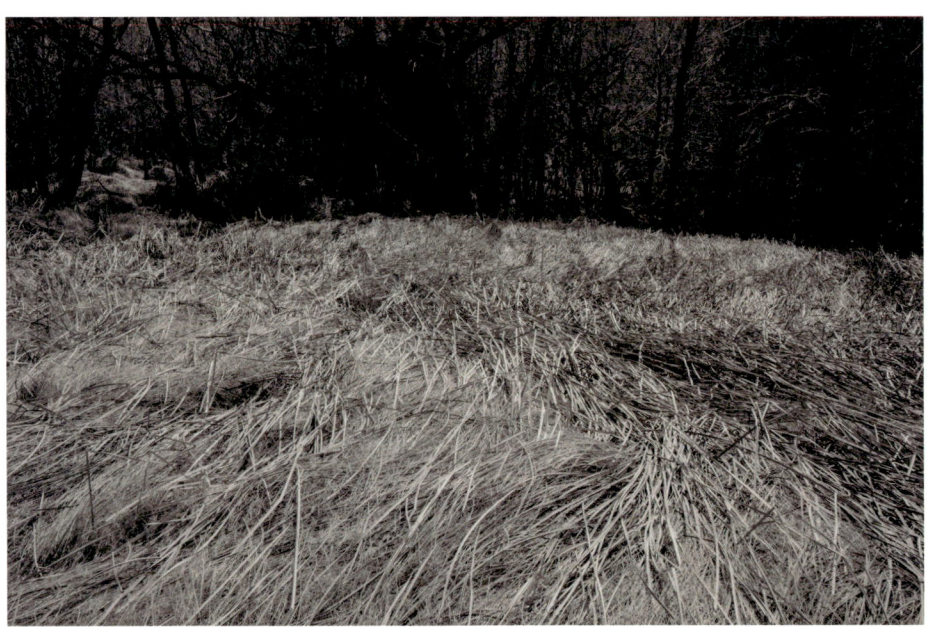

Michael Berman *Ojo Calienta, Sierra San Luis, Chihuahua, Mexico, 2020*

Boundary, Everglades National Park, Florida, 2004
From the series "Everglades"
Pigment print, 17½ × 21⅞ inches. S-1210.2022
Canal

Michael Berman Born New York, NY, 1956 – lives Silver City, NM

Cajón Bonito, Sierra San Luis, Chihuahua, Mexico, 2020
Pigment print, 11¹⁄₁₆ × 16⁹⁄₁₆ inches. S-1212.2022
Borderland

Ojo Caliente, Sierra San Luis, Chihuahua, Mexico, 2020
Pigment print, 11¹⁄₁₆ × 16⁹⁄₁₆ inches. S-1211.2022
Ciénega

Andrew Borowiec Born New York, NY, 1956 – lives Akron, OH and New York, NY

Meigs County, Ohio, 1998
From the series "Along the Ohio"
Pigment print, 13⁷⁄₁₆ × 20 inches. S-1214.2022
Wilderness

Laramie County, Wyoming, 2014
From the series "The Lincoln Highway"
Pigment print, 13⁵⁄₁₆ × 20 inches. S-1213.2022
Shortgrass prairie

Barbara Bosworth Born Novelty, OH, 1953 – lives Stow, MA

Moon Rising, the Night the Bird was Singing, Carlisle, Massachusetts, 2006
From the series "The Meadow"
Pigment print, 32 × 40 inches. S-1278.2022
Meadow

Along the St. George River, Maine, 2014
From the series "Summer Days"
Pigment print, 40 × 32 inches. S-1279.2022
Forest

Joann Brennan Born Philadelphia, PA, 1962 – lives Denver, CO

North Platte River Reclamation, Walden, Colorado, 2000
Pigment print, 14¾ × 18⅜ inches. S-1215.2022
Pool and riffle

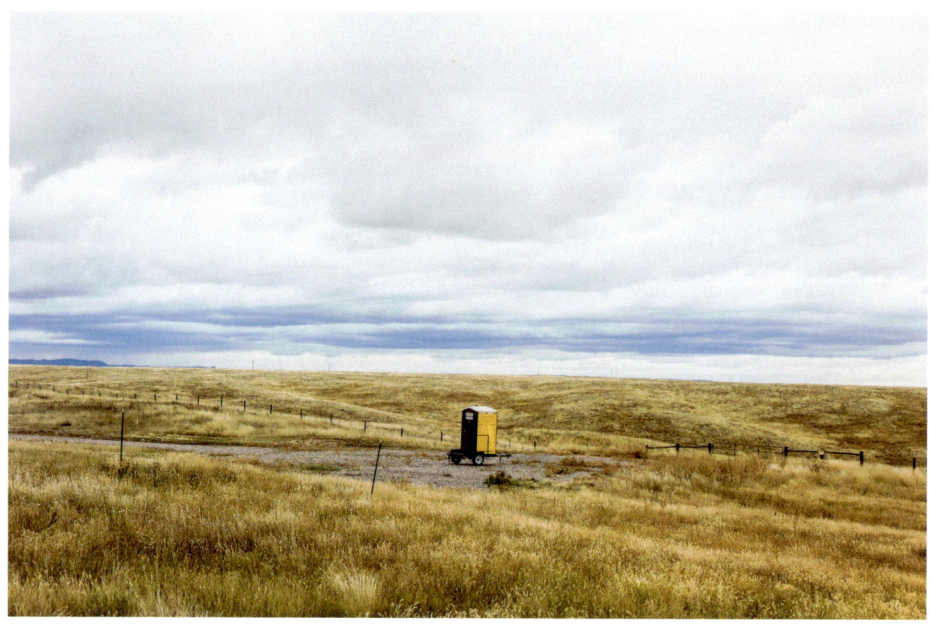

Andrew Borowiec *Laramie County, Wyoming, 2014*

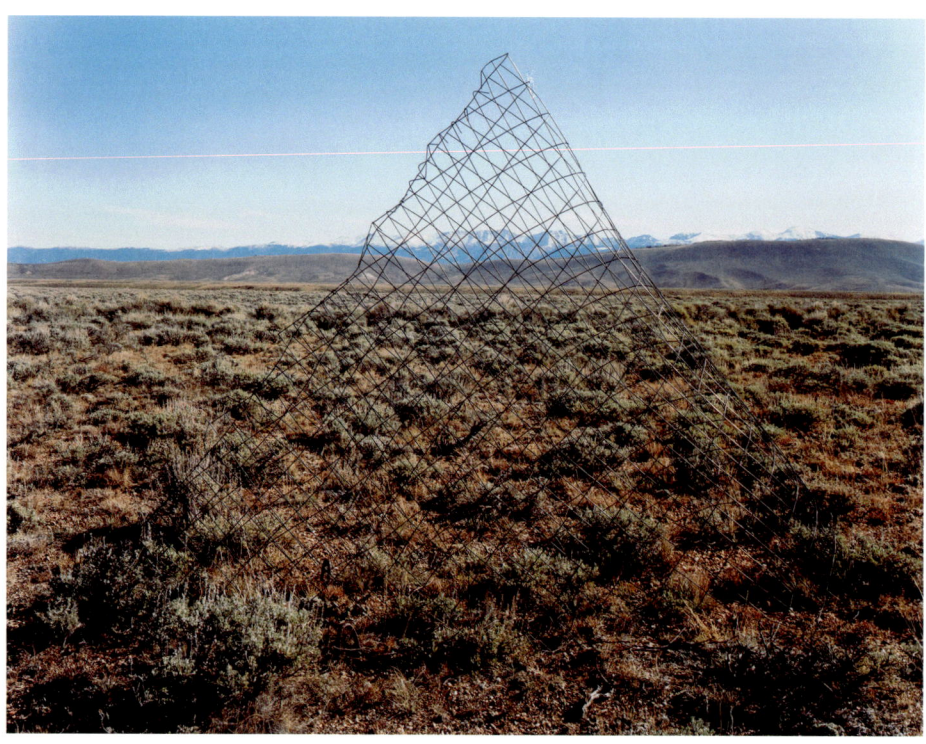

Joann Brennan *Research Cone Placed around a Control Group of Sagebrush, 2000*

*Research Cone Placed around a Control Group of Sagebrush.
Owl Mountain Partnership, Walden, Colorado*, 2000
Pigment print, 14⅞ × 18⅞ inches. S-1216.2022
Scrub

Lois Conner Born Rockville Centre, NY, 1951 – lives New York, NY

Arches National Park, Utah, 1990
Platinum print, 8⅜ × 18¹⁵⁄₁₆ inches. S-1220.2022
Arch

Badlands National Park, South Dakota, 1996
Platinum print, 7⁷⁄₁₆ × 18⅜ inches. S-1221.2022
Badlands

Gregory Conniff Born Jersey City, NJ, 1944 – lives Madison, WI

Madison, Wisconsin, 1979
Gelatin silver print, 12 × 16 inches. S-1217.2022
Yard

Central Park, New York City, 2018
Pigment print, 14 × 14 inches. S-1218.2022
Desire path

Linda Connor Born New York, NY, 1944 – lives San Francisco, CA

Lava, Hawaii, 1979
Gelatin silver print on printing-out paper, 8 × 9¹⁵⁄₁₆ inches.
S-1219.2022
Pāhoehoe

Thomas Joshua Cooper Born San Francisco, CA, 1946 – lives Glasgow, Scotland

The Snake River / Cauldron Linn, No. 2 / Jerome County, Idaho,
2003–2004
Gelatin silver print, 4⁹⁄₁₆ × 6½ inches. S-1223.2022
Cauldron

*Lingering Twilight–The First View / Shoshone Falls, Centre Rim
Top, The Snake River Basin / Idaho*, 2003–2004
Gelatin silver print, 4½ × 6⁹⁄₁₆ inches. S-1222.2022
Dry fall

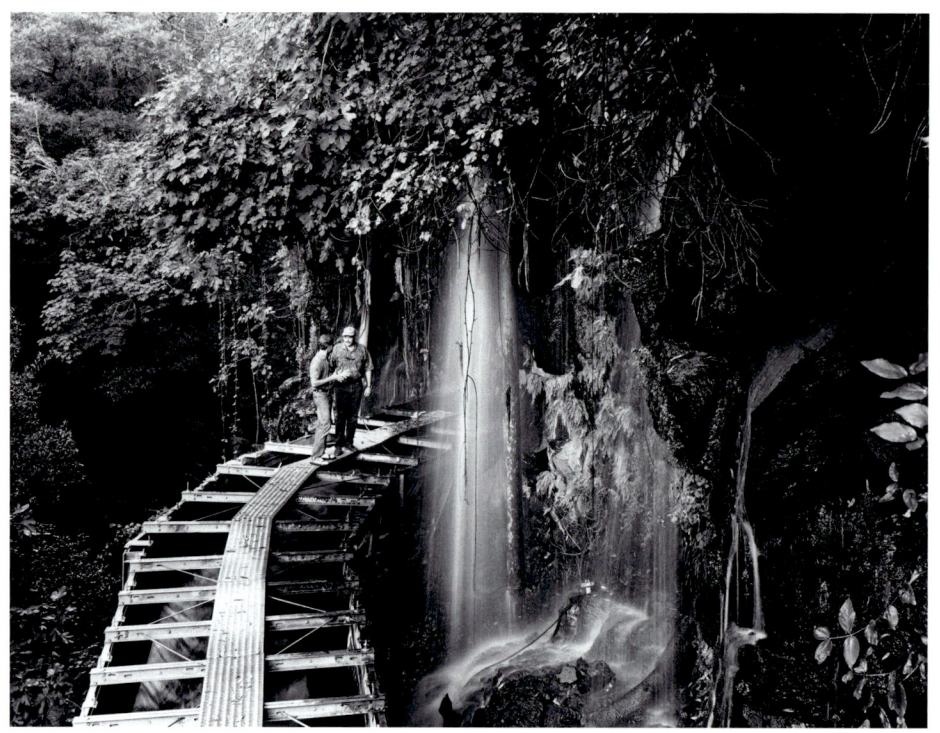

Robert Dawson *Two Scientists Discussing the Demise and Restoration of California's Salmon, Sacramento River, California,* 1997

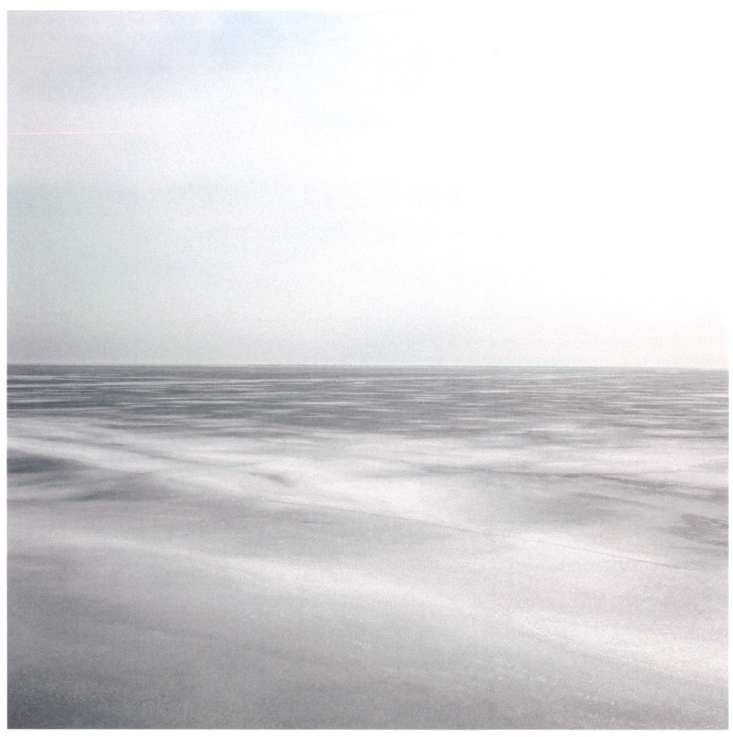

Lucinda Devlin *Lake Huron, 3-17-2011 1:49pm,* 2011

Checklist

Robert Dawson   Born Sacramento, CA, 1950 – lives San Francisco, CA

Spillway, Lake Berryessa, California, 1986
From the "Great Central Valley" Project
Gelatin silver print, 10⅝ × 18⁷⁄₁₆ inches. S-1225.2022
Glory hole

*Two Scientists Discussing the Demise and Restoration of
California's Salmon, Sacramento River, California*, 1997
From the "Farewell, Promised Land" Project
Gelatin silver print, 14⁷⁄₁₆ × 18⁷⁄₁₆ inches. S-1224.2022
Flume

Peter de Lory   Born Fall River, MA, 1948 – lives Seattle, WA

*Canyonlands Saunter: Slick Rock Pool; The Narrows; Peek-a-Boo
Canyon, Canyonlands National Park, Utah*, 1997
Gelatin silver print, 15 × 14⅞ inches, each image. S-1226.A-C.2022
Slot canyon

Lucinda Devlin   Born Ann Arbor, MI, 1947 – lives Belmont, NC

Lake Huron, 5-10-2011 8:43pm, 2011
From the series "Lake Pictures"
Pigment print, 20 × 20 inches. S-1228.2022
Horizon

Lake Huron, 3-17-2011 1:49pm, 2011
From the series "Lake Pictures"
Pigment print, 20 × 20 inches. S-1227.2022
Horizon

Rick Dingus   Born Appleton City, MO, 1951 – lives Bend, OR

Visitor Center, Monahans Sandhills State Park, Texas, 2004
Pigment print, 15 × 36½ inches. S-1230.2022
Sandhill

*Ponderosa Pines in Whychus Creek Canyon (Upstream from
Where Whychus Creek Merges with the Deschutes River),
Oregon*, 2020
Pigment print, 13⁵⁄₁₆ × 20 inches. S-1229.2022
Barranca

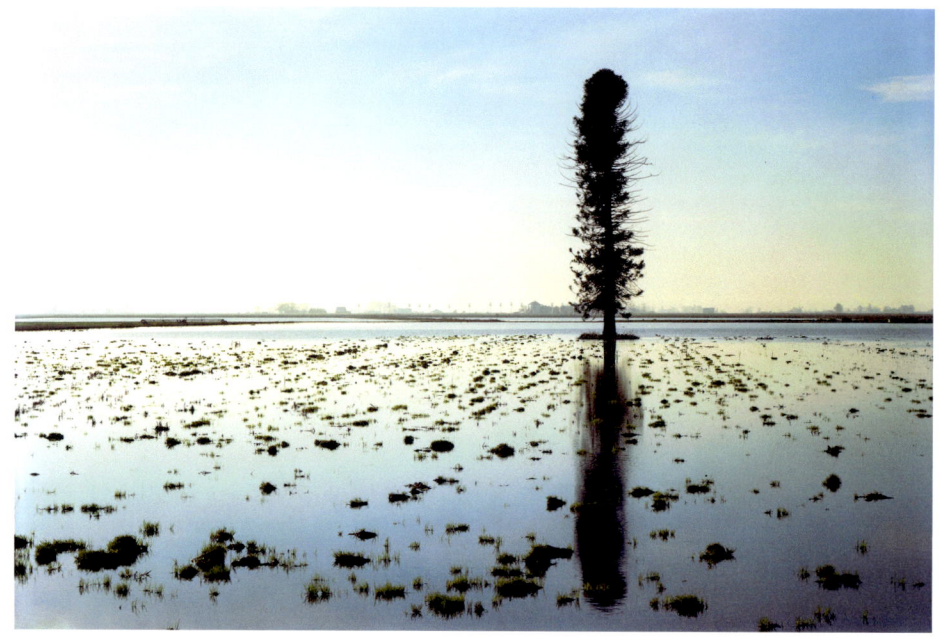

Lukas Felzmann *Rice Field, Sacramento Valley, California,* 2009

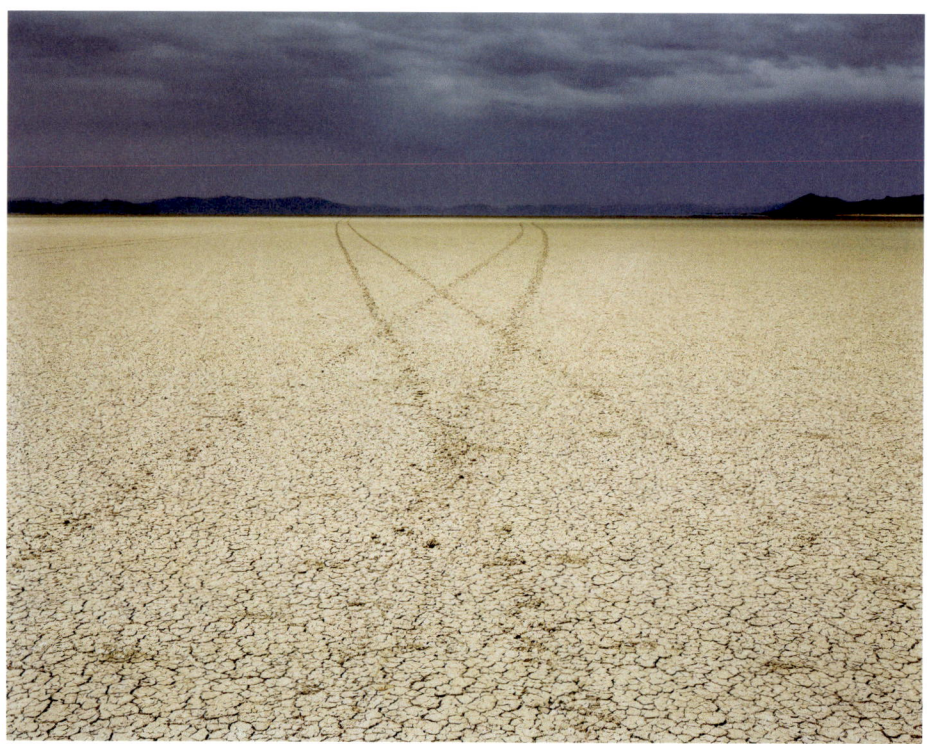

Peter Goin *Intersecting Tracks, Black Rock Desert, Nevada,* 1988

Checklist

Terry Evans Born Kansas City, MO, 1944 – lives Chicago, IL

Platte River, Nebraska, 1990
Pigment print, 19¹⁄₁₆ × 19 inches. S-1232.2022
Meander

Train North of Matfield Green, Chase County, Kansas, July 2009,
2009
Pigment print, 16 × 16 inches. S-1231.2022
Prairie

Lukas Felzmann Born Zürich, Switzerland, 1959 – lives San Francisco, CA

The Western Edge of the Sacramento Valley, California, 2009
Pigment print, 16½ × 23⅞ inches. S-1234.2022
Foothill

Rice Field, Sacramento Valley, California, 2009
Pigment print, 16½ × 24 inches. S-1233.2022
Field pattern

Steve Fitch Born Tucson, AZ, 1949 – lives Santa Fe County, NM

*Jaguar with a Rattlesnake Tail Petroglyph, Overlooking the
Tularosa Basin and Trinity Site, Three Rivers, New Mexico,
January 10, 1983*, 1983
Pigment print, 15¹⁄₁₆ × 19 inches. S-1235.2022
Basin

*Radio Tower on the Llano Estacado between Caprock and
Maljamar, New Mexico, June 29, 2005*, 2005
Pigment print, 15¹⁄₁₆ × 19 inches. S-1236.2022
Staked plain

Frank Gohlke Born Wichita Falls, TX, 1942 – lives Tucson, AZ

*Looking Southeast across Lahar (mud flow), Six Miles Southeast
of Mount St. Helen's, Washington*, 1983
Gelatin silver print, 18 × 21⅞ inches. S-1237.2022
Lahar

Peter Goin Born Madison, WI, 1951 – lives Reno, NV

Intersecting Tracks, Black Rock Desert, Nevada, 1988
Pigment print, 20 × 25 inches. S-1204.2022
Desert

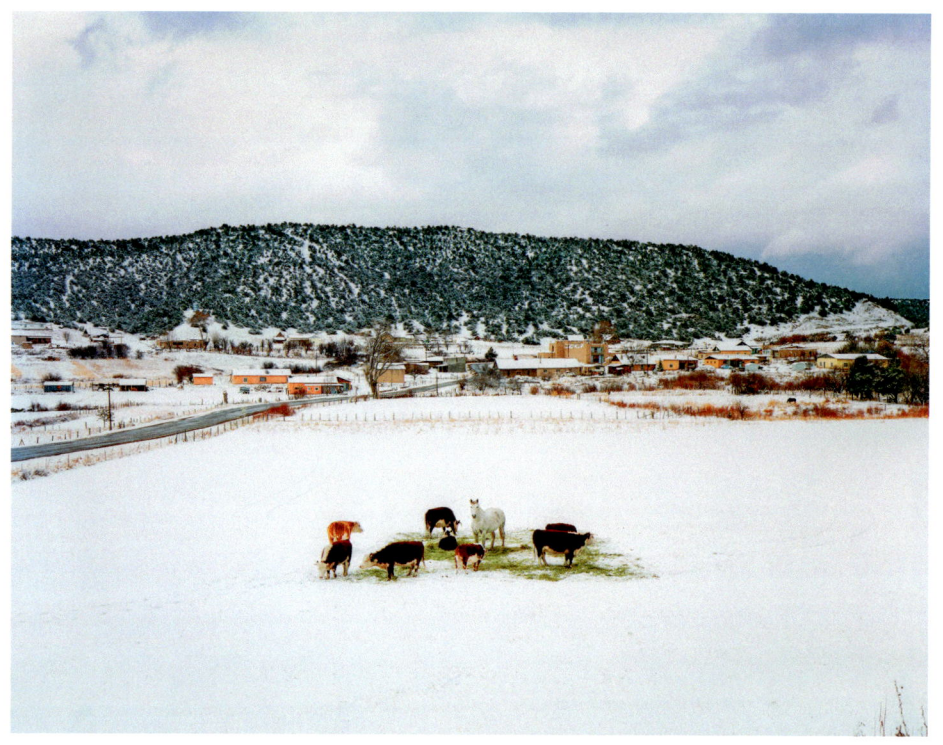

Alex Harris *Las Trampas, New Mexico, March 1984*, 1984

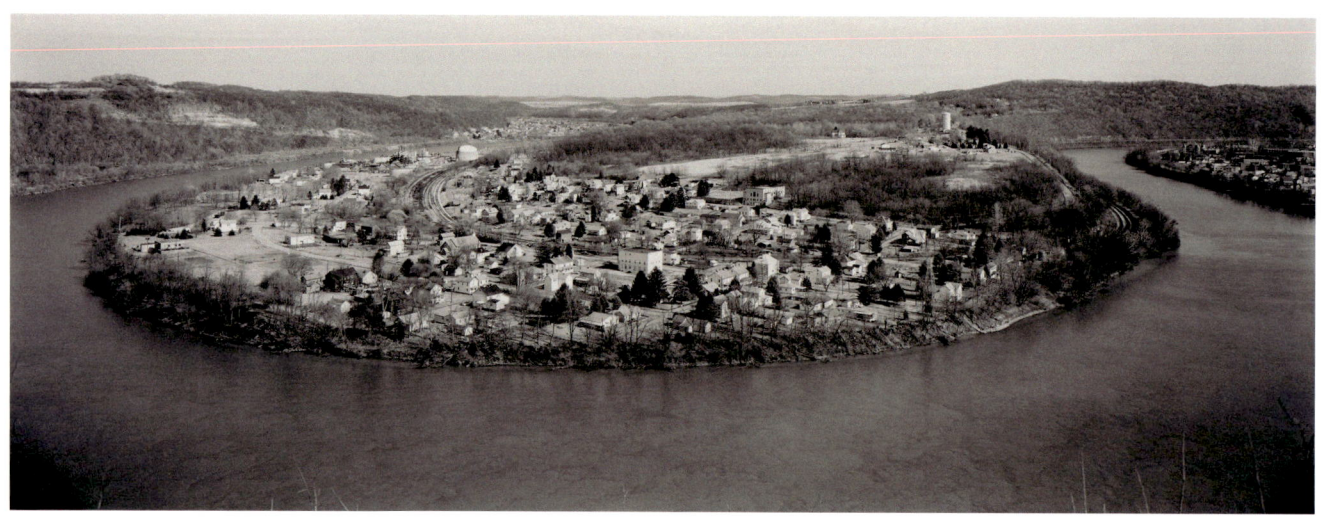

Allen Hess *Monongahela River, Newell, Pennsylvania*, 1989

Tapestry Wall, Colorado River, Lake Powell, Utah, 2013
Pigment print, 16 × 46 inches. S-1203.2022
Tapestry wall

Emmet Gowin Born Danville, VA, 1941 – lives Newtown, PA

*Alluvial Fan, Natural Drainage, near the Yuma Proving Ground
and the Arizona-California Border*, 1988
Gelatin silver print, 9¹¹⁄₁₆ × 9⅝ inches. S-1198.2022
Alluvial fan

Wayne Gudmundson Born Fargo, ND, 1949 – lives on Bad Medicine Lake, MN
and Tucson, AZ

South of Marmarth, North Dakota, 1983
Gelatin silver print, 12¹³⁄₁₆ × 16¼ inches. S-1239.2022
Looking-glass prairie

Red River, North of Georgetown, Minnesota, 2013
Gelatin silver print, 13⁷⁄₁₆ × 16¹³⁄₁₆ inches. S-1238.2022
Floodplain

Owen Gump Born Kentfield, CA, 1980 – lives Northern CA

Mine Tailings, Lyon County, Nevada, 2018
Pigment print, 12⅝ × 18⅞ inches. S-1241.2022
Tailings pile

*Martin Canyon, Future Site of Alphabet, Inc. Research Complex,
Storey County, Nevada*, 2018
Pigment print, 12⅝ × 18⅞ inches. S-1240.2022
Tool mark

David T. Hanson Born Billings, MT, 1948 – lives Fairfield, IA

Coal Strip Mine, Power Plant and Waste Ponds, 1984
From the series "Colstrip, Montana"
Pigment print, 14⅝ × 18 inches. S-1243.2022
Strip mine

*Yankee Doodle Tailings Pond, Tailings Dam, and Leach Pads,
Butte, Montana*, 1991
From the series "The Treasure State"
Pigment print, 14¹¹⁄₁₆ × 18 inches. S-1242.2022
Tailings pond

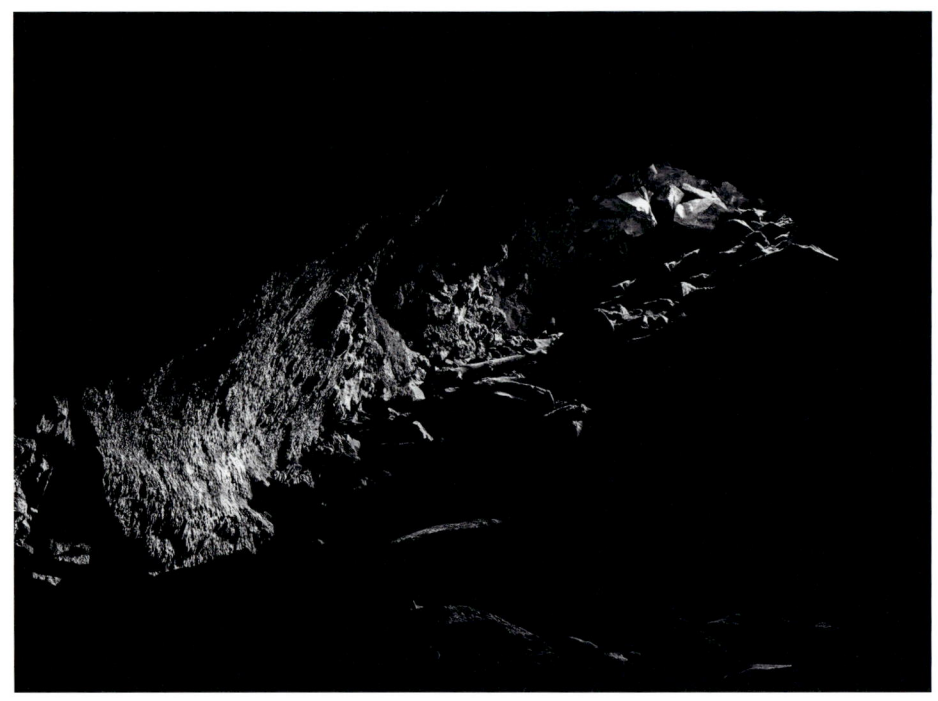

Ron Jude *Lava Tube #1, 2017*

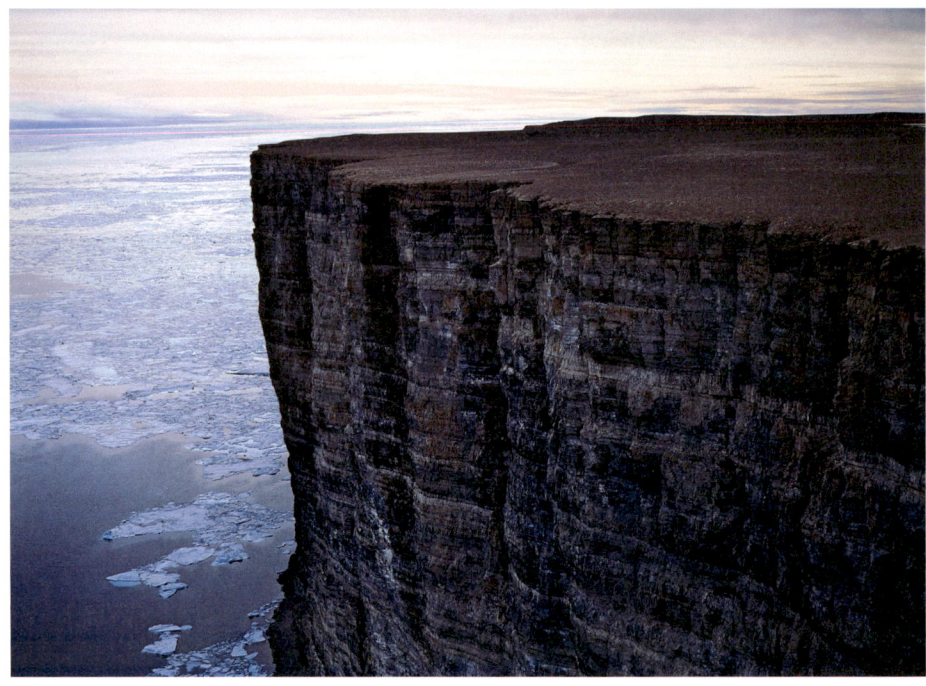

Robert Glenn Ketchum *Rookery Cliffs at the Edge of Lancaster Sound, Nunavut, Canada, 1994*

Checklist

Alex Harris Born Atlanta, GA, 1949 – lives Durham, NC

Las Trampas, New Mexico, March 1984, 1984
Pigment print, 22 × 27¹³⁄₁₆ inches. S-1245.2022
Valle

*Black Mesa, New Mexico, Looking East from Fred Cata's 1957
Chevrolet Belair*, 1987
Pigment print, 22 × 27½ inches. S-1244.2022
Mesa

Allen Hess Born Dayton, OH, 1950 – lives Bethlehem, PA

Monongahela River, Newell, Pennsylvania, 1989
From the series "The River's Green Margins"
Pigment print, 12 × 31¼ inches. S-1206.2022
Lookout

*Levee Break, Quincy, Illinois, Mississippi River Flood, August 27,
1993*, 1993
From the series "The River's Green Margins"
Pigment print, 12 × 16½ inches. S-1205.2022
Levee

Ben Huff Born LeClaire, IA, 1973 – lives Juneau, AK

Kulluk Bay Neighborhood, Adak, Alaska, 2017
From "Atomic Island"
Pigment print, 20 × 25¼ inches. S-1247.2022
Volcanic plug

Above the Gilkey Trench, Camp 18, Juneau Icefield, Alaska, 2018
From "The Light That Got Lost"
Pigment print, 20 × 25¼ inches. S-1246.2022
Nunatak

Ron Jude Born Los Angeles, CA, 1965 – lives Eugene, OR

River, 2017
From the series "12 Hz"
Pigment print, 15 × 20 inches. S-1248.2022
Turbulent flow

Lava Tube #1, 2017
From the series "12 Hz"
Pigment print, 15 × 20 inches. S-1249.2022
Lava cave

177

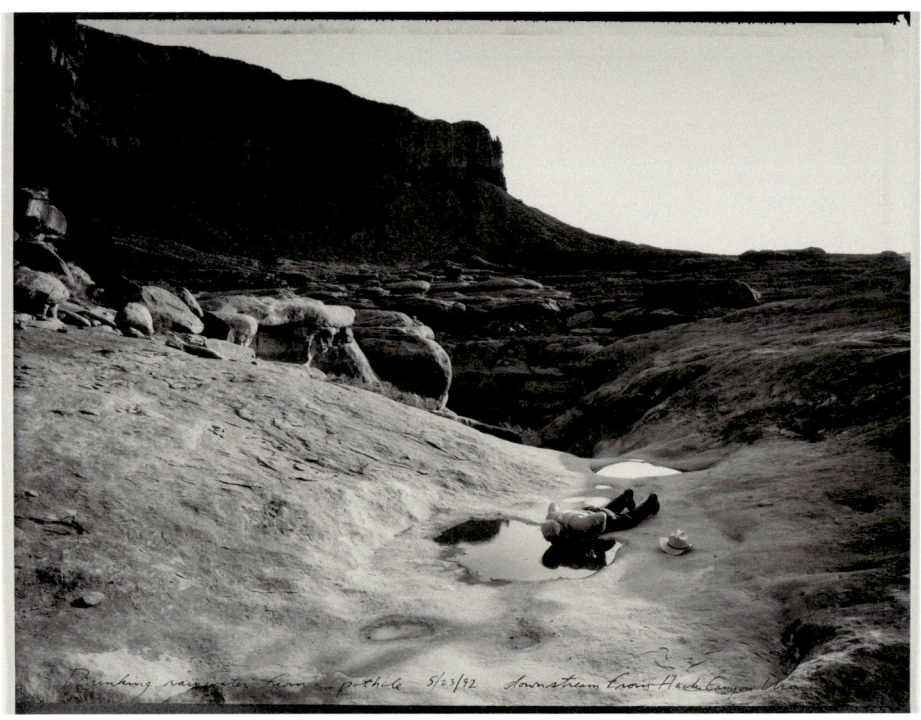

Mark Klett *Drinking Rainwater from a Pothole Downstream from Hack Canyon Uranium Mine, Arizona 5/23/92*, 1992

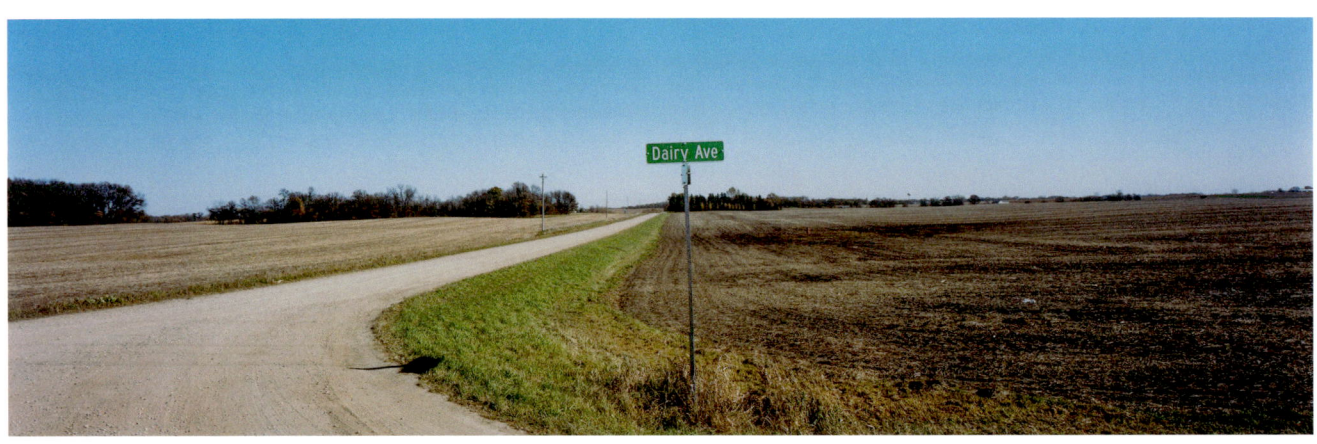

Stuart Klipper *Dairy Avenue, near Lester Prairie, McCleod County, Minnesota*, 2018

Checklist

Robert Glenn Ketchum   Born Los Angeles, CA, 1947 – lives Los Angeles, CA

Glacial Outflow, Otto Fjord, Ellesmere Island, Canada, 1994
Cibachrome print, 24¹⁄₁₆ × 30 inches. S-1250.2022
Glacial valley

Rookery Cliffs at the Edge of Lancaster Sound, Nunavut, Canada, 1994
Cibachrome print, 30 × 40 inches. S-1251.2022
Headland

Mark Klett   Born Albany, NY, 1952 – lives Tempe, AZ

Drinking Rainwater from a Pothole Downstream from Hack Canyon Uranium Mine, Arizona 5/23/92, 1992
Gelatin silver print, 15⅞ × 20 inches. S-1253.2022
Pothole

My Camera at the Head of Sinbad, San Rafael Swell, Utah 5/22/93, 1993
Gelatin silver print, 15¹⁵⁄₁₆ × 19¹³⁄₁₆ inches. S-1252.2022
Swell

Stuart Klipper   Born New York, NY, 1941 – lives Minneapolis, MN

Confluence of the Buffalo River (Flooded) and the Red River, Clay County, Minnesota, 2013
From the series "The World in a Few States"
Chromogenic development print, 12 × 37¼ inches. S-1195.2022
Confluence

Dairy Avenue, near Lester Prairie, McCleod County, Minnesota, 2018
From the series "The World in a Few States"
Chromogenic development print, 12 × 36⅞ inches. S-1196.2022
Section-line road

Peter Latner   Born New York, NY, 1950 – lives Minneapolis, MN

Mississippi River Valley at Dusk, La Crosse County, Wisconsin, 2000
Gelatin silver print, 17 × 21½ inches. S-1194.2022
Swale

Little Bighorn Battlefield, Montana, 2007
Gelatin silver print, 14⁹⁄₁₆ × 17⅞ inches. S-1193.2022
Viewshed

179

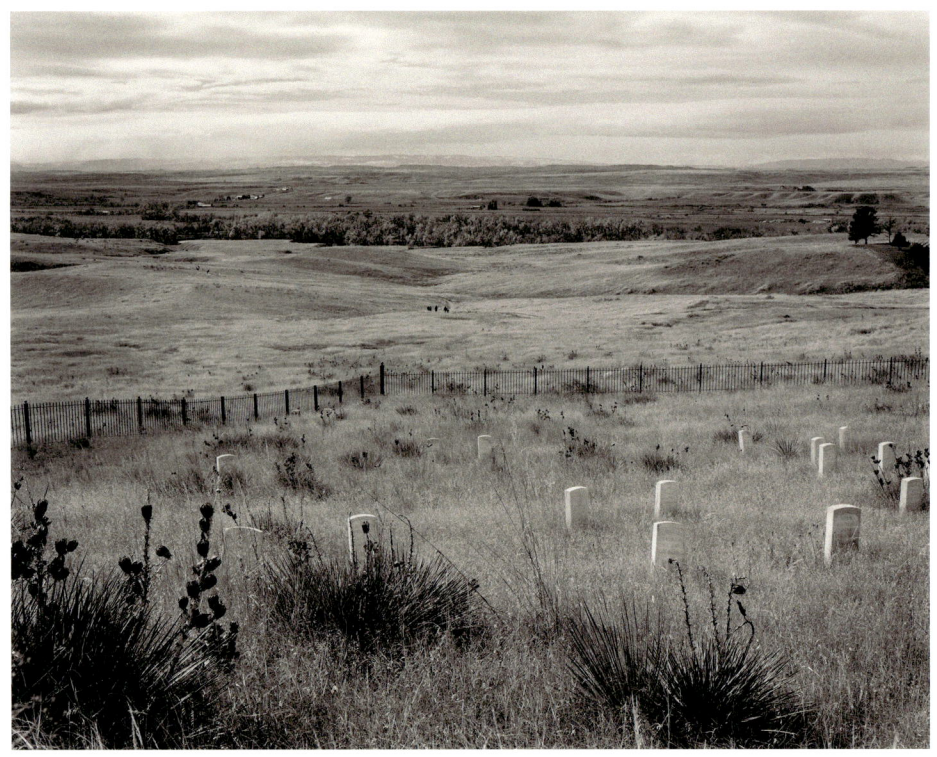

Peter Latner *Little Bighorn Battlefield, Montana,* 2007

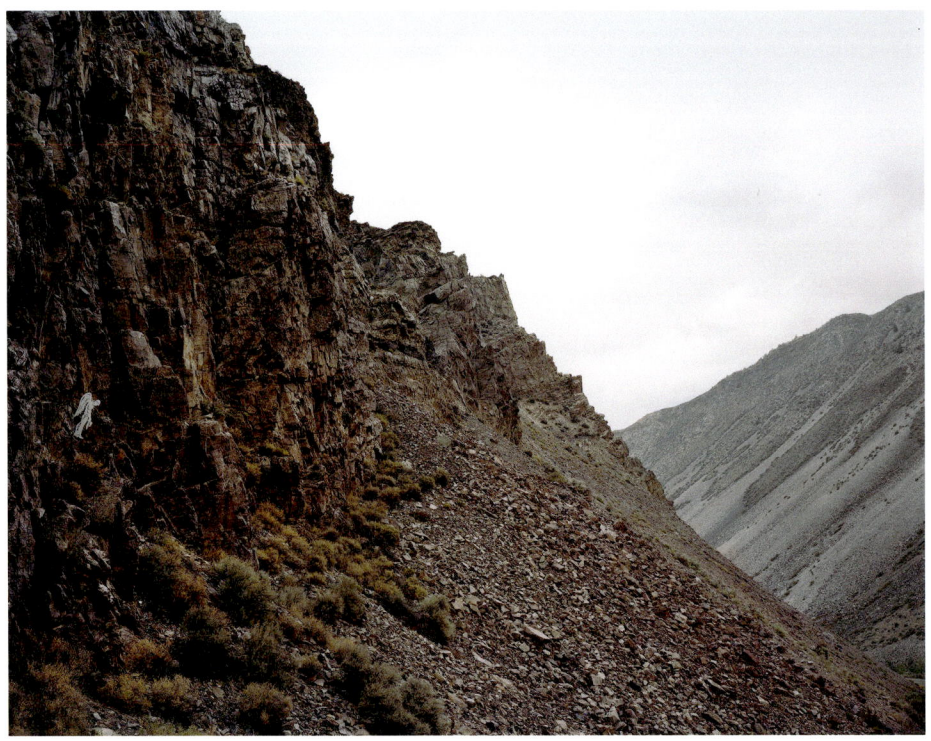

Laura McPhee *Salmon River Canyon, Near Bayhorse, Custer County, Idaho,* 2015

Checklist

David Maisel   Born New York, NY, 1961 – lives north of San Francisco, CA

Terminal Mirage 14, 2003
Pigment print, 29 × 29 inches. S-1280.2022
Salt lake

Laura McPhee   Born New York, NY, 1958 – lives Wood River Valley, ID and New York, NY

*Irrigator's Tarp Directing Water, Fourth of July Creek Ranch,
Custer County, Idaho*, 2004
Pigment print, 31⅝ × 40 inches. S-1282.2022
Sawtooth

Salmon River Canyon, Near Bayhorse, Custer County, Idaho, 2015
Pigment print, 31⅞ × 40 inches. S-1281.2022
Talus

Andrew Moore   Born Old Greenwich, CT, 1957 – lives Kingston, NY

Broken Pivot, Cherry County, Nebraska, 2013
Pigment print, 30 × 40 inches. S-1284.2022
Aquifer

Riding Fence, Sheridan County, Nebraska, 2013
Pigment print, 29⅜ × 40 inches. S-1283.2022
High plains

Eric Paddock   Born Boulder, CO, 1954 – lives Denver, CO

Monument Hill, Colorado, 1991
Pigment print, 12 x 17¹³⁄₁₆ inches. S-1254.2022
Grade

Loveland Pass, Colorado, 1994
Pigment print, 12 × 17⁹⁄₁₆ inches. S-1255.2022
Shoulder

Mary Peck   Born Minneapolis, MN, 1952 – lives Santa Fe, NM

*Following the Route of the Keystone XL, Syncrude Tailings Pond,
North of Fort McMurray, Alberta*, 2017
Pigment print, 22 × 28⁵⁄₁₆ inches. S-1256.2022
Boreal forest

*Following the Route of the Keystone XL, Niobrara National Scenic
River North of Newport, Nebraska*, 2017
Pigment print, 22 × 27⁷⁄₁₆ inches. S-1257.2022
Ecotone

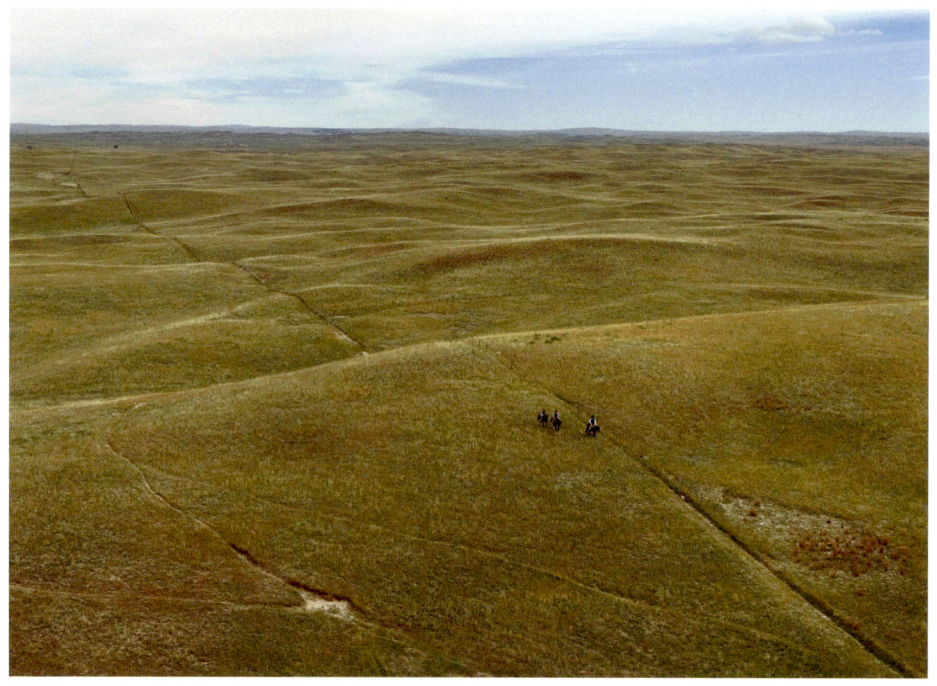

Andrew Moore   *Riding Fence, Sheridan County, Nebraska*, 2013

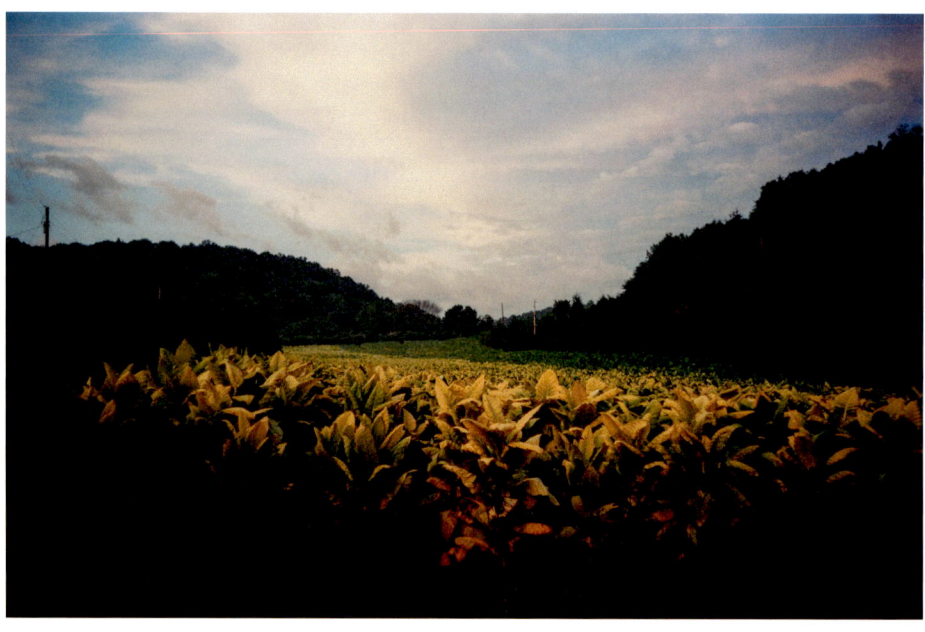

Mike Smith   *Piney Flats, Tennessee*, 1987

Checklist

Edward Ranney

Born Chicago, IL, 1942 – lives Santa Fe, NM

Hungo Pavi to Fajada Butte, Chaco Canyon, New Mexico, 1982
Gelatin silver print, 12³⁄₁₆ × 18⁷⁄₁₆ inches. S-1259.2022
Chaco

Canyon del Muerto, Arizona, 1987
Gelatin silver print, 12¹³⁄₁₆ × 18⅜ inches. S-1258.2022
Canyon

Jeff Rich

Born Atlanta, GA, 1977 – lives Atlanta, GA

Slough and MS-25 Bridge, Iuka, Mississippi, 2013
From "The Watershed Project"
Pigment print, 19 × 23¹³⁄₁₆ inches. S-1260.2022
Slough

North Platte River Headwaters, Jackson County, Colorado, 2018
From "The Watershed Project"
Pigment print, 19 × 23¹³⁄₁₆ inches. S-1261.2022
Headwaters

Meghann Riepenhoff

Born Atlanta, GA, 1979 – lives Bainbridge Island, WA and
San Francisco, CA

*Littoral Drift #1223 (Chattahoochee River, Atlanta, Georgia
09.26.18, Draped on Long Island at Confluence of White Water
Creek)*, 2018
Dynamic cyanotype, 11¹⁵⁄₁₆ × 9 inches. S-1262.2022
Littoral drift

Mark Ruwedel

Born Bethlehem, PA, 1954 – lives Long Beach, CA

Hells Canyon Creek, Snake River Drainage, 1999
Gelatin silver print mounted on board, 7½ × 9½ inches.
S-1264.2022
Hell

Lower Colorado Desert, The Horse Intaglio, 2005
Gelatin silver print mounted on board, 7⁷⁄₁₆ × 9⁷⁄₁₆ inches.
S-1263.2022
Desert pavement

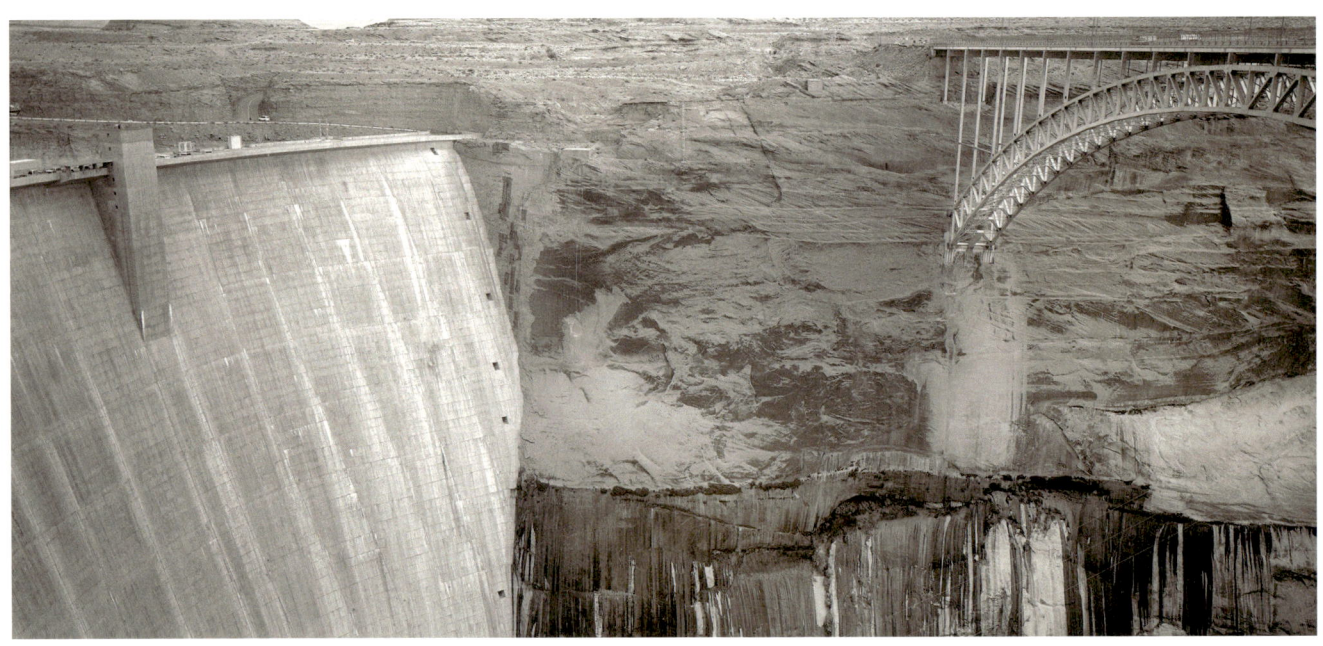

Martin Stupich *Dam and Bridge at Glen Canyon near Page, Arizona*, 1992

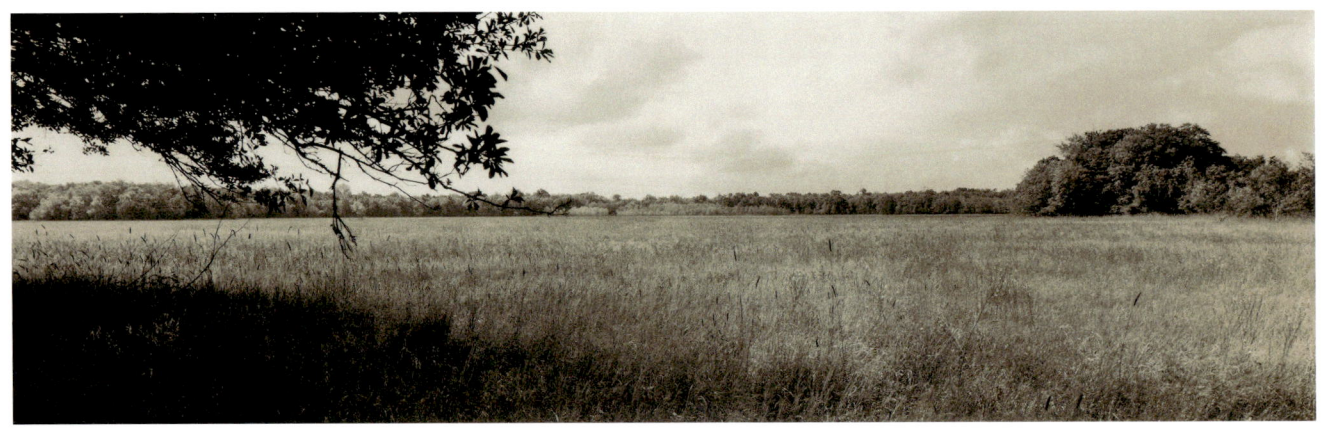

Geoff Winningham *Fisher's Farm and Buffalo Bayou Treeline, Houston, Texas*, 2001

Checklist

Mike Smith   Born Heidelberg, Germany, 1951 – lives Johnson City, TN

Piney Flats, Tennessee, 1987
Chromogenic development print, 14 × 21 inches. S-1265.2022
Flat

Blue Hole, Carter County, Tennessee, 2011
Pigment print, 7½ × 9⅜ inches. S-1266.2022
Blue hole

Joel Sternfeld   Born New York, NY, 1944 – lives New York, NY

Rim View Trail, Page, Arizona, August 1983, 1983
Digital chromogenic development print, 16⁹⁄₁₆ × 20¹¹⁄₁₆ inches.
S-1267.2022
Plateau

Martin Stupich   Born Milwaukee, WI, 1949 – lives Albuquerque, NM

Sand Mountain, Nevada, 1980
Pigment print, 14¹⁄₁₆ × 55¹⁵⁄₁₆ inches. S-1202.2022
Dune

Dam and Bridge at Glen Canyon near Page, Arizona, 1992
Pigment print, 14 × 29 inches. S-1201.2022
Abutment

William Sutton   Born Toledo, OH, 1956 – lives Boulder, CO

Comb Ridge, Bureau of Land Management, Utah, 1989
Pigment print, 7 × 9 inches. S-1268.2022
Comb ridge

Strawberry Crater, Coconino National Forest, Arizona, 1989
Pigment print, 6¹⁵⁄₁₆ × 9 inches. S-1269.2022
Crater

Bob Thall   Born Chicago, IL, 1948 – lives Evanston, IL

Chicago (Chicago River. View East from the Roof of the IBM Building), 1989
Gelatin silver print, 13⁹⁄₁₆ × 16¹⁵⁄₁₆ inches. S-1270.2022
Portage

Chicago (Chicago River. View West from Wabash Avenue), 2007
Gelatin silver print, 13⅝ × 16⅞ inches. S-1271.2022
River

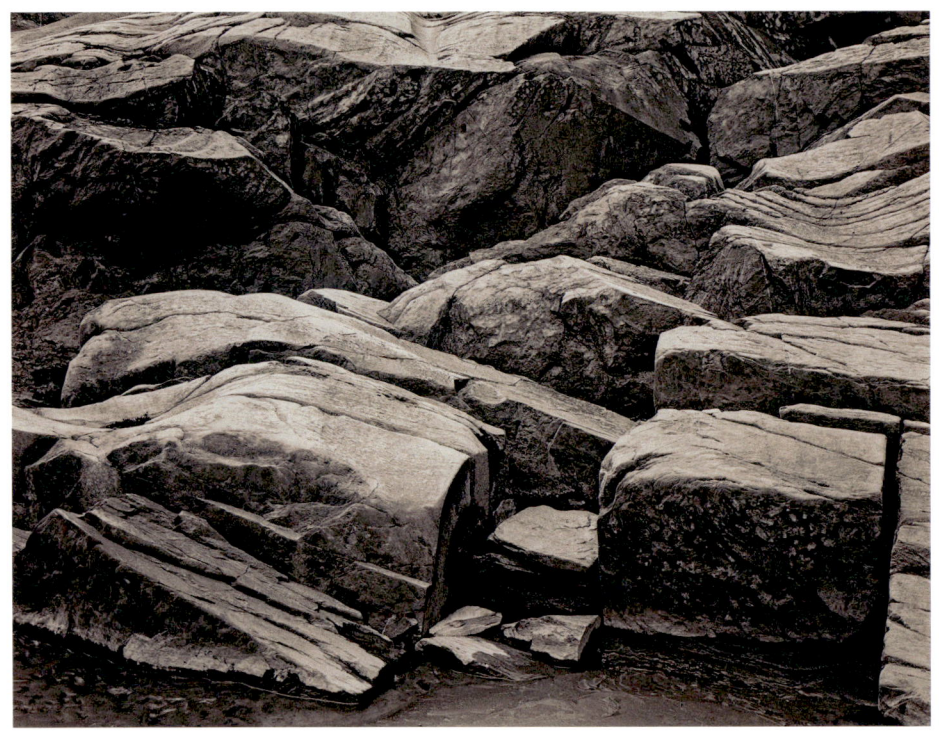

Dennis Witmer *Glaciated Rocks, Bird Point, Turnagain Arm, Alaska*, 1994

Checklist

Terry Toedtemeier Born Portland, OR, 1947 – died Hood River, OR, 2008

View from the Rimrock below Fairbanks Gap, One Mile West of Celilo Drawbridge, Columbia River Gorge, Oregon, 1987
Gelatin silver print, 8 9/16 × 18 7/16 inches. S-1273.2022
Gorge

Palomino Lake, Malheur County, Oregon, 1993
Gelatin silver print, 8½ × 18 5/16 inches. S-1272.2022
Basin and range

Geoff Winningham Born Jackson, TN, 1943 – lives Houston, TX

Allen's Landing on Buffalo Bayou, Houston, Texas, 2001
Photogravure, 7⅛ × 22 inches. S-1199.2022
Bayou

Fisher's Farm and Buffalo Bayou Treeline, Houston, Texas, 2001
Photogravure, 7 × 22 inches. S-1200.2022
Pasture

Dennis Witmer Born Lancaster, PA, 1957 – died Spokane, WA, 2022

Glaciated Rocks, Bird Point, Turnagain Arm, Alaska, 1994
Gelatin silver print, 8 × 10 inches. S-1208.2022
Glacial polish

Hanging Valley, Brooks Range, Alaska, 1996
Gelatin silver print, 9 × 9 inches. S-1207.2022
Hanging valley

William Wylie Born Harvey, IL, 1957 – lives Charlottesville, VA

Narrows in Upper Canyon, Cache la Poudre River, Colorado, 1997
Gelatin silver print, 13½ × 17 7/16 inches. S-1275.2022
Narrows

Cache la Poudre River, Colorado, 2000
From the series "Stillwater"
Gelatin silver print, 17 3/16 × 21 9/16 inches. S-1274.2022
Stillwater

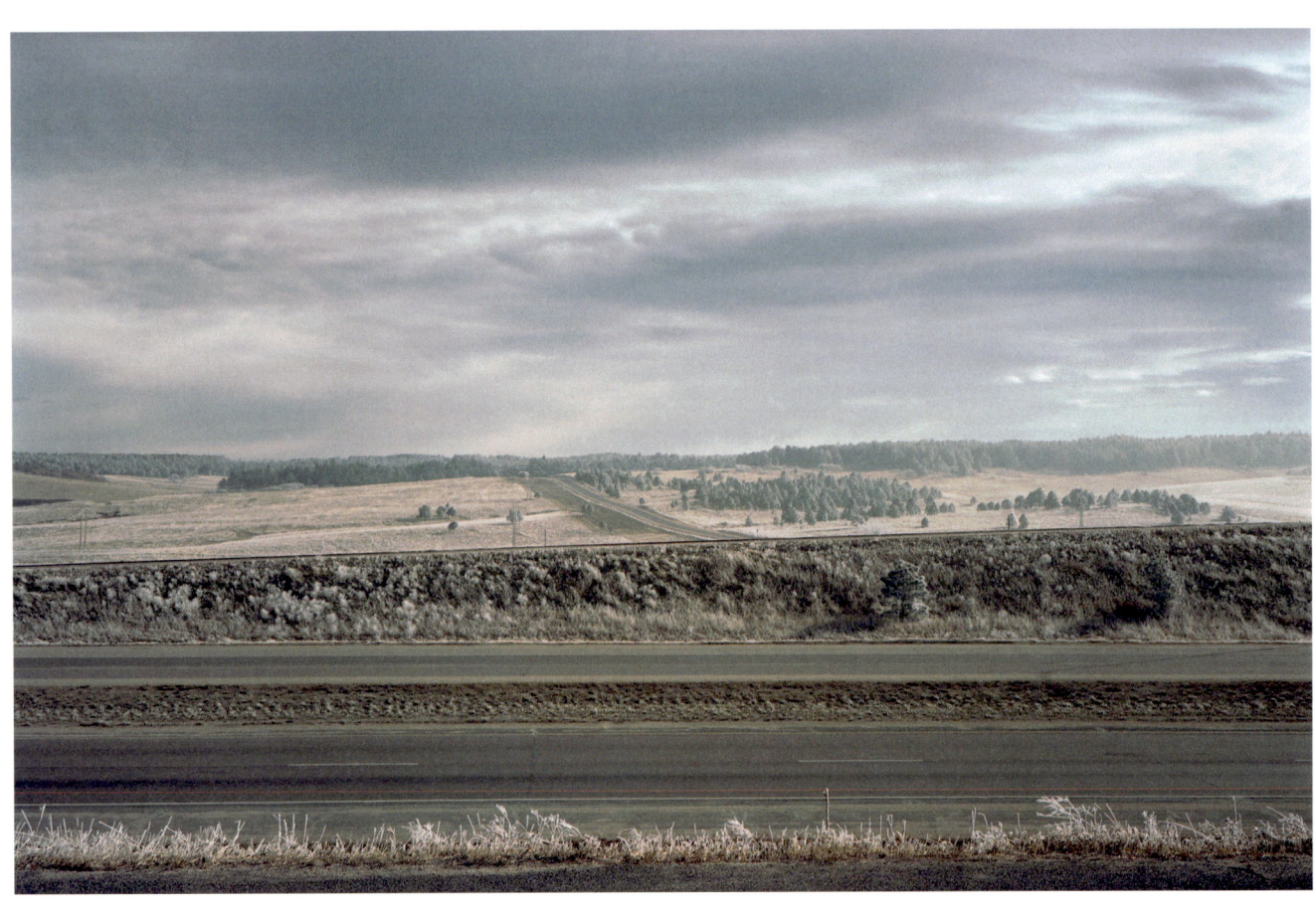

Eric Paddock
Monument Hill, Colorado, 1991
Sheldon Museum of Art, the Home Ground Collection

Grade

Barry Lopez Foundation for Art & Environment Acknowledgments

I want to begin by thanking the fifty photographers who generously donated their work to create the Home Ground Collection in Honor of Barry Lopez—when asked, their response was immediate and enthusiastic. I believe everyone was happy not only to help mark Barry's life but to be in the company of other friends with shared affinities. Just as *Home Ground: A Guide to the American Landscape* sustains a vocabulary based upon our sense of place, their work reminds us of the unique ability of a photograph to capture "the factual testimony of the land" in a manner both exact and inspiring. Barry's absence is the one lacuna in this celebration—as Robert Macfarlane so graciously notes, "I wish, of course, that he were here." But Barry watched as the collection took shape and was humbled by the kindness of his friends and colleagues. Likewise, I am also fortunate to call many of the artists in this collection friends. Some I have known for decades, others I've come to know only recently, but much of what I understand about photography I owe to their cumulative generosity and good nature during many conversations and days shared in their studios or better yet in the field.

The Home Ground Collection would not have become what it is without Virginia Beahan, who was quick to volunteer her assistance and was an indispensable partner from start to finish. Sandra Phillips was working on a parallel exhibition with Barry that became the weighty and ominous *American Geography: Photographs of Land Use from 1840 to the Present*, and many good ideas were passed back and forth. Eric Paddock and I have sustained an ongoing conversation about landscape photography for more than two decades—his thoughtful recommendations were essential to the project and kept my wheels out of the ditch. Laura McPhee helped Virginia and me apply the final polish, and the collection owes much to her insights. Martin Stupich gave digital assistance, and Gregory Conniff tightened the last screw. In Santa Fe, I would like to thank Kate Ware for her friendship, keen eye for geology, and careful remarks on my essay, which was much improved by her efforts, and Mary Peck for our conversations along the trail.

Robert Macfarlane joyfully agreed to start things off—thank you for your heartfelt introduction to Barry and for giving us a personal glimpse of how he moved through the world. It is fair to say that Debra Gwartney, Barry's wife, has been a part of this project since before it began, working side by side with him to realize their vision of a geographic dictionary celebrating our national landscape. I would like to have seen the map she describes as it filled with names and phrases as *Home Ground* took shape—perhaps it's a practice we should all adopt, beyond simply collecting images of where we've been on our phones. Debra would also like to thank Barbara Ras, former director of Trinity University Press, for her critical role in bringing *Home Ground* to print.

The Home Ground Collection took shape before the Barry Lopez Foundation for Art & Environment was established, and I would like to thank the board for enthusiastically welcoming this project and for their guidance and support during the foundation's first two years: Dr. Hugh M. Davies, Chair; A. Michael Hewins, Treasurer; Dr. Emily Ballew Neff, Secretary; Dr. Rachel Leibowitz; and William Wylie.

I want to extend my appreciation to everyone at Lucia|Marquand in Seattle—Adrian Lucia, Leah Finger, Meghann Ney, Kestrel Rundle, and especially Melissa Duffes for keeping a careful watch on the text and Tom Eykemans for designing a book that asks to be picked up and read. This is the fourth catalogue we have worked on together, each better than the last—thank you for making beautiful books. Beth Stinson, who volunteers with the Barry Lopez Foundation, was of immeasurable help in preparing the catalogue entries and checklist.

The exhibition and catalogue would not have been possible without the support of Wally Mason, director and chief curator of Sheldon Museum of Art, University of Nebraska–Lincoln. Wally lights up when he spots a good photograph, and he eagerly embraced the chance to bring this project to Sheldon. It is fitting that a collection of images celebrating our geography should find its home so close to the center of the country, and the foundation could not have asked for a better partner. The project's success was ensured by the generosity of Susan O'Connor—thank you for your support of the Barry Lopez Foundation and your desire to help honor Barry and his life's work.

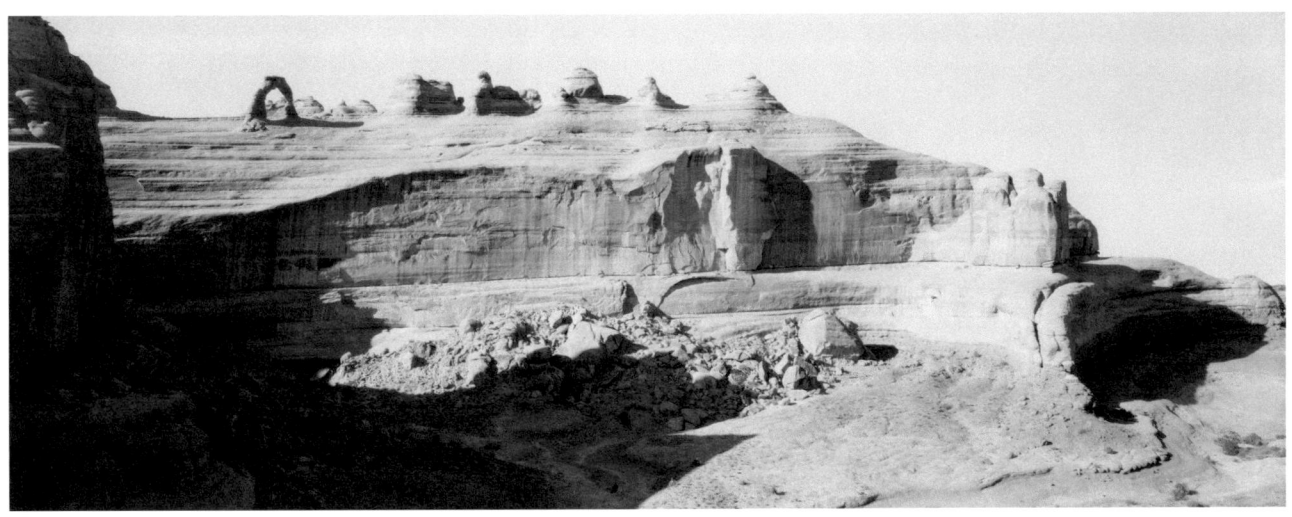

Lois Conner
Arches National Park, Utah, 1990
Sheldon Museum of Art, the
Home Ground Collection

Arch

Margaret Kirkeby provided the initial support to get the Home Ground Collection underway. For the past decade, she has been a steadfast presence in my life and more generous and forgiving than I deserve. A native of South Dakota, she has an appreciative eye for the Plains and makes a fine navigator for an afternoon drive to the middle of nowhere—thank you for everything.

Lastly, I want to recognize Barry Lopez. I first reached out to him over twenty years ago after coming across his essay, "A Scary Abundance of Water," about growing up in the San Fernando Valley. He was not only kind enough to reply but to welcome a correspondence. A few years later, we had our first conversation about creating an exhibition to accompany *Home Ground*, proving, I suppose, that good ideas can be stubborn things. Thank you, Barry, for your friendship and for the invitation to do meaningful work together.

Toby Jurovics
Director
Barry Lopez Foundation for Art & Environment

191

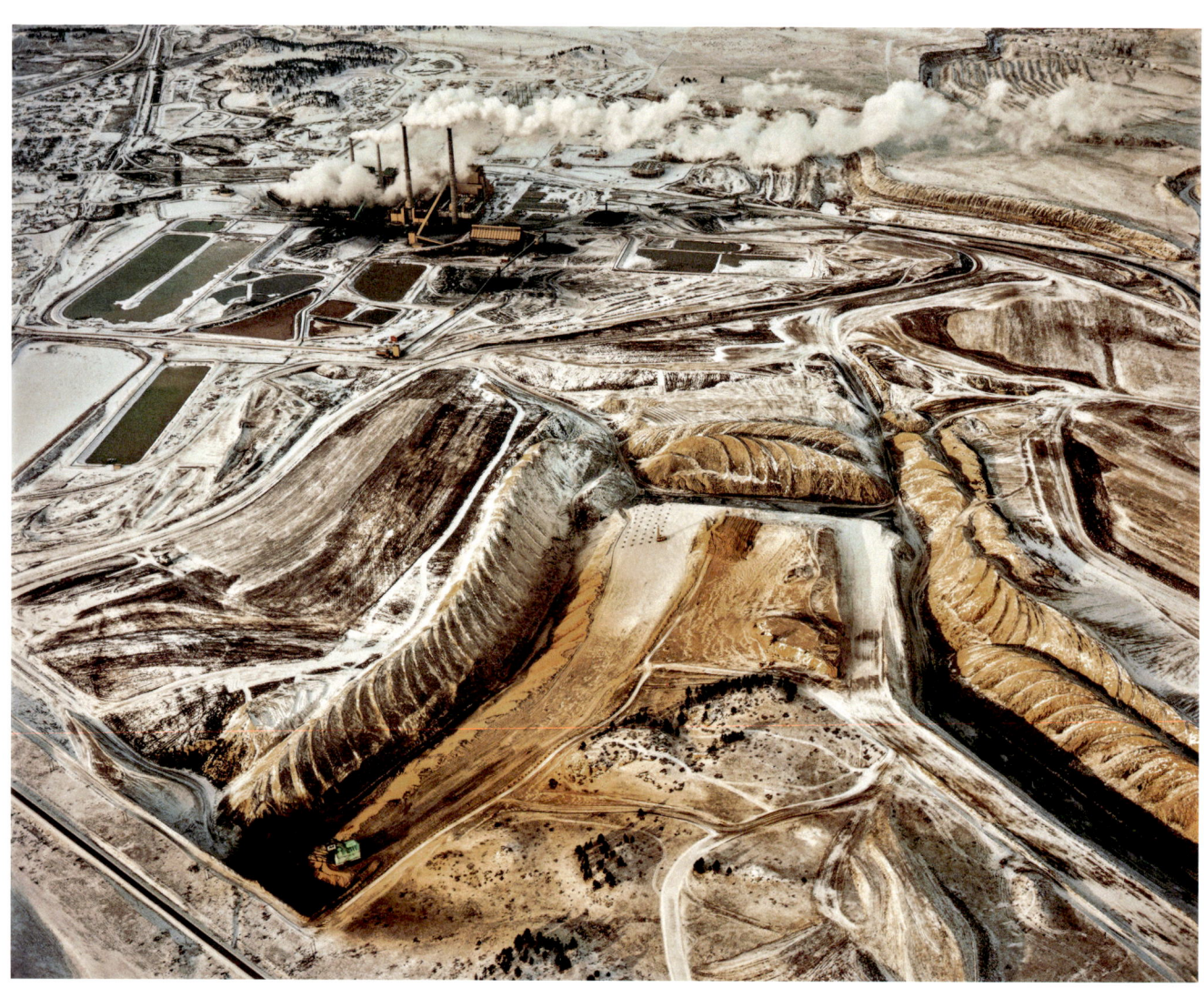

David T. Hanson
Coal Strip Mine, Power Plant and Waste Ponds, 1984
Sheldon Museum of Art, the Home Ground Collection

Strip mine

Home Ground Author Index

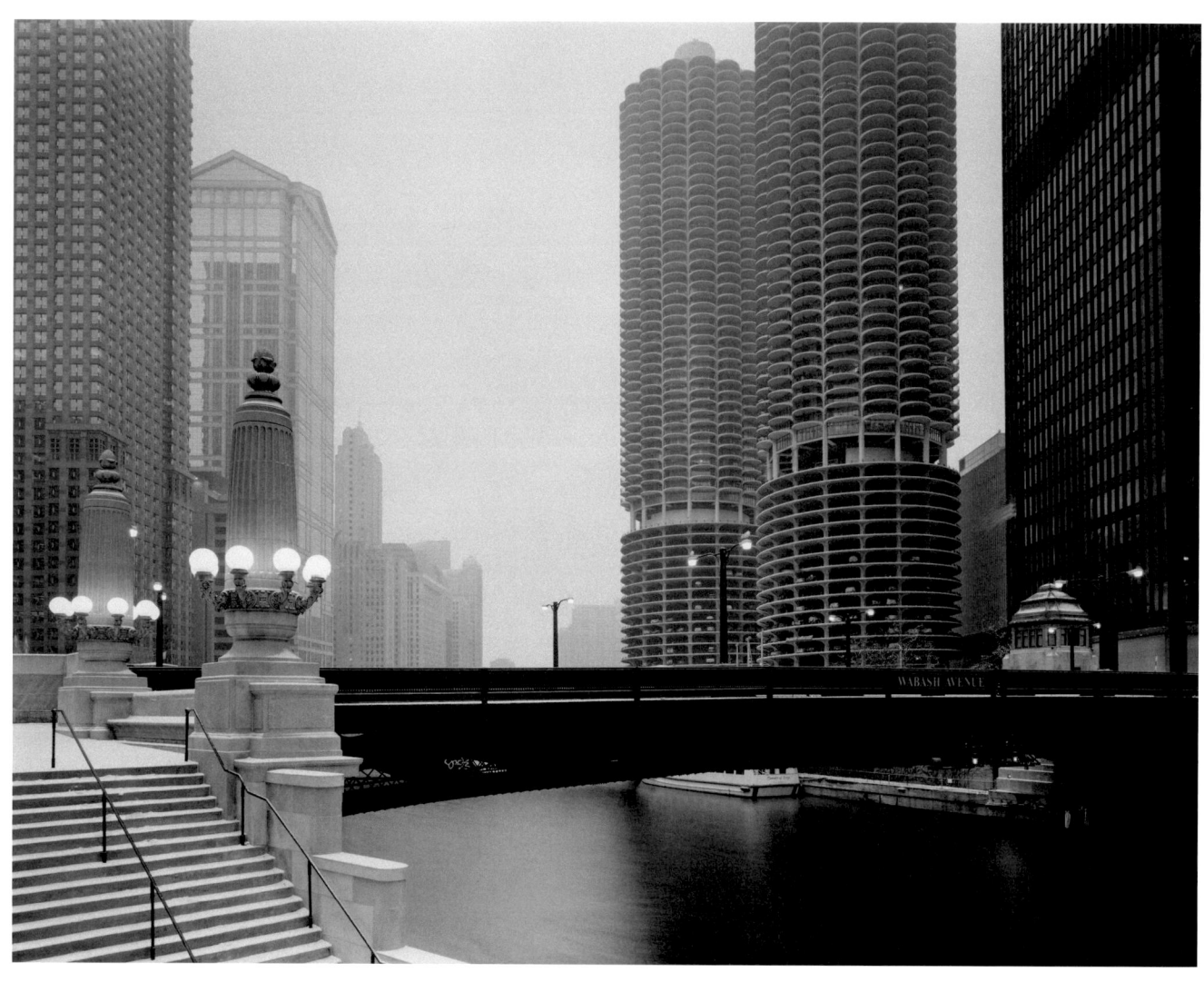

Bob Thall
Chicago (Chicago River. View West from Wabash Avenue), 2007
Sheldon Museum of Art, the Home Ground Collection

River

Contributor Biographies

Debra Gwartney is the author of two memoirs, including *I Am a Stranger Here Myself* (2019), winner of the River Teeth Nonfiction Prize and the Willa Award for Nonfiction. Her first book, *Live Through This* (2010), was a finalist for the National Book Critics Circle Award. Gwartney co-edited *Home Ground: A Guide to the American Landscape* (2006) with her husband Barry Lopez. She has published widely in journals including *Granta*, *The Sun*, *Tin House*, *American Scholar*, *The Normal School*, *Creative Nonfiction*, and *VQR*, and she is the recipient of a 2020 Pushcart Prize. Gwartney lives in western Oregon.

Toby Jurovics is the founding director of the Barry Lopez Foundation for Art & Environment. He was chief curator and curator of American Western Art at Joslyn Art Museum from 2011 to 2020, prior to which he was a curator of photography at the Smithsonian American Art Museum and the Princeton University Art Museum. A specialist in nineteenth- and twentieth-century American landscape photography, he has curated over fifty monographic and group exhibitions of photography, painting, works on paper, and new media, including shows on Robert Adams, Lewis Baltz, Virginia Beahan, Barbara Bosworth, John Divola, Emmet Gowin, Edward Ranney, Andrew J. Russell, and William Wylie. He is the author of *Framing the West: The Survey Photographs of Timothy H. O'Sullivan* (2010) and has published essays on Thomas Joshua Cooper, Rick Dingus, Steve Fitch, John Gossage, Andrew Moore, William Sutton, and the New Topographics.

Robert Macfarlane is the author of celebrated books about people, place, and nature, including *Mountains of the Mind* (2003), *The Wild Places* (2007), *The Old Ways: A Journey on Foot* (2012), *Landmarks* (2015), and, most recently, *Underland: A Deep Time Journey* (2019). His books have been translated into thirty languages and won prizes internationally, including the Philip Leverhulme Prize in Modern

European Languages and Literature (2011), the E. M. Forster Prize for Literature 2017, awarded by the American Academy of Arts and Letters, and the Wainwright Prize for Nature Writing (2019). In addition, his work has been widely adapted for film, television, stage, radio, and music, and his most recent film, *River* (2022), was scored by Radiohead and voiced by Willem Dafoe. Macfarlane is a Fellow of Emmanuel College, University of Cambridge.

Barry Lopez was born in 1945 in Port Chester, New York. He grew up in Southern California and New York City and attended the University of Notre Dame before moving to Oregon, where he lived on the McKenzie River from 1968 until his passing in December of 2020. Lopez was the author of *Of Wolves and Men*, a National Book Award finalist in 1978, which was awarded the John Burroughs and Christopher medals; *Arctic Dreams: Imagination and Desire in a Northern Landscape*, which received the National Book Award for Nonfiction in 1986; and eight works of fiction, including *Desert Notes* (1976), *River Notes* (1979), *Winter Count* (1981), *Field Notes* (1994), and *Resistance* (2004). His essays are collected in three books, *Crossing Open Ground* (1988), *About This Life* (1998), and the posthumous *Embrace Fearlessly the Burning World* (2022), and he co-edited *Home Ground: Language for an American Landscape* (2006) with Debra Gwartney. His long-awaited memoir, *Horizon*, was published in 2019. Lopez was a regular contributor to *Harper's*, *Granta*, *The Georgia Review*, *Orion*, *Outside*, *The Paris Review*, *Manoa*, and other publications in the United States and abroad.

Lopez was the recipient of Guggenheim, Lannan, MacDowell and National Science Foundation fellowships; Pushcart Prizes in fiction and nonfiction; the St. Francis of Assisi Award from DePaul University; the Denise Levertov Award from Image magazine; and honors from the Academy of Television Arts and Sciences, the Association of American Geographers, the New York Public Library, The Nature Conservancy, and the American Society of Magazine Editors. In 2020, Lopez received the Award in Literature from the American Academy of Arts and Letters and was awarded The Sun Valley Writers' Conference's inaugural Writer in the World Prize in recognition of his singular voice in the landscape of American literature.

Published in conjunction with the exhibition *From Here to the Horizon: Photographs in Honor of Barry Lopez*, presented at Sheldon Museum of Art, University of Nebraska-Lincoln, from January 27 to May 26, 2023.

sheldon

BARRY LOPEZ FOUNDATION
FOR ART & ENVIRONMENT

Funding was provided by
Phyllis Acklie
Assurity
Kristen and Geoff Cline
D F Dillon Foundation
Duncan Family Trust
The Charles Engelhard Foundation
Melanie and Jon Gross
Institute of Museum and Library
　Services
Kathy and Marc LeBaron
Patricia and Joel Meier
Nebraska Arts Council and Nebraska
　Cultural Endowment
Peck Stacpoole Foundation
Roseann and Phil Perry
Rhonda Seacrest
Lisa and Tom Smith

Catalogue photography by Bill Ganzel.

Images for Virginia Beahan, Barbara Bosworth, Lucinda Devlin, Terry Evans, Steve Fitch, Peter Goin, Mark Klett, David Maisel, Laura McPhee, Andrew Moore, Eric Paddock, and Martin Stupich provided by the artists. Ansel Adams, *Winter Sunrise, the Sierra Nevada from Lone Pine, California*, 1944, courtesy the Center for Creative Photography, University of Arizona. George N. Barnard courtesy the Metropolitan Museum of Art. James Casebere courtesy the artist and Sean Kelly, New York. Dan Holdsworth courtesy the artist and Denver Art Museum. Timothy H. O'Sullivan courtesy Prints and Photographs Division, Library of Congress. Portrait of Barry Lopez courtesy Ron Jude.

Cover: Mark Klett, *My Camera at the Head of Sinbad, San Rafael Swell, Utah 5/22/93*, 1993

Texts by Debra Gwartney, Toby Jurovics, Robert Macfarlane, and Wally Mason © the authors

Library of Congress Control Number: 2022941506
ISBN 978-1-59534-993-4

Published by Sheldon Museum of Art and the Barry Lopez Foundation for Art & Environment
sheldonartmuseum.org
barrylopezfoundation.org

Distributed by Trinity University Press
tupress.org

Produced by Lucia | Marquand, Seattle
luciamarquand.com

Edited by Melissa Duffes
Designed by Thomas Eykemans
Typeset in BW Nista International
　by Brynn Warriner
Proofread by Ted Gilley
Color management by I/O Color, Seattle
Printed and bound in China by Artron
　Art Group